DAVID LEA
An Architect of Principle

Adam Voelcker

Artifice
books on architecture

Adam has created a record of 50 years of work. I thank him for putting this before us and for calling up my memories of all those projects and of the people involved, associates, assistants, clients, consultants, builders, teachers, philosophers, family and friends. Without them all the work would not have been possible, nor would I have my memories of co-operation, discussion, friendship and love. They will know who they are, and I thank them all.
David Lea

Contents

PREFACE 4
by Adam Voelcker

INTRODUCTION 7
by Peter Blundell Jones

DAVID LEA: AN ARCHITECT OF PRINCIPLE
A Conversation between David Lea and Adam Voelcker 15 to 63

Housing, London Borough of Merton 66
Land Use Studies, Edgbaston 68
Sheltered Housing, Churt 69
Housing, Takeley 76
New Office, Ogoronwy 78
Bledisloe Court, The Royal Agricultural College 82
Library Extension, The Royal Agricultural College 84
Pembroke College, Oxford 86
The Walled Garden, Coates 88
Timber-Framed Gwynedd House Project 92
Darwin College, Cambridge 94
Artist's Studio, Somerset 95
Coad Court, The Royal Agricultural College 100
Gonville and Caius College, Cambridge 104
Visitor Centre, Wakehurst Place 106
House in Wiltshire 108
Robinson College, Cambridge 110
The Oasis of Peace, Porthmadog 112
Kingswood Project, Somerset 116
Visitor Centre, Sir Harold Hillier Garden and Arboretum 118
House Extension, Blaen Camel 122
Bridge Pottery, Cheriton 126
Magdalene College, Cambridge 128
Community Centre, Slaidburn 130
Penlee Quarry, Cornwall 132
House in North Wales 134
House in Dorset 136
WISE building, Centre for Alternative Technology 138
Schnapps 146

QUOTATION SOURCES 148
CATALOGUE OF WORKS 150
LIST OF PUBLICATIONS 154
INDEX 156
IMAGE CREDITS 158
ACKNOWLEDGEMENTS 159

Preface
by Adam Voelcker

Figures such as Edward Cullinan, Richard MacCormac and David Lea, seen as modern successors to the Arts and Crafts movement, were more important for the recovery of credibility during the 1990s than the big names of High Tech, Postmodernism or Classicism. Of these three, Lea has been the least prolific but probably the most high principled, admired for his rigorous use of sustainable materials with the kind of sophistication of space and detailing that were usually missing from the emergent Green Movement in architecture.

"… the least prolific but probably the most high principled…." is how Alan Powers rated Lea in his book *Britain*, a critical appraisal of modern British architecture, published in 2007. It is true that Lea has not built much, yet most of what he has built has been featured in the architectural journals (and not only in Britain—see List of Publications). However he has remained in the wings of the architectural stage since first establishing a modest reputation in the early 1970s with a timber-framed sheltered housing scheme in Surrey, and then in the 1980s with new Cotswold-inspired buildings at the Royal Agricultural College, Cirencester. Both projects were very different, yet they shared a sensitivity to place and to local materials, and each was a thoughtful response to the needs of the respective users. To be in harmony with nature and to conserve the earth's natural resources, yet at the same time to create good architecture, were fundamental aims in both schemes, making Lea an "architect of conscience" and an early apostle of the green movement long before sustainability became the key concern it is today. This concern has continued to play a crucial part in all of Lea's projects, built and unbuilt.

It would oversimplify things to consider architecture separately from Lea's broader concerns, as they are all deeply held and integral to each other. For this reason a book focusing only on his projects, although undoubtedly a feast, would miss the target. This is because architecture, for Lea, is just part (admittedly a big part) of a life devoted to the integration of the many, often contradictory, aspects of modern civilisation. Fundamental to Lea's philosophy of life is "the profound, ever-renewing, enduring beauty of nature". From an early age he was intensely aware of the natural world around him, of the thin, fragile layer of air and earth that magically sustains life on our planet. He was also dismayed, even angered, by the sheer disregard that modern man has for the planet—by the way humans plunder the earth and exhaust its finite resources, by the waste they leave behind, by their inability to share fairly, by the social and economic imbalances caused by capitalism, centralisation, and by the increasing rift between brain and manual work. Lea's life has been a quest to address these concerns. He has done more than pay lip-service to the failings of the modern world. In 1976 he moved from London to North Wales so that he could lead the sort of integrated, balanced life he believed in—living as a member of a decentralised, rural, relatively self-sustaining society in harmony with nature. Quite what this radical move would bring Lea on the architectural front, he had no inkling. In time, jobs did materialise, good ones too, but it remains a minor tragedy that so many of his projects failed to go ahead. Nor was life on the land easy. The climate and terrain of Wales is often harsh and wet, the area where Lea settled is the heartland of the Welsh language, and it was sheer hard work to establish a smallholding. But Lea persevered. One can but admire him for following his principles doggedly, some would say stubbornly to the point of self-sacrifice. If more architects followed Lea's ethical stand, they might lose out on professional opportunities and the fulfilment of purely architectural ambitions, but surely the world would be a better place.

...

Göran Schildt, who began his great biography of Alvar Aalto some six years after Aalto had died, wrote in his preface how much he regretted passing up his chance to become Aalto's Boswell. With David Lea still happily alive, this is not a regret I need have myself. On the other hand, the challenge of writing about someone still living is considerable, especially when that person is as particular as Lea. From the beginning I knew that my plan to write a book about him—the idea occurred to me when returning home from the formal opening of the Wales Institute for Sustainable Education (WISE) building at the Centre for Alternative Technology (CAT) in 2010—could work only with his full co-operation. This I got wholeheartedly and with surprising enthusiasm. But as my text developed, it became clear that certain reservations were building up. I don't think he minded that I was never very keen on one of his Cambridge college projects, but when I began to form a link between his approach and that of the Arts and Crafts movement, he reacted with surprising vehemence, saying he didn't want to be claimed as an inheritor of those values I had thought he treasured. However, the real issue at stake was that I was not offering Lea the opportunity to say what he believed himself. This came to a head one day when he said, more flippantly than I think he intended, "the whole thing reads as if I'm already dead". It was at this point (which might have occurred earlier if Schildt had been around to advise me) that I realised that an extended conversation might be the answer. We had initially taken the decision not to use a tape recorder, not least because our discussions tend to be punctuated by long gaps of silence. But once we decided to give the interview format a go, encouraged by the example of Martin Gayford's conversations with David Hockney, the process unfolded rather smoothly and pleasurably. We had four interview sessions and a few subsequent ones to edit the transcribed text. They took place in Lea's kitchen at Ogoronwy, usually in the company of his cat and always with coffee and lunch (invariably of bread, cheese and home-made soup using produce from the garden). Birdsong accompanied the fourth and last interview because we could at last sit out on the terrace (the spring and early summer of 2013 were particularly chilly). The end result is not what I had originally intended, and actually has very little of me and my views in it. But the subject matter is David Lea, after all—his ideas and his projects, his views rather than mine. It is far better that his voice is taken advantage of when it can still be heard. A retrospective analysis can follow one day....

Fig 1

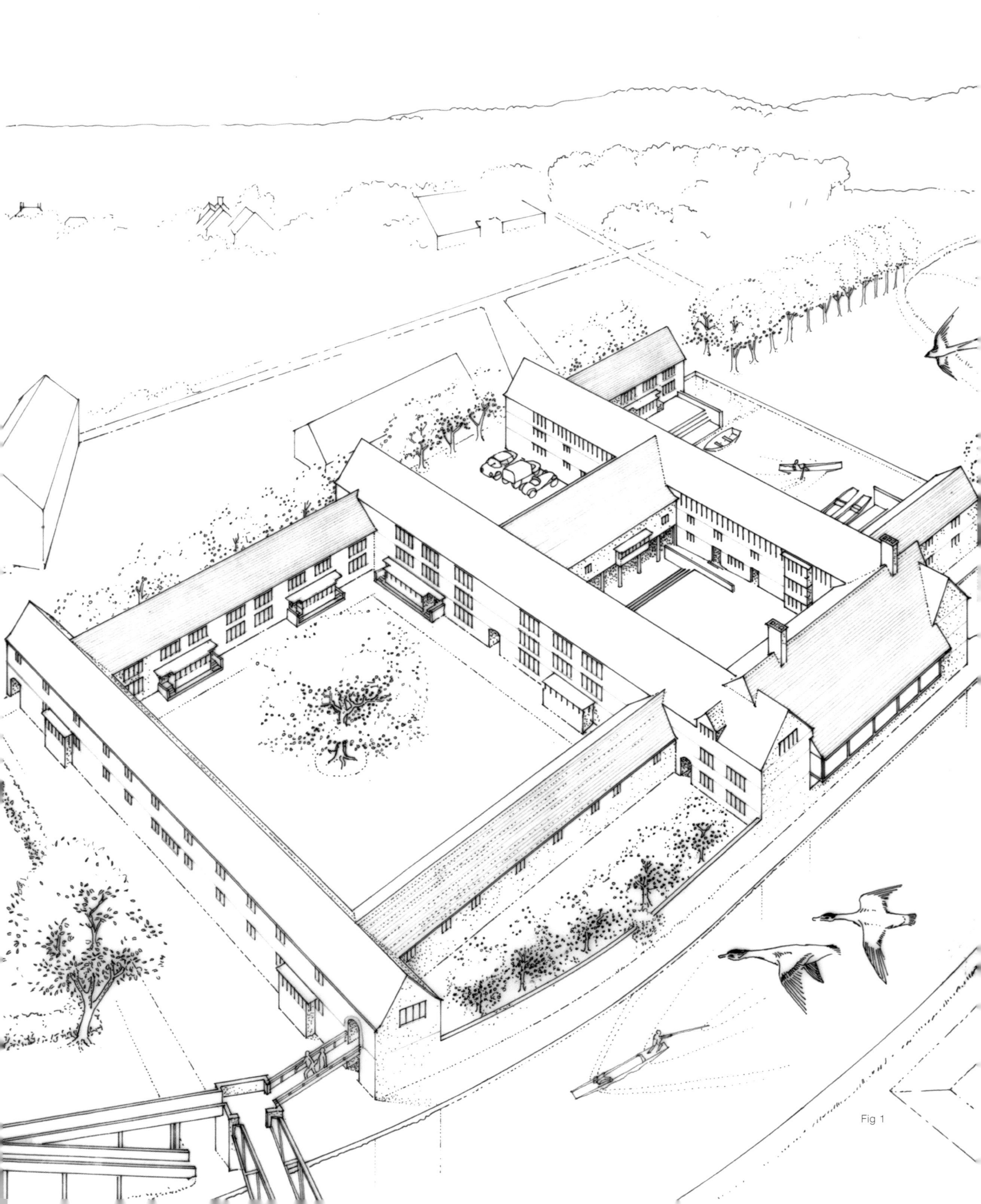

Introduction
by Peter Blundell Jones

In the interview of this book I found myself cited for calling David Lea's competition design for Pembroke College Oxford "timeless", and praising it for "getting everything in the right place". That article in *Architects' Journal* is now nearly 30 years old, so I had to find it and read it again, but on reviewing the drawings I am still seduced by the limpid clarity of Lea's proposal. I am also still convinced that it was the best on offer, all the more so on seeing how much the postmodernist styling of the others has dated.[1] It was a curious period, when a generation of architects brought up as rational modernists were experimenting playfully to reincorporate historic towers and gables, some of them dangerously close to Disney. They were egged-on by an Oxford College that not only expected stone walls and quadrangles but had actually ruled out flat roofs as technically unsound. Lea, having reopened a quarry for new stone roofs at Cirencester, was hardly immune to this turn to tradition, but his act of reclamation was more a deeply held matter of principle, as he sought an enduring simplicity and continuity of craft rather than expressive rhetoric. I would qualify my claim that his design was "timeless" only by adding "insofar as anything can be", for it does seem the least dated of the group, and had it been built it would be the hardest to assign to a period. Since it demonstrates many of the essential virtues of Lea's work, it will serve here as an example for me to expand on my other claim about "getting everything in the right place". Two of Lea's drawings tell almost the whole story: the bird's-eye view of the complex with the river winding past, and the section through a student kitchen-diner in which a newspaper reader finds himself at home. The contrast between them indicates the wide range of scales which the project embraces (figs 1 and 3.)

Oxford and Cambridge colleges derive from the monastic tradition, the courtyard or quad being descended from the cloister, which was at once a space of contemplation, a paradise garden, and the main distributor of circulation. In Medieval monasteries the cloister was precisely square, often with a refectory on the south axis and a chapter house on the east, as at Rievaulx Abbey (fig 2). It was not just an empty space but the social centre, and the very starting point of the monastic plan defining its geometry. Lea based his Pembroke plan on a series of courts, three of them square and the fourth half-square, managing to keep the whole thing orthogonal without forcing it onto the site. By deploying the courts in their varied sizes with consummate skill, he found a seemingly effortless way to respond to the irregular curve of the river bank, supplying a high-level bridge link, adding a curved and elevated riverside garden, and making an appropriate climax of social rooms with jettied balconies, the highest roofs, and chimneys. He completed the west end with a water court, facing downriver to enjoy the long view while preventing intruders. The courts were to be varied in size and character, the largest one green with a central tree, the southern one open for approach and parking. The central court was paved and stepped with a monastic central fountain, the western one stepped down into its captive lake. No other competitor created such definitive inner spaces, most merely leaving residual gardens between the more positive forms of their buildings, many also deploying circulation internally by corridor. Lea decided to avoid corridors by placing all access at ground level through the courts and grouping rooms in sixes around double stairs. Everyone would have to descend past the shared kitchen/diner and make their way through the open air courts to the communal facilities,

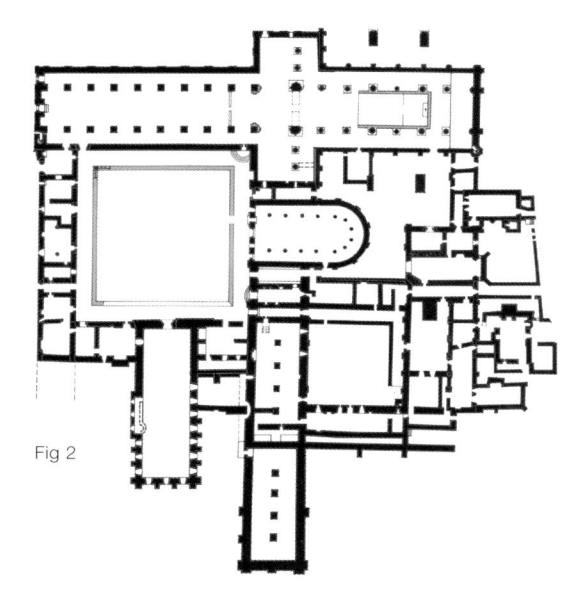

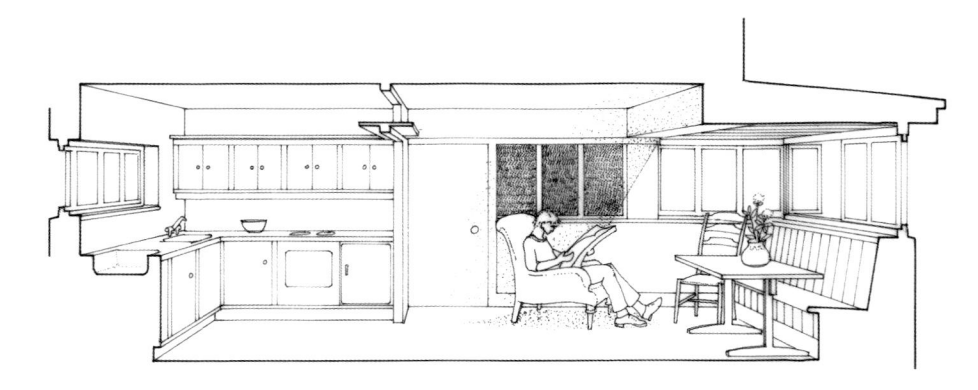

Fig 3

exactly as they do in traditional Oxford and Cambridge colleges. It is no great hardship to brave the cold and rain for a few moments on your way to breakfast, particularly if thereafter you are going to walk half way across town to a lecture, but perhaps there was a gut reaction among the clients that this arrangement was primitive, corridors being a necessary part of modern life. Since the mid-twentieth century they have certainly become the norm in institutional buildings, but at what cost? The increased area built and heated is only the start. Corridors do not encourage encounters like the cloister: if set on several levels they separate people rather than bringing them together, which improves neither the sense of community nor safety. Worse still, most corridors are double-loaded, dark and airless, and rooms then have only one aspect. Even if a corridor is glazed onto a courtyard, the air and sound of the outside world are still cut off, reducing the external space to a mere light well.

Lea's room grouping manages not only to give all rooms views to both sides, but even allows windows in bathrooms and lavatories. The double outlook gives contrasting views, stronger light, cross-ventilation in summer, and two chances of catching the sun. In addition each group's kitchen/diner at ground level gains a yet wider view of 180° through a projecting bay, at once marking that group in the facade and projecting their social presence into the more public life of the court. All this produces a clear social scale. A student belongs first to the group of six with whom he or she shares stairs and communal room, then to the court, the largest of which is surrounded by nine groups. The courts are then organised in another perceptible system, the great court and water court deployed at opposite ends of the east-west axis with central archways placed as intuitively expected, linked through the centre court where one arrives in an open undercroft. At this point we need a third drawing, a perspective of the centre court looking west, to permit discussion of the main progression (fig 4).

The experience of pedestrian movement through a building complex has always been of concern to sensible architects, but it was too often subsumed in the later twentieth century under the more technical heading of "circulation", sometimes treated blindly like plumbing. Some of the worst offenders are modern hospitals, where due to the sheer complexity and priority given to structure and services, people constantly get lost and must rely on signs to navigate from department to department, which wastes time and provokes anxiety. On the most basic level we all need to know where we are going in order to remember how to get out again, but the order of an institution also presents itself to us serially and hierarchically through its layers and levels.[2] This order must be readable spatially to seem manageable and friendly. There must be a point of arrival and greeting, progress to places of social congregation should be clear, and the general distribution of functions should be made manifest. The role of entrance halls, staircases, courts and foyers tends to be underrated, perhaps because we spend considerably

Fig 4

less time in them than we do in the rooms where we work or sleep, but they are the most social spaces in a building: spaces of threshold and encounter. They also mark the transitions from one state of being to another—from person in the street to member of college and on to member of room-group, for example—thereby giving us the strongest sense of what the institution is.

Lea's Pembroke plan develops hierarchically around two plan axes. We have already met the east-west axis which joins the great court to the water court via the cloistered side of the main court. On both sides the linking archway is placed in the middle, precisely where one would expect it, and on moving through there would be dramatic views into another world: the tree in the great court one side and the long view up the river the other, like those moments at Cirencester where arches allow sudden glimpses from courts to the world beyond (fig 5).

Although in the Pembroke plan the east-west axis is the longer, the south-north one spells out the main progression, starting with the open car court to south, moving through its central arch up into the main court, then climbing steps to the fountain (fig 4). Ramps and stairs lead on up again to a big conference room on the north side, which is completely glazed onto the river. A stair at its east end rises once more to the common room, the climax of the progression. The gradual rises are hierarchically appropriate for moving onto more important territories, as in a monastery, but the increases in height also solve the problem of leaving the Thames towpath public without compromising the college's security. That Lea could at the same time make a high-level garden link from the north west Thames bridge to the social rooms at the heart was an added bonus, answering a necessary demand of the site, as both the city and the rest of the university lie across the river. In the bird's-eye view (fig 1) the common room roof with its two chimneys and half-hips masters all other roofs, sitting neatly between the ends of accommodation wings, and the top floor is jettied out over the towpath as a balcony. The chimneys serve hearths at the ends of the room to give a sense of comfort and intimacy. Lea's internal perspective shows a timber-trussed hall in the Medieval tradition, revealing its structure and carpentry in contrast with lesser roofs with flat-ceilings. This appropriately traditional rhetorical device would probably have been developed in execution as elegantly as Lea's Blaenau sports hall, in which the internally visible roof structure is the main glory (fig 6).[3]

Fig 5

Fig 6

To summarise the virtues of Lea's Pembroke, it works at every scale from relating to the landscape down to a bed or chair, and it follows traditional monastic hierarchies of building and space, with great attention to the experience of the inhabitant moving through. Despite being orthogonal and set on a consistent pair of axes, it does not seem stiff or forced, as the decision to prioritise the courts was justified by the nature

Fig 7

of the institution, and instead of forcing the right-angle of the drawing board, it accepts the irregularity of the site edges with alacrity. Although this college outpost was intended as secondary to the original Pembroke College, it could never have developed much social cohesion on its own as a mere group of rooms, so playing up the common room as its hall and centre promised coherence for the whole. The emphasis on court as outdoor room and the design of the room-group were elements retained by Lea and further developed in later projects (see pp 86–87 for further illustrations of Lea's Pembroke scheme).

A much smaller Lea project of the same period shows similar virtues in a less formal setting. The Royal Agricultural College, Cirencester owned a large house in the nearby village of Coates which they wished to develop, so asked Lea to design a series of five houses (see pp 88–91 and fig 7). They are L-shaped, each embracing a garden to the south and comprising three wings deployed as theme and variations, the principal wing gaining an added bedroom storey. Four were set within the old walled garden, making use of existing walls and preserving trees, each in itself orthogonal but swung around at slightly different angles to make best use of the site, the garage wing being placed differently in each case. This response to existing site lines gave individual identity to each house and made the whole development more genuinely village-like than the standard cul-de-sac lined with identical houses like soldiers on parade which we now see in village extensions everywhere. With their plain tiled roofs, rendered walls and simple mullioned timber windows, Lea's houses have an Arts and Crafts look, almost Voysey, but on the garden side is a fully glazed veranda for maximum contact with the garden, a modernist touch that Lea admits is inspired by Frank Lloyd Wright and Japanese architecture. The exposed structure was made of reclaimed pitch pine, its newly planed and untreated surfaces creating a delicate aroma, and there were naked tongue and groove boarded doors, simple wooden shelves and fittings, even a wooden settle.[4] This solid local joinery is reminiscent of William Lethaby's instructions for simple cottage furniture, beautiful in its plain unadornedness and the honesty of its workmanship:

> *It would be quite vain to try to teach the practice of a craft in print: that can only be done by actual contact with a workman who holds it as a tradition received from some other, and so back and back. The tools, too, are shaped by the experience of thousands of years.... To plane level, to shoot a joint straight and glue it together: to tongue clamps across the grain, to rebate, mitre, and frame rails into uprights with closely fitted mortise and tenon; to frame up panelling and fit dovetail angles—all this forms but the alphabet.*[5]

Lea is not only a skilled draftsman as the accompanying drawings indicate, but has also been all his life a maker, ready with tools to hand, willing to experiment and with a profound feeling for detail. This sensibility allowed him early on in his career to extend Walter Segal's minimal building method with a Japanese twist for his sheltered housing at Churt (see pp 69–75), just as later it led to a new use for saplings, thatch and render in the tiny thatched cottage for a painter friend on which he contributed labour himself (see pp 95–99). I remember from years back Lea's steady insistence on using naked wood, retaining a sense of the tree it had been instead of crushing the life out of it and imposing a mechanical homogeneity. He knows his trees, and he once told me that when he employs others to draw for him, it is the trees he insists on drawing himself, because he knows how to depict their different species and habits. In recent years and in collaboration with Pat Borer he has experimented with rammed earth, hemp-lime, wool insulation, green oak, and many other natural materials in a bid to improve thermal performance, encourage local sourcing, and to reduce energy wastage, always with a sense of direct confrontation with the substance, its capabilities, its smell and texture, its weight, its new possibilities.

The return in the 1980s to the pitched roof reflected a widespread hunger for a recognisable roofness, at least on rural and suburban buildings. But it also marked, after well-publicised failures of flat roofs, a new recognition of the longevity of slates and tiles. These discrete overlapping units which can slide over each other when movements occur with changes of weather and temperature need a pitch of around 30°. Pitched roofs are limited in span and if done properly confer a strong discipline on the plan, so Arts and Crafts architects tended to design as much from the roof down as from the ground plan up. That Lea has a feeling for this is obvious from both Pembroke and Coates, but he has not always wanted to give the roof so much of a voice. His design with Ekkehard Weisner for the Hillier Garden visitor centre (see pp 118–121) from the mid-1990s was intended to have a flat roof finished in stainless steel panels, for the generous spans of the main spaces would have produced huge obtrusive barn-like volumes, instead of which he proposed crisp low horizontal roof edges, allowing the brick walls to dominate. This conveniently preserved a modernist freedom of plan, but it also fulfilled the idea of making the whole building like a walled garden, and therefore not competing with the landscape and the trees, which are the soul of the place. Sir Harold Hillier (1905–1985) was a nurseryman and author of the definitive plant catalogue, who built up an arboretum on land around his own modest house near Southampton. It is now owned by Hampshire County Council and open to the public. In the mid-1990s they sought to improve it partly by improving the landscape design, partly by adding a visitor centre. This needed to be the usual entrance, cafe and shop, but also stood in for the expected house which one finds at every National Trust property, Hillier's own house being

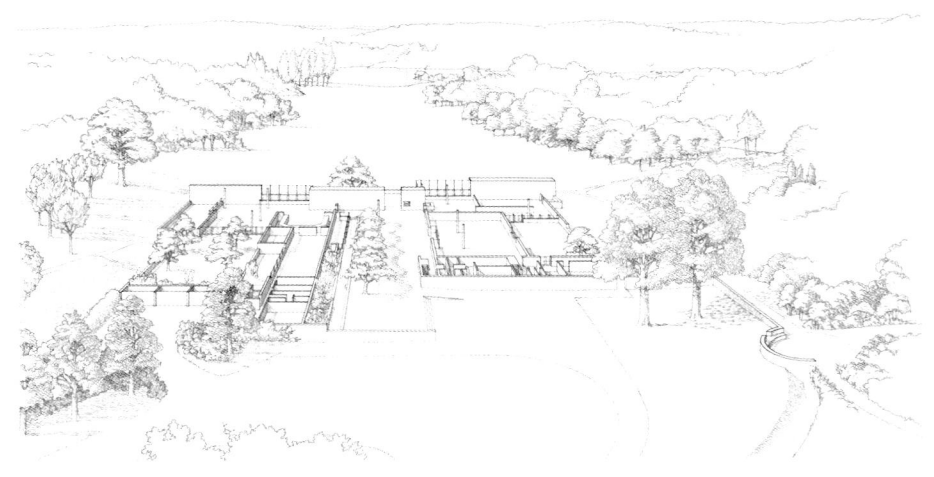

Fig 8

small, marginal and not on show. Lea and Weisner won a limited architectural competition in 1995 and went on to refine the project over the next three years, though in the end were refused lottery money, not because of the design but for doubts about the economic viability of the institution. This should surely have been tested first, before investing and wasting so much time and effort.

The visitor centre was intended to set up a threshold between the public car park and a long clearing leading down to the lake (fig 8), the most commanding view in the whole park. The architects made a long central court with trees and a pond, leading to the threshold of the park and suddenly opening up the view next to the ticket kiosk. To the left was the restaurant, to the right the shop and exhibition, revealing in different ways the long views onto the park, and open courtyards were added behind to each side, while lavatories and services were discreetly hidden in the apparent thickness of the front wall. Much depended on a playful asymmetry of the plan, derived at least in part from Ludwig Mies van der Rohe, as Lea had been much impressed by a visit to the resurrected Barcelona Pavilion. But there was also once more in this project an acute sense of the experience of moving through, with concealment followed by sudden exposure. Lest clients and judges should miss the point, this was explored in a series of analytical diagrams showing precisely what could be seen from where.

The interior perspectives show once again Lea's tactile sense of materials, suggesting a calm and noble place, surely just what was needed to create a sense of arrival and hospitality, to prove the very issue at stake: that people would come and then come again for a day out, as they do at National Trust sites.

It is a relief that in the second decade of the new millennium we finally have one substantial building complex by Lea that we can experience in reality, this time designed in collaboration with Pat Borer (fig 9 and pp 138–145). The five-year-old Wales Institute for Sustainable Education building at the Centre for Alternative Technology in Wales has courtyards, flat roofs, terraces, spatial progressions and special views as with the other projects so far discussed, but it also results from long studies about energy usage, in terms of both daily consumption and the energy locked into materials by manufacture and transport to the site. Because of the concerns of the Centre, a very strict brief was set, which went as far as including the fuel used by visiting consultants' cars. Lea was happy to go along with this. He has for decades been concerned about our overuse of energy and our failure to look after the planet. This is shown not just by his continuous attempts to use local and sustainable materials for buildings, but also in his experiments with farming and gardening at his home in Snowdonia (see pp 78–81). Our society has become dominated increasingly by the worship of money and the valuing of nearly everything in crude economic terms, while our political system seems to have lost all

Fig 9

means to engage with anything beyond the next five years. Yet we are taking great risks with the planet and living profligately, and the gap between rich and poor widens year by year. The need for economic growth and the ability to find technical fixes for the problems we ourselves have created are now so much taken for granted that we fail to reflect on how fortunate we are, how fruitful the earth, how much longer we now live, and how we might share these benefits with the rest of the world instead of fighting each other and always demanding more. Lea has, in protest against this, consistently promoted the idea of a modest, efficient and humane architecture, with generous daylighting, good way-finding, priority to on-foot, avoidance of unnecessary services and adherence to a small scale if possible. Behind all his projects lies the utopian vision of a stable and dignified state of existence, which would be at once generous, resilient and sustainable, making wise use of the earth's bounty. In this there are distinct echoes of William Morris.

1 Blundell Jones, Peter, "College collage", *Architects' Journal*, no 24 vol 183, 11 June 1986, pp 29–49.
2 Mark Meagher and I recently published a book on the experience of movement in architecture to which Lea contributed a chapter based on a lecture he gave at Sheffield in 2011: see Lea, David, "Move to the Light", in Blundell Jones, Peter and Mark Meagher, eds, *Architecture and Movement: the dynamic experience of buildings and landscapes*, London: Routledge, 2015, pp 72–80.
3 Blundell Jones, Peter, "Traditional games", *Architects' Journal*, 20 September 1989, pp 40–47.
4 Blundell Jones, Peter, "A modern vernacular", *Architects' Journal*, 17 September 1986, pp 64–69.
5 Lethaby, WR, *Simple Furniture*, written 1892, published as Dryad Leaflet no 5 in the 1920s and reprinted for the Lethaby Exhibition of 1984.
6 Blundell Jones, Peter, "Woodland retreat", *Architects' Journal*, 27 September 1989, pp 26–31.
7 Blundell Jones, Peter, and Jan Woudstra, "Hillier's Visitor Centre, Romsey, a project by David Lea", *Architectural Research Quarterly*, vol 4, no 3, 2000, pp 204–217.
9 Blundell Jones, Peter, "Wales Institute for Sustainable Education", *The Architectural Review*, January 2011, pp 35–41.

David Lea: An Architect of Principle
A Conversation between David Lea and Adam Voelcker

AV: Over the last 40 years, whenever any of your projects have featured in the journals, the one recurring theme is your concern for the natural environment. One might go as far as to say it is the bedrock supporting everything you do. Do you remember how and when this concern began?

DL: Yes, that's a long story, which goes back to my earliest memories of the countryside. I suppose I first became conscious of natural beauty when I was about seven or eight. It must be a rather conventional experience but I remember a particular sunset when on holiday in mid-Wales, which completely overawed me, and I just sat there for ages. I suppose it was from that experience that I really began to enjoy natural beauty. It was a very essential part of my life.

You often talk about farming and agriculture but was this something you were aware of when you were a boy at school? I imagined it coming a bit later.

I was certainly aware of the countryside. I used to paint views of the countryside endlessly, along with painting and drawing more mechanical things like trains and aeroplanes. There were two strands when I think about it, the countryside and the interest in machines. I suppose my interest in land and buildings grew from that period. I remember being quite outspoken about this with my parents: I felt everything being done in our age was ugly and the good things of the past were being destroyed.

When I met your sister Fiona, she told me how she remembered your mother's worries that you would end up having a very unhappy life if you took these concerns so much to heart.

Yes, I remember that conversation very well. It was on a drive somewhere and I said that I hoped I'd never lose this critical attitude because it's really important to hang onto it. In a way that is where William Morris comes in; he followed the same route. It starts by being an aesthetic concern about the destruction of beauty, and then there's the question of why and how that's happened and can anything be done to alter it. That leads you into the political and social aspects of life....

That's a big topic, which I'm sure we'll come back to. You mention the architecture, and the countryside on the one hand, and the machines on the other, but there's no actual link to architecture in this as such. I'm still wondering where the interest in buildings came from.

The architecture came as a result of doing Art for O and A levels, so I suppose from the age of 13 when I went to Clifton College [in Bristol] my interest in it gradually grew because I had a very good teacher who made sure that we looked at buildings, and architecture was an important part of the history aspect of Art A level. So I was certainly looking at old buildings with some interest from the age of 15 onwards. When I was 16, that was the year I decided to become an architect, after being strongly warned against it by the architect parents of a close friend of mine.

The present course of civilization will destroy the beauty of life— these are hard words and I wish I could mend them, but I cannot, while I speak what I believe to be the truth.
William Morris

The roots of our understanding of architecture lie in our childhood, in our youth; they lie in our biography.
Peter Zumthor

Given your very practical approach to building, things like model-making presumably featured in your life.

I always loved making models but they were usually aeroplanes. I had a very good friend, Tim Cooper, who also went on to become an architect, and we used to spend most of our holidays making models and flying or sailing them, so constructing things was very much part of my upbringing and life. Then there was my keen interest in flying. I tried to get a flying scholarship but my eyesight wasn't good enough.

But you continued liking fast cars and good machines.

Yes, I did. Now fast cars don't… you know I don't take any notice of that… it's in the past. But I like sailing, which has some connection, and I like boats that sail well, and fast.

From what you've told me previously, your childhood sounds happy and uneventful, and your father was a rather conventional establishment figure who didn't like rocking boats. I'm just wondering what caused you to be more rebellious by nature.

I hardly knew my father till I was about four or five years old because he was away at war. I travelled for the first three or four years of my life. My earliest memories are of the west coast of Scotland, up in Poolewe in Wester Ross where my father was stationed with his anti-aircraft guns and searchlights. I think that wild landscape with its rushing rivers and deserted beaches must underlie my sense that the western seaboard of these islands is my home. It was a time of upheaval. My mother and I travelled constantly, taking rented accommodation or a room in someone's house from Cornwall up to Scotland so it wasn't a settled early life. Then when my father came back and re-established his job as a stockbroker [in Birmingham], our lives became much more steady and conventional. In fact I'd say entirely conventional, and very orderly. I think that didn't seem to be a great difference to me; looking back I can see it was very different from the first years, but at the time it just seemed to be the way things were.

At Clifton I had some good teachers in English and History; they taught us to question everything. I think that it's ironic that a place like Clifton was set up to maintain the status quo in a big way, a training ground to run the empire. You didn't rock the boat but at the same time you were encouraged to question everything. When I had discussions with my father later on, I thought if he didn't want me to question things why did he send me to a school like that? The questioning was all part of my perception that things are not organised right. Nature is being destroyed and ugliness invades everywhere.

Do you think that below the surface there might have been a bit more of a rebel in your father? At one point you did say that later on he started to question things more himself, so maybe he was a victim of his times.

I think that's a good way of putting it. He was an extremely conscientious man, he wanted to do the right thing and I guess there was a lot of frustration in him. He was

1: School of Architecture extension, Cambridge (Leslie Martin and Colin St John Wilson) **2:** Harvey Court, Cambridge (Leslie Martin and Colin St John Wilson) **3:** Sandy (Colin St John) Wilson

basically very kind but he could be testy and irritated quickly if things didn't work out right. But he would never explode in a way that I do sometimes.

You went to Cambridge to study architecture in 1959, just a couple of years after Leslie Martin had become head of the school. Was he (and his rationalist, analytical approach) an important influence on you, or were others more so?

Leslie was a remote figure, patrician and distant in many ways, but he did have wonderful gatherings at the Mill, his home just outside Cambridge. He was very generous then and he had a lot of time for people and wanted to get to know them, but in the day-to-day teaching he would give maybe one lecture each term or would attend one crit a term. He was never there day-to-day in the way Sandy [Colin St John] Wilson and Colin Rowe were. These two had a much more direct influence on me. Sandy was the first-year tutor and had Leslie's rational approach. Everything had to stand up to rational scrutiny but he also had more passion. I found him a very inspiring person. He had tremendous interest in architecture, a real passion for it. It was always interesting to talk about architecture with him, in much the same way that it was with Richard MacCormac, whom I got to know in my third year. I came away from these conversations encouraged.

Just to put this in context, what had Sandy built by this stage, as it was fairly early on in his career?

Yes, he had come with Leslie Martin from the LCC where they had built little Corbusier-inspired *unités d'habitation* in Bentham Road, Hackney, quite a lot of housing [lower-rise as well as the *unités*], the new building at the School of Architecture which was being built when I was there, and also Harvey Court [for Gonville and Caius College] and the William Stone Building [for Peterhouse College]. So there was a lot going on, and he was able to demonstrate his ideas in reality, which was terrific. They started a brick tradition, which I don't think has ever been bettered or even followed through and developed, which is a pity. Then there was Colin Rowe, who was a rather different sort of person. They both had a deep sense of history, of architectural history and historical context. I always found that an essential part of things. In fact, if you don't have a sense of history and work outside a historical context, you can do anything, and easily fall prey to a kind of idiosyncratic expressionism. It seems that many architects have little idea of historical context and this leads to a general falling apart of the environment and destruction of shared cultural values. Who knows what effect this will have long term?

Nowadays students tend to do their first year-out in the middle of their training but you did yours at the end, with Harry Weese in Chicago. Do you think your year in the US was of any significance to your development?

What was of significance was my trip there by boat. There were five of us and we took six months to sail from Spain down to the Canary Islands, across to the West Indies and up to Nassau where the boat was sold. It was a wonderful experience but by the end of it I felt I needed to get down to some work somewhere, a feeling I think in

The architect must always start with an eye on the best architecture of the past.
Louis Kahn

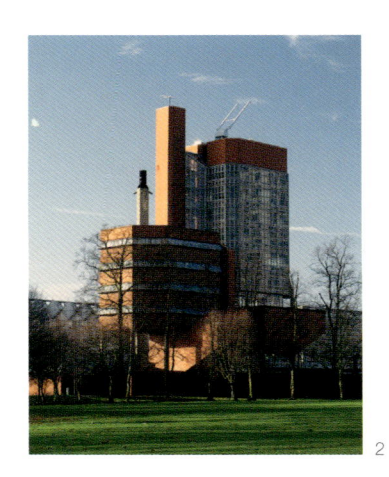

retrospect was a mistake. What I do remember more than anything else was that the voyage across the ocean made me realise that fundamentally life is extremely simple. I thought that I would never worry about anything ever again. The sun comes up, goes overhead, drops into the sea again, and the next day it comes up again and at night the stars go overhead…. It was an amazingly simple existence. But America itself was of course the opposite of this, and I don't think I carried away from working with Harry Weese anything of lasting influence except my work with Bob Bell who had trained under Louis Kahn. I suppose that influenced me to some extent, but I found I wanted to redesign all Harry Weese's buildings. They were all rather bland. Everything of interest seemed to be happening in Britain. Jim Stirling had just finished the Leicester Engineering Building and I had a picture of this above my drawing board. It looked much more interesting than anything going on in the States, much more expressive and inventive. Travelling to see the Usonian houses was certainly significant. I thought they were very good, particularly the hexagonally-planned Hanna house, and the Bazett house. That was a lasting influence and one I've returned to later on, with deeper appreciation.

Did you by any chance see any of the Shaker villages? I ask because when I look at any building of yours I think of Shaker simplicity.

That interest came later. I'll tell you what really impressed me more than anything else in Chicago was Mies's Lake Shore Drive. It is such a powerful statement and so incredibly well done and so simple. And the way the two buildings relate to each other as you move past them—the relationship changes, a bit like a Henry Moore sculpture. It seems odd in retrospect. In comparison with that, Frank Lloyd Wright's Prairie houses, which I visited, seemed to be almost part of the previous century. Looking at Mies now I think that his Barcelona Pavilion is probably the greatest modernist building, but after he went to America his work became generally more rigid and axial, and not so interesting.

There's a link here to the next stage in the story, which is that Sandy Wilson came to lecture in Chicago, you helped raise an audience and he asked you if you'd join him in Cambridge.

Yes, that was a very good evening. I had got to know a group of young architects working in Chicago and they brought their friends. Sandy talked about the British Library project [1962–1964], which was planned at that time to be right opposite the British Museum in Bloomsbury. It was a development of the Harvey Court plan with a roof over the courtyard and a stepped section. It looked like a very exciting project. Sandy said he'd be setting up a practice and if I wanted to I'd be welcome to come and join him. That worked out, except that we didn't work on the British Library at that point because it was in abeyance, but Sandy did separate his practice from Leslie Martin's, set up on his own in his new house in Cambridge and started building up an office. I was actually the first person he took on, shortly followed by MJ [Long] who had been a student of his at Yale. And then the office grew to around ten people from all over the world. Shortly after I joined him he got the Liverpool Civic Centre job, a vast scheme, and we

4

1: Barcelona Pavilion (Ludwig Mies van der Rohe) 2: Leicester Engineering Building (James Stirling) 3: Shaker interior 4: Liverpool Civic Centre (Colin St John Wilson)

worked mainly on that. I'm not quite sure what happened to the British Library project at this time. I think Leslie Martin had handed it over to Sandy by that point.

The Liverpool scheme—am I right in thinking there was a huge amount of fact-finding that went on before it was even designed on paper, so much so that Sandy actually regretted it later on—the process had got the better of him.

Yes… it was partly Christopher Alexander's influence. Alexander was an ex-student of Sandy's and he had just recently written *Community and Privacy*, where every single activity of the day-to-day life in a household was analysed and given a weight, and then it was fed into a computer. So Sandy thought we should do the same sort of operation to decide on the best form for the connectivity between various Liverpool council departments. We used to go up to Liverpool for days at a time to go through everything with the departments, which were spaced out over the city. We had to bring them all together under one roof so they would all meet around the central hall and it'd be easy for people to find the departments. The whole building was planned around the idea that there had to be the shortest possible distance between individual employees who wanted to meet. The idea that actually it might have been good for everybody to go for a long walk and that it was probably better to have them spread out, got completely overlooked. I don't think it resulted in a terribly good building. I never felt quite happy with it—I don't think anybody did, in fact. Then there was a change of local government and it was thrown out, so the entire thing was wasted—or not wasted but came to nothing.

Were there other schemes you worked on with him?

Graduate housing for St John's College [Cambridge], a development of the Harvey Court stepped section.

What about Sandy's liking for courtyards, as this is something that stayed with you?

Yes, in a way that's part of historical sense. It's partly to do with collegiate courtyards and at a bigger scale it's part of the planning of urban space, buildings as containers of urban space rather than objects in landscape. Maybe it's also part of the idea that you don't have to build high. You can have quite dense housing on the ground around open space which I think Sandy, Patrick Hodgkinson and Leslie Martin were beginning to explore in their St Pancras housing, a very complex scheme of interlocking maisonettes. The first proposal for the British Library was basically a covered courtyard, and Liverpool Civic Centre contained an urban space in quite a grand way, but the St John's housing didn't—it was arranged in three linear blocks orientated to the south, which is a bit boring actually, and maybe one of the reasons why St John's didn't proceed with it. But Cambridge colleges have a habit of getting a long way with schemes and then just dropping them.

There's a convenient link here between these ideas of perimeter planning and your next move, when you went to a local authority to design housing which

… first, the pattern of needs— that is the programme; second, the appropriate pattern of the built form (which has a range of its own); and third, the technical means. These are inseparable, interacting and interlocking. The work of architecture is the 'fit' between them. And in all this there is no special need to search for expression of 'symbol'.
Sir Leslie Martin
(Martin's paradigm of architecture)

A great building must… begin with the unmeasurable and go through the measurable in the process of design but must in the end be unmeasurable.
Louis Kahn

The notion of a closed room, open to the sky, as a unit of both composition and way of life in a community's development over time, is one of the great archetypes of civilization.
Colin St John Wilson

picked up on some of these ideas. But why did you decide you wanted to leave an interesting office?

Well, I left Sandy because I had felt for some time that being back in Cambridge might be a mistake on a personal level when all my friends had moved on and most of them were based in London, so I felt I was left stranded on the beach. Apart from working in Sandy's office, there wasn't much in Cambridge except for things that reminded me of a past that had gone, so I wasn't happy there on that level and felt I had to get out. I had been discussing with Richard MacCormac for some time our intention to do some housing in a good local authority because that seemed to be something of great interest and something we were concerned about. In fact most young architects at that time felt they had a duty to contribute to local authority housing. This was a good experience and very worthwhile. Then the Merton job came up within a year of going to work for Sandy, so I thought I'd have to take it as it seemed to be what was opening up before me. Also, at Sandy's it was not possible to really take responsibility for a job because he controlled everything and if you felt you wanted to do anything different, you couldn't do it there.

At the Architects' Department of the London Borough of Merton (pp 66–67), there were three of you, Richard MacCormac, Peter Bell and you—three strong-minded, talented young students suddenly came together. How did you manage to get on and co-operate? When I asked Richard about this he said it was all a bit like a rugby game, in which each player tries to grab the ball for himself and run with it.

That may be Richard's idea of a rugby game!

Did you parcel up the work so that each of you had a different territory, or was it not that clear-cut?

We all worked on the design but Peter was the person who got things done. Richard and I would decide what we wanted, and Peter would make sure it was done. He had an incredible gift for getting his way and was an absolute master at it. God knows how he did it… humorous… he was very good at putting down with a joke people who were in opposition, so the atmosphere with him around was quite light, but very determined. Richard and I were left to design it, and I suppose we had a few arguments but basically we were both after the same thing.

What sort of thing was that? Was it a social vision or an architectural vision, or a bit of both?

A bit of both. Richard was more concerned about the social side than I was at that stage. He'd been doing work with Peter Willmott at Bethnal Green, on people's needs in new housing and how relationships were built up and that kind of thing. He felt that we ought to talk to future tenants but we weren't allowed to do that by the housing department; they told us to get on with the design. We were both aware of what

The authentic artist and architect must engage in an ideal world, architecture makes concrete an ideal view of life. And architecture is lost at the point that this vision and aspiration for an ideal is abandoned.
Juhani Pallasmaa

1: Graduate housing, St John's College, Cambridge

Lionel March had been doing in Cambridge with the perimeter development theories, and I think we were both keen to try that out, we wanted to achieve the relatively high densities required in houses on the ground—though we didn't start like that. We started with maisonette blocks on the Pains Fireworks factory site and it was only later, after we'd worked through a number of options that we found we could give every family a house on the ground with a garden and a garage. Nick Alexander joined us and he developed the Pains site using this house type.

Richard is often given credit for the perimeter idea, yet he had left Cambridge after three years and gone to the Bartlett School of Architecture. So I wasn't sure if he was still involved with the Cambridge ideas, or whether in fact they came more from you.

My memory is that I had been having lots of conversations with Lionel March. I had worked alongside him briefly at Leslie Martin's, doing the Whitehall project drawings in the winter of 1964–1965 and Lionel had talked at length about his theories about perimeter and linear development which he publicised in articles like "Homes beyond the Fringe". I had got excited by the potential of this approach, for example it could reduce the need to build much above three or four storeys. I think I told people at Merton about it, and we started investigating it, but Richard probably knew about it from reading. To begin with, we proposed maisonette blocks around the edge of both sites and then I started talking to Walter Segal about density. That was very early on. I think I rang him up and he said you can get densities in two-storey houses of 400 bed spaces per acre but it starts getting a bit intense. So we then started looking at houses and you remember that corduroy scheme that was just rows of terraces... it was at that point that Richard said to me, "Well, if that's what we're going to build, I'm not interested, I'm off." So we started trying to put them around squares and he suddenly produced the Greek key pattern in which everything seemed to work beautifully. It also coped with levels in an ingenious way. There was quite a slope on the site so each square was at a different height from the next. I think that's why he is given the credit, because he invented that plan in the final scheme and then went on afterwards to explore it further and write about it. I was just a sort of channel between Lionel and the end result.

Later on, in the mid-1970s, when the City of Birmingham decided to triple the population of Edgbaston by building in the gardens of large Edwardian houses, Barratt Homes proposed to fill up these sites with their irrational road layouts and random planning. The roads alone took up 7 per cent of the site area. I gave a talk to the local residents' association demonstrating that all the proposed houses could be placed around the perimeter on reasonably wide plots leaving enough land in the centre for allotments which would keep the residents in fruit and vegetables, or even for a dairy farm supplying 2.5 pints of milk a day to each house. This kind of study seems essential to me now in the context of transition towns and a resilient way of life in the future (p 68).

One thing that Richard said to me was that you drew scheme after scheme to explore the possibilities, something that reminded him of what he'd forgotten during his two years at the Bartlett where that kind of approach had been neglected.

But look, suppose people lived in little communities among gardens and green fields, so that you could be in the country in five minutes' walk, and had few wants, almost no furniture for instance, and no servants, and studied the (difficult) arts of enjoying life, and finding out what they really wanted: then I think one might hope civilization had really begun.
William Morris

1

2

The motive for Pollards Hill was the realization that radical housing forms, high-rise and middle-rise, had failed. In attempting to define housing criteria we continually found ourselves falling back upon those met by the terrace house and we began to realize that people's expectations of housing are inevitably formed by their experience—the identifiable house, terraced or otherwise, entered off the street and with a back garden. Therefore Pollards Hill represented a change from a revolutionary to evolutionary view of housing design.
Richard MacCormac

He used to make ingenious little models. I remember him making a tiny model he took on our trip to Finland, an interlocking thing, I think it was an artist's studio. He'd take it as a kind of passport to various offices we visited. He'd produce it and the Finnish architects would look at it, turn it around and around and ask what it was all about.

Another thing Richard said was that, of the three of you, you were the one who was particularly concerned with what the housing looked like. It's a very crisp, International Style aesthetic you used. He said he might have been more interested in a brick architecture. With hindsight, it was quite a contrast to your later schemes.

Oh, I thought we all wanted to do a crisp International Style scheme. We wanted to make a definite statement about modern architecture. We kept referring to Georgian terraces and said this was a modern version. But I do remember Richard at a later point producing a little drawing showing how it could be done in brick. I rather liked it and thought perhaps we'd got it wrong, perhaps this could be good—but then we agreed it was too late to change.

There's an interesting passage in Sarah Menin and Stephen Kite's book on Sandy Wilson where they say, "The three men attacked the housing cliché of the tall block and examined how housing could be worked onto a site in low-rise high-density configurations, citing Georgian squares as a precedent." They were referring to Sandy Wilson, Leslie Martin and Patrick Hodgkinson, but it could apply exactly to the three of you some ten years later.

Yes, indeed, that's amazing… it was an extraordinary opportunity. Merton had got themselves into a corner because they had not produced the housing they were supposed to, they hadn't fulfilled their housing quota and were going to lose the money if they didn't get them built. So they were desperate and were looking for a team of people to do it.

They obviously got the ideas from you but what about the actual detailing, the buildability of the scheme, because you were all fairly fresh from your training.

Halfway into the project we discovered they had entered into a design-and-build arrangement with Wimpey, so we were shipped off to the Wimpey office to work on details with the staff of New Zealanders and South Africans who seemed to be incredibly good and competent. They thought we didn't know a thing about construction, which we probably didn't.

But was this something you enjoyed, getting to the detail level?

Yes, I did. I didn't enjoy the working conditions there, but it was an interesting experience. We had tried to develop a cladding system with Christopher Bailey [friend from Cambridge and later Bursar at the Royal Agricultural College, Cirencester], this would be produced by his packaging firm. It was a timber-framed panel with a compressed board

1 and **2:** Pollard's Hill Housing, Merton **3:** Fredensborg Houses, Denmark (Jørn Utzon)

cladding plus a plastic gritty finish. The Wimpey staff would have nothing to do with it. They thought it was tatty and they preferred to use enamelled steel sheet, which we had to go along with. I think we were quite glad they took the responsibility. But certainly we weren't determining every detail. We were trying to make sure that the appearance of it didn't stray too far from our intentions.

So, you saw the Merton schemes through and then you....

No, I didn't see them through, as we all left before they were finished.

You left to do what?

We all left to start our own practices and work on our own. Peter Bell regretted this. He thought we should have stuck together and formed a practice, but I felt that I had things to explore, which I couldn't with Richard around because he was such a dominating personality. I was very lucky to have a job coming up at this point with a cousin of mine. Without it, I wouldn't have left so soon.

What was the scheme your cousin had in mind?

Ruth Douglass was one of those women who had worked overseas for most of their lives and she was retiring from missionary work in Africa where she ran a teachers' training college. She thought there were a lot of people in her position, particularly women, who had not married because of the slaughter of men in the two world wars. Lacking close family, they might like to have a place they could come to in their retirement where there was a community of like-minded souls. So she bought a big timber-framed medieval house in Churt, Surrey. Her idea was to convert it into flats and to build more houses in the grounds. She was a sympathetic client and was prepared to take a risk employing me. It all worked according to plan, and we converted the house into seven flats, we repaired the barn with the help of voluntary labour from various sources, and then we put in a planning application for the first five houses in the grounds (pp 69–71).

You chose timber-frame for the construction. Was this a decision you made early on, or did it come later as you began to think about the detail?

One reason was that I felt I could build it myself because of my model-making and carpentry in the past, and I knew enough about timber construction to be able to control it pretty confidently, and not be faced with awkward contractual situations where I actually knew less than the contractor, so I thought this a good way into the whole business of construction.

But arguably the houses could have been as straightforward and simple in brick, couldn't they? I'm thinking of Jørn Utzon's courtyard housing in Denmark which I think you had seen by this time—and also of the brick architecture in Cambridge you mentioned earlier. After all, brick is not exactly a complex technology! Was the fact that you could actually build the buildings yourself particularly important?

It was one aspect of it. I suppose another aspect was that I was building right next to timber-framed buildings, and it seemed appropriate to find a modern way of doing that. Yet another was that I was becoming interested in Japanese buildings and also at the same time I had been watching what Walter Segal was doing with his lightweight timber-framed construction which was rational, very well worked out, simple, and very minimal. That all appealed to me. I saw there was a similarity in methodology between Segal's work and the traditional Japanese construction where everything was standardised but at the same time had a very free kind of grid planning so each building would be different from any others, but using standardised components, and that attracted me as an idea. All these things went together, so I planned these houses as Segal-type houses using his method and virtually every detail including his sliding windows which I thought were very clever. It was a consistent way of building, and very flexible too. I liked the flexibility, the fact that you can put up a roof and then show the future residents the house without its walls and can discuss with them where they want walls and windows and partitions. It was all quite possible to build like that and you could also change it later on if things weren't right. You just unbolted and bolted together again because there were no wet trades above foundation level. It was all dry construction. And Segal was building extremely cheaply. This was a big issue: how we were going to raise money. We tried to get grants from the Housing Corporation. We went along with the plans of the Segal-type houses which were on a 2ft 2ins grid (that's 2ft with a 2ins skip dimension for the joints) and they said they couldn't provide any grants if it wasn't on a 300mm grid. We had to tell them that we could not change the grid as that would mean a completely different scheme. Ruth said let's just build one house to start with and we'll sell the lease on that and build the next one. We were lucky to find a couple of good carpenters in the village who were happy to take this on, and a very enjoyable working relationship developed with them over a number of years.

Do you think your environmental concerns played a large part, or was it more to do with building economically and cutting down wastage, rather than a wider environmental concern?

This was 1968 and it wasn't such a pressing issue until 1972 when *The Limits to Growth* was published. So in 1968 I think it was more a question of building economically, rationally and minimally. What was important was that it should be a really lovely place, so each house had its own little courtyard garden that opened out onto the main garden, and extended porches that gave a kind of cloistered feeling to it. Also important was the way plants would climb up the fences, and details like that.

The buildings were frame structures resting on pad foundations, touching the earth lightly, but was that more an economic concern rather than wanting to minimise the damage to nature?

There was that, and one only needed to dig 2ft-square footings. There was very little site disturbance, and I must have appreciated that. It was part of the Walter Segal method too, that the building just rested on the ground.

1: Sheltered Housing, Churt, Surrey, Phase 1 **2:** Japanese construction (tea-house in Tokyo)

But ironically, for old people, it was not the most sensible decision perhaps, to step up off the ground, and indeed in the later phases you did change to a concrete slab (pp 72–73). Was that to do with the stepping-up problem, or were your ideas moving on by then in terms of construction?

The concrete slab first appeared in the terrace houses, which needed to have party walls. Those party walls I thought were better done in masonry to stop sound, and since one was putting concrete footings in there it seemed silly not to join them up with a slab. That also resulted in having a more level access. We had a raised footpath to the first five houses, so you just had one step from the footpath into the house. But on the other hand, if you wanted to get from the house into the garden, you had to go down two steps. Yes, that's a problem for some older people.

When the third phase went ahead (pp 74–75), the system had developed even further and become rather unlike Segal's in the sense that it wasn't so much boards with cover-strips but bigger expanses of wall, which you plastered. By this time you'd been to Japan and presumably come back with ideas.

It was a step-by-step progression, which started with pure Segal—but with pitched roofs—then it went to the terrace of five houses which I thought were better done with masonry party walls. At that point I was looking for an alternative to the 2ft 2in grid because it didn't give you a 3ft [or 900mm] doorway. I also decided to use the full height of the volume at the centre and that resulted in a departure from Walter Segal's ideas. But it was all quite rational; it wasn't driven by aesthetics. The 900mm panels were done by laying the 600 by 1800 woodwool slabs horizontally rather than vertically and using 900mm plasterboard, so it all worked very rationally. But the next step was to get rid of the cover-strips and use a plastered finish for the infill panels. That again was a progression. The warden's house came first and in fact had stud walls within the main structural frame, but what I was after was a material which could be used in its standard sizes, like woodwool slabs, and then plastered. I eventually found a way of doing that by glueing two woodwool slabs together with a narrow gap between them. The reason for doing that was partly to do with the inspiration of my trip to Japan. I realised that it was more expressive of how the building was built to show the structure alone. I don't know that you could call it a purely aesthetic decision to do it that way. It seemed to me better because it gave us a heftier structure. The Segal structure with its 2ins wide posts was actually so lightweight that they could deflect. I felt that this really wasn't solid enough, and we should try to get back to square posts and heavier beams so that the main structure would be the primary thing.

Yes, with Segal's houses, you've always got the very wide and heavy-looking battens every board junction. These compete with the structure and the end result is very heavy. Anyway, let's talk more about aesthetics. I always feel that Segal's buildings, or at least some of them, have a certain elegance to them but actually many of them are rather clunky, especially the Lewisham houses. I've always felt

The feature that distinguishes Japanese residential architecture from any other architecture, past and present, is ORDER.
Heinrich Engel

1

We should understand that beauty is not a mysterious veil thrown over a building but a logical result of having everything in the right place.
Erik Bryggman

Every building that is treated naturally, without disguise or concealment, cannot fail to look well.
A W N Pugin

I prefer casual visual relations when built, which do not show the conscious effort.
Walter Segal

that you've been much more concerned with the look of your buildings, although you argue that the look comes from the method and the construction.

Both things are true. I *am* concerned about the way things look and the look *does* come from the method and construction. To me the two aren't separate. It *has* to look good but the method and construction have to be the structure on which it's expressed clearly and beautifully. I think it's very important not to try to prize those apart.

Yes, but there must be instances where there is competition or a clash between the two….

In what sense?

When, if you were to follow the rational line of thought, it might produce a detail which was rather awkward-looking. You know, another part of your brain says this doesn't look very nice….

… like modern timber windows, in which the frames look far too thick….

Yes, there's a reason for this, but the result….

Yes, that's the result and I detest them, so I try to design around that somehow. If we compare them with traditional sash windows, they are clumsy, to my eye anyway. The way things look has to come out of the way things are built, but I always look for something which is really clear and direct, and to my eyes harmonious.

Segal admitted that he was a "limited and pedestrian" designer, and when the Lewisham houses were finished, he rubbed his hands in delight because he had eventually achieved the architect-free elevation.

I think he was being partly tongue-in-cheek. To the extent that he was successful, I think the Lewisham houses show that. But they are fairly inelegant structures, aren't they?

There's the whole issue of self-build, where you've got a certain amount of detail that's built and designed by the owners, and this would depart from the purity of the original ideas. What are your feelings about self-build, and the control you might lose over the details, because this is incredibly important to you. As soon as people start fiddling around with your details, you get very unhappy. Yet at the same time this process allows them self-expression, which, from a Ruskin or Morris point of view, is all rather important.

I don't think Ruskin or Morris would have thought it a good idea that people, with no formal sense, should be allowed to build whatever they wanted wherever they wanted. I think they wanted a proper understanding of craft and architectural language and form, but, wearing a social hat, one must applaud the whole idea of self-build and think it's a

1: Self-build Housing, Walters Way, Honor Oak Park, Lewisham (Walter Segal) **2:** Ryoan-ji, Kyoto

very good thing. But the results one doesn't have to applaud. I've only done one self-build house and that was one of the Coates houses. The clients built it themselves but they followed the plans exactly. There's no problem with that at all. I suppose now I can say quite honestly that I like the *idea* of self-build for its social aspects but just because it's self-build doesn't necessarily make it a good building or piece of architectural design. One must surely think that all our training and experience counts for something. It reminds me of a question that arose when I drove down to South Wales with the poet RS Thomas to attend an anti-nuclear rally. Because the car was neutral ground, he was prepared to speak English with me, and he spent the journey railing against what was happening in the environment as we drove past. We had a great time condemning everything we saw. I said everyone thinks they can design and can be an architect… so what makes one person's choice better than another's? And he said "you have a right to your decision about architectural form based on your many years of training and a lifetime of consideration about these matters, and it must count for something", implying "I've been writing poetry my entire life and reckon I've a right to what I think about my poetry and the way it should be. I don't want people to come along and tell me it should be done differently".

We should talk more about Japan, because that's so important in your work. I think it's possible to look at very different buildings of yours (say, the Churt housing, Bledisloe Court at the Royal Agricultural College and the WISE building at CAT) and see a Japanese element in all of them, even though they are so different from each other. It'd be interesting to talk about this 'essence' of Japan, which pervades them. But you mentioned you'd also been struck by Wright's Usonian houses. There must be a degree of influence here, because the Usonian houses were also experiments in construction using uncut boards etc. Presumably you picked up on that—as much Wright, then, as Segal.

Yes, that's true.

Had you seen Wright's details at first hand, or was it through John Sergeant's book?

I had seen them and Wright himself illustrates them in his own book, *The Natural House*. John Sergeant's book was published later. In a Usonian house you see how it's made, like a Segal house. It's screwed together with horizontal boards and vertically placed ply boards on a 1.2m grid. The other thing that I feel is important about Wright's houses is the way they use this very simple construction to achieve amazing flowing lines and spaces in an extremely inventive way. Segal had nothing of that at all. Also the planning is brilliant, the way the hearth backs onto the kitchen which backs onto the bathroom, and the kitchen looks out over the dining table, and when you sit at the dining table you can see the fire burning. It's a marvellous spatial connection there. And the way the houses address their sites and surround their gardens, I imagine Japanese temple courtyards and precincts must have played a part in that. I think my awareness of Japanese architecture started in San Francisco, where I bought a very fine book with lovely pictures of Japanese buildings, and I remember reading a book called *The Tao*

… everything made by man's hands has a form, which must be either beautiful or ugly; beautiful if it is in accord with Nature, and helps her; ugly if it is discordant with Nature, and thwarts her; it cannot be indifferent….
William Morris

Apart from the desire to produce beautiful things, the leading passion of my life has been and is hatred of modern civilization.
William Morris

To discover wabi, one must have an eye for the beautiful, yet it is not an aesthetic understood only by the Japanese of old, but a quality that can be recognized by anyone, anywhere who is discriminating and sensitive to beauty.
Itoh Teiji

Beauty should not be displayed and pronounced but should be hidden humbly behind the surface of things, to be discovered and brought forth by the beholder himself.
Heinrich Engel

of Creativity quite early on when I first moved to London. So I was beginning to get to know more about Taoism and Zen by the time I started to read Engel's magisterial book on Japanese buildings, and then it was a couple of years after that that I went to Japan. I liked the simplicity and basic construction of its timber-framed housing. It seemed to work on so many levels in such a beautiful way, and the whole attitude to nature was very profound. There was an influential article in *Architectural Design* on the concept of *ma*, I think by Gunter Nitschke, in which he analysed the spaces of temple courtyards. Later a Japanese friend told me that *ma* also means "relationship between" as well as space. Then there's the concept of *wabi*, with its complex of meanings: perfected artlessness, voluntary poverty of means, ageing and naturalness. That was all becoming important to me. Those are the sort of qualities running through the projects you mentioned if you think you see some kind of link with Japan. But Japanese buildings are at a much more sophisticated level, a different level of achievement, which is really unmatchable because of the intensity of their vision and the skill of their craftsmanship.

You were living in London at this time [1967 to 1975] and had a few small jobs in addition to the Churt project, including the Melling vicarage which was also based on the Segal method. You might have remained and started a practice there but in fact you decided to move to the country. Why such a big change?

I always thought of London as a temporary abode and I couldn't imagine I'd spend the rest of my life there. I suppose it was a number of things. Some friends and I bought a cottage, Nant Pasgen Fawr in North Wales, and we used to go there whenever we could. I loved that. Also the investigations by Lionel March into the relationships between buildings and land started me thinking about how land is used. Taking that to Merton, then finding out the possibilities for allotments and urban farming, reading *The Limits to Growth* and early issues of *The Ecologist* magazine, all these things made me question the whole way of urban life. The commune movement was in full swing. Some idealistic people were moving back to the country and buying smallholdings and starting their 'agricultural' careers, some of them more successfully than others. All this appealed to me. I started looking for somewhere to live. I looked all over Britain and eventually found my present home at Ogoronwy in North Wales, after spending six months at John Seymour, the self-sufficiency guru's farm in Pembrokeshire where I thought I was going to learn about smallholding but in fact spent most of my time building with them. I found Ogoronwy quite by chance. It fell into my hands really, and I could spend six months renting it during the winter before buying it.

Let's just go back a step because in 1975, when you went to Japan, the purpose of your trip was actually to go to China, and I'm wondering how important that was to you. Presumably this was all part of the jigsaw of ideas….

It was very much a central part of the jigsaw. People like me were inspired by decentralist ideas and were questioning the way we organise society. Public discourse never refers to the fact that only 0.76 per cent [2012 census] of the population are employed in agriculture or that only about 0.01 per cent [about 6000 people] own 70

1: Katsura Palace, Kyoto
2: Melling vicarage
3: Snowdonia, North Wales
4: Chinese agriculture

per cent of all the land. This extreme imbalance lies at the heart of many of the social, economic and ecological problems of capitalist societies. China was doing it in a completely different way, and trying in their planning policies, as they said, to resolve the problems of the contradictions between city and country, mental and manual labour and agriculture and industry. So I thought I must find out more about this. I joined the Society for Anglo-Chinese Understanding [SACU] and we went on a study tour of communes and were there for three weeks travelling about 4000 miles up and down China. We travelled on trains and buses and could look out of the window and keep our eyes open. You could see that the general level of development was very similar throughout the country. It wasn't just a matter of being shown what people wanted us to see, although I think we knew nothing about the turmoil and violence of the Cultural Revolution, so we didn't really know what had preceded this apparent order. I remember crossing the border between Hong Kong and China and there was a total change of atmosphere from the frenetic advertising and high-pressure western way of life in Hong Kong into an absolutely peaceful rural environment where everything seemed so ordered and calm, and very beautiful. And that impression remained with me right the way through China— wonderfully tended fields, ordered crops, inter-cropping, water control….

Was this a vision, then, that you took up to North Wales in 1976?

It was certainly a vision which suggested that if the agriculture was properly managed it would be beautiful. The key to this is a countryside full of people, whereas you can drive from the north to the south of Wales and not see a single person in the fields. In China there were always communities in the fields, and that seemed to me to be the picture of harmony between people and nature, which I thought we should move towards. Although we now know something of the human cost of the Chinese experiment I have never doubted that it is possible for humanity to find appropriate social and political frameworks to bring such harmony about. There are many, but geographically limited examples of this throughout the world. This vision became the context for my work.

What part did you think the architecture would play in this vision?

At this time my focus wasn't on the architecture. I wanted to explore the land use and smallholding/agriculture side of things and thought the architecture would look after itself for a bit. But I did see it as being part of life in the country so there would be a harmonious relationship between working with our heads and our hands. I'd always wanted to spend time outside throughout my life. If the sun came out, I felt drawn outside by an irresistible force. I remember days at school doing exams, which always seemed to be timed for the most beautiful time of the year when one desperately wanted to be outside. I thought that was an incredible cruelty enacted on young people, a sort of vicious kind of restraint… I wanted to have a life where I could spend half of it at the drawing board and half in the fields and woods….

A life of small-scale farming may appear to be primitive, but in living such a life it becomes possible to contemplate the Great Way.
Masanobu Fukuoka

Wherever men have tried to imagine a perfect life, they have imagined a place where men plough and sow and reap, not a place where there are great wheels turning and great chimneys vomiting smoke.
W B Yeats

I went to the woods because I wished to live deliberately, to front only the essential facts of life, and see if I could not learn what it had to teach, and not, when I came to die, discover that I had not lived.... I wanted to live deep and suck out all the marrow of life, to live so sturdily and Spartan-like as to put to rout all that was not life.
Henry David Thoreau

You've said before how much you admired Frank Lloyd Wright's work. Was Wright's community at Taliesin in your mind when you established your home and office in North Wales?

I don't remember that. I was certainly aware of Taliesin, and of Broadacre City, his version of decentralisation, but I don't remember thinking "let's build a Taliesin" although I suppose many of the ideas are similar. But I'm not Frank Lloyd Wright and it didn't develop in that way. What I thought I wanted was a commune where things were done *well*. I visited a lot of communes which were chaotic, frankly, and always sinking to the lowest common denominator as far as caring for the place. There was much discussion at that time about what made these communities work and they always seemed to require a religious base or some kind of spiritual centre to them if they were going to flourish and last for any length of time. Otherwise people's personalities destroyed them. But once I had got to know the community living around me I began to think of the village as the larger unit, the 'commune', and to see that intentional communities often isolate themselves from the surrounding society.

What was it that you found at Ogoronwy when you arrived and how did you develop it?

Ogoronwy was the house, some outbuildings, some of which had collapsed down to ground level, and a little cottage, which needed a new roof and total refurbishment (pp 78–81). All the field walls were down, and the land had become a bit of rough grazing, part of the sheep farm surrounding it. There were five acres around the house, within a kind of fence and they could be parcelled off from the rest of the land, which was owned by the local landowner. It was those five acres I bought. We proceeded to mend the walls and do some draining and digging and put up fences and buy a few sheep and grow vegetables.

You say "we"…

That was me plus architecture students to begin with, and friends, and then assistants like you, and later, Emlyn Cullen. I also had strong links with the community based on Hoxton Hall in Shoreditch through Terence Goodfellow who was the director there. He used to bring groups of children to Ogoronwy twice a year for many years. Some of them became very attached to the place and returned year after year to help with projects like the hydro installation.

I came across a brief you'd written for yourself before you moved to Wales, which described your requirements for a place in the country. You mentioned you'd like to live in a seventeenth-century stone house and there would be buildings you could convert for use by students. So obviously students were an important part of this vision.

1: Ogoronwy, North Wales
2: Tea-break, while building the new office

Yes, I'd been doing occasional teaching at Bristol, sometimes at Cardiff, and I'd been invited to take part in the winter schools which had been started at Hull. These were all about grass-roots initiatives and different ways of organising society. So I always tried to get landuse into my projects for students. In fact, one we did at Bristol was actually a way for me to find out what was going on in our area of North Wales. The students came to live at Ogoronwy and we went around all the neighbouring farms and introduced ourselves and asked them about their farming practices and what scope there was for co-operation, and all these sorts of rather idealistic ideas.

It's interesting that you're planning to do exactly that at this very moment, nearly 40 years later, with your students at CAT, looking at the future of Porthmadog.

Yes, it's still the same kind of concern but more widely shared now….

Frances and I joined you in 1979, despite your warnings about the wet weather and the harsh reality of living conditions in a remote but beautiful corner of Britain. We all spent much of our time on the land and building the new office, and I remember how keen you were on *The One-Straw Revolution* by Masanobu Fukuoka. Rereading it recently, I thought how like you Fukuoka sounds in his writing. How realistic was it to apply his ideas to North Wales rather than Japan, or do you think he had a deeper message, about life generally?

Fukuoka's message was based on the principles of working with, rather than against, nature, and it took him 30 years of experimentation and very close observation to reach his particular farming method which was no digging, no cultivation, returning straw to the land, no composting, allowing nature to do that. The only composting was done by ducks running over the straw, their manure helped to break it down. Then he sowed the seed of the following crop into the preceding crop before it was harvested, and he also grew clover to boost the nitrogen. That was his particular system for his particular part of the world where they could grow two or three crops a year. So it was the principles that were important and many people have tried transposing those principles to other parts of the world with varying degrees of success. We tried a few of the things like spreading straw and pelleting seeds to stop birds eating them, but we very quickly got crops of weeds, and I think I personally wasn't that focused on it, because the architecture was beginning to take up more of our time. So we couldn't really spend the time it required to make his principles work in our climate. There's another thing, too. Fukuoka thought that 'do-nothing' farming would give time back to people. There's a wonderful bit in the book where he describes going into a local shrine and finding farmers of previous ages had written lots of poems and left them there, and he asked "what farmer today has time to write a poem?"

Looking back over the time you've been at Ogoronwy, nearly 40 years now, do you think you have achieved your vision?

Serve nature and all is well.
Masanobu Fukuoka

The ultimate goal of farming is not the growing of crops, but the cultivation and perfection of human beings.
Masanobu Fukuoka

Not as a long-term thing, because conditions change. I can think of a certain point when, with my wife Irene and my children when they were young, we did run a pretty productive concern here. We had the sheep, produced milk and yogurt, grew vegetables and fruit, and even wheat and rye for a short time, which are difficult to grow in this climate—they worked one year at least. So we were doing what we set out to do and Irene shared that vision too. We also shared our work in CND, the anti-nuclear waste movement and our interest in organic farming. But then when conditions changed, we split up, my office shrank to one or two and my children grew up with other interests. I went back to just a bit of vegetable growing and chopping wood. I think living in the woods and mountains of Snowdonia has had a profound effect on my outlook and given me an independence, which I might not have had if I had stayed within the London orbit. The world certainly looks different from here where nature is still powerful. This is not just to do with the effect of the landscape but also very much to do with the history and unique culture of the Welsh people. I was very fortunate to come here when an older generation of farmers was still working the land, people whose lives were still rooted in pre-industrial farming practice. They had a particular quality of quiet assurance and balance, which touched me very much. But it was not all quietness. The energy of the music and singing attracted me too, and the Welsh capacity to cut through pretence.

And all this applies to architecture too. Certain ways of designing and building are out of bounds to me. I am suspicious of formalisms and like to search for the 'is-ness' of things.

Let's talk about the architecture more. It didn't take very long for you to realise you didn't want to be involved with small back extensions and the sort of argy-bargy these jobs bring. By luck (and this of course is why we joined you) you landed a substantial job which ironically was back in England, at the Royal Agricultural College in Cirencester. How did this piece of good fortune happen?

It was through Christopher Bailey whom I had known when we were students at Cambridge where we'd had many discussions about architecture, farming and so on. When I was living in London, he had a market garden in Takeley, Essex. I did a couple of projects for him there—a development of three- to four-bedroom houses which went up to planning stage but didn't get approval (pp 76–77), and a small garden pavilion planned on a hexagonal grid like some of Wright's Usonian houses. Also I worked with him at Merton because, before that, he had been running a packaging factory. We tried to develop the low-cost cladding system using his packaging material, which we have already spoken about. Then, when he became Bursar at the Royal Agricultural College and needed buildings designed, I was a natural person for him to turn to because I was the architect he knew best, and he knew of my work at Merton and Churt.

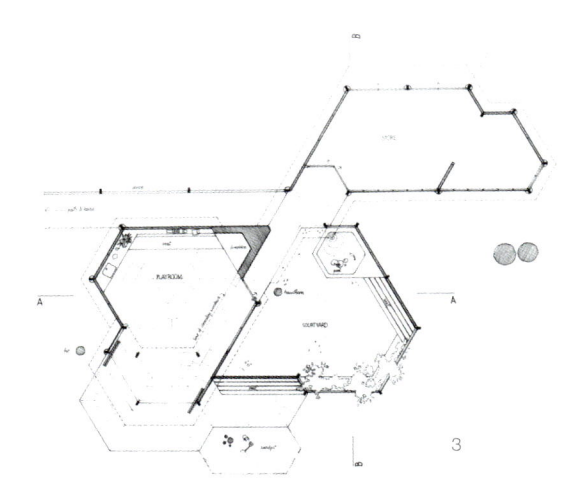

I know, from talking with Christopher Bailey, that he was quite nervous taking on someone like you in a bastion of conservatism. You hadn't built much, you would be at some distance from the job and your political/social persuasions might ruffle a few college feathers. On the other hand, he admired your thorough and committed

1: Ogoronwy in the snow
2: Fireplace in the new office
3: Takeley garden pavilion
4: Westwood Manor, Wiltshire

approach and thought your lack of track-record meant you didn't have a set approach or office style. Were you nervous too?

I think it was a big risk for him. We were let in very gently by having various small tasks to do before we embarked on the bigger buildings, so I don't remember being particularly nervous about it. I thought we could do it.

It's amazing that Bailey could come just to you, and not go out to competitive tender and all that sort of business.

They were completely different times. He introduced us to the staff and governors, we stopped their machinery block roof leaking, then they asked us to extend the library (pp 84–85). We did it in a very thorough way, interviewing everyone and then we presented our proposals to the governors who seemed to be half asleep. They just passed them, with very few questions. Their line was that they employed the bursar to handle these things. It was a completely different set-up then and we wouldn't get anywhere near the job today.

I remember that the library extension almost designed itself but when we designed Bledisloe Court [the first phase of student housing] (pp 82–83), it all became much more complex. Naively I had imagined we'd put Segal-method student chalets in the college woods—maybe we did even consider this—but the final design was entirely different, a very solid traditional building in Cotswold vernacular style, totally alien to your Merton way of thinking and your modernist training. How do you account for this?

That's a very interesting question, and I'm trying to remember how I started on it. I think to begin with I was open-minded about what it might be, but while we were working on the library, I was travelling around the Cotswolds looking at the buildings there, and those wonderfully homogeneous buildings started to exert their power—the basic simplicity of doing everything with stone—stone walls, stone window frames, stone roofs. I remember searching for precedents, which might indicate a very simple basic way of using that architectural language.

The houses at Bibury were important, weren't they?

Yes, and then there was also Alec Clifton-Taylor's *The Pattern of English Building*. I went to see one of his examples, Westwood Manor in Wiltshire, which had very simple details and rendered walls. That was a big influence because we couldn't afford to build walls of stone at the college and indeed there was a sort of moral/ethical question here about using fake or real materials. That particular building was a key to this because I could see that the actual wall material didn't matter so much if it was rendered. Many of my buildings are rendered because they are built of materials you can't expose to the weather. This, as I now see it, is a kind of fudge, which we could talk about later. Thinking about modernist alternatives we went to see Ted Cullinan's conference centre at Minster Lovell, with its roofs of Cotswold stone tiles. There was something I didn't like about it. By cutting up the roofs it looked as if he was straining to make his building

1

Try to get the most out of your material, but always in such a way as honours it most. Not only should it be obvious what your material is, but something should be done with it which is specially natural to it, something that could not be done with any other.
William Morris

different, suggesting that maybe Modernism resided in that difference. That sort of thing always made me feel uneasy. I thought, why not just accept one of the chief glories of Cotswold buildings, which is the magnificent roofs? And since we had concluded that the roof was the key, we found an old mason, Bill Berry, who said he could open a quarry and provide stone tiles for the roofs at reasonable cost, and they'd last longer than any concrete imitation.

The whole question of 'authenticity' was critical, I recall. There was tremendous pressure to roof the building with mock-stone tiles and build the walls with reconstituted blocks, yet you were adamant about using natural local materials, and being honest. How did that battle get won?

I thought that was a key question about materials. We went to a factory that made imitation products and it showed how fake they are. In fact, the more realistic they become, the worse the lie is. It seemed ethically unacceptable, and I couldn't see that that was a way forward, so we *had* to win that battle, or else change the material and use something quite different. The genuine stone tiles weren't actually that much more expensive. Bill was very economical. He worked with his family and did everything by hand except for a little digger for removing the overburden above the stones, which you could see sticking out of the sides of the railway embankment. He started his quarry right there on the line of the old railway, which ran to the east of Cirencester, so it was a very short distance to bring them to the site. And he used everything he brought out of the ground, because it's all graded from small to large. At that time we supposed, and everybody said, they'd outlast concrete tiles by a century because concrete tiles would grow brittle over time and would lose their colour. So there was quite a lot of argument against using those imitation materials.

There is a delicious juxtaposition between old Mr Berry and his family digging these things out of the field, and the nylon golf tees he suggested for fixing the tiles.

His argument was sound. He drove an up-to-the-minute Jaguar and said you just have the best piece of kit for whatever job you're doing. If you want to have a good roof, you get a good stone tile; if you want to hold it with something that will last, you use a nylon peg; if you want to drive around, you have the best car you can get…. That was an interesting sort of philosophy.

Berry made Christopher Bailey nervous because he would never sign a contract and would never guarantee anything.

Actually Chris did outface him on one occasion. He stood there with the contract and said, "Okay, if you don't sign this, you don't get paid". So in the end Berry did sign it, but he had already started the work by then.

The planners liked the building, so did the college governors and so did Prince Charles, who praised Bledisloe Court in his TV programme and subsequent book. How do you feel about this stamp of royal approval?

I feel very uneasy about it. What I did like about Prince Charles was his holistic vision, that things like food, health, the environment are all inter-related, and this was something that people who were at the receiving end of his criticism often didn't appreciate fully. But his knowledge of architecture and his appreciation of the gains of Modernism — well, he didn't know anything about that, and he wasn't really prepared to learn. So he developed his name-calling method of architectural criticism and he did a lot of damage. By lumping together the work of very good, sincere architects with that of commercial developers, he actually put back the cause of good modern architecture. So I didn't like his attention for those reasons. But there's another reason too: the way he interfered with architectural competitions like the one for the National Gallery and overrode the democratic process for making these decisions. That's bad for the political life of Britain. People should be allowed to say what they think about proposals, but he used his position of power in a very undemocratic way.

At around the same time, you entered a competition for Pembroke College, Oxford (pp 86–87). Your scheme was in the same vein as the Bledisloe building and Peter Blundell Jones, who liked your scheme the best out of 16 entries, called it a "timeless proposal". Did you set out to achieve "timelessness" or do you think this isn't a meaningful concept in architecture?

Is it a question of style, or of essence? If the word is applied to lasting values like serenity, durability, naturalness, the harmonious relationship to nature and so on, then that sort of timelessness has a profound meaning. But if a building is called timeless because it's just referring to something in the past, then that's of no interest to me.

What do you think Peter Blundell Jones meant?

It's a mixture, because there were definitely elements of the Pembroke scheme which could have been built at any time since the Middle Ages, but underlying that I hope there were the more fundamental essential aspects of timelessness. I suspect that people say it's timeless when the first thing they latch onto is the fact that it's a traditional looking building and has pitched roofs and small windows and so on, but I would hope that they would look behind that.

I think that Peter was making this comment in the context of the other entries and also because he knew you and your work. I think you could apply what you've just said to some of the other entries. One of the competition requirements was that every scheme should have a traditional quadrangle. The entry by Joanna van Heyningen and Birkin Haward, for instance, was one huge quadrangle, with a clock tower, pitched roofs, dormer windows, chimneys and so on. Stylistically it perhaps looked back rather than forwards but I wouldn't call that scheme 'timeless' and I'm sure Peter wouldn't

Simplicity, sincerity, repose, directness and frankness are moral qualities as essential to good architecture as to good men.
C F A Voysey

either, so there must have been something else in your building that he identified as being timeless. Probably that was to do with him knowing about your approach.

He said that everything in my scheme was in the right place, and the sequence of courtyards….

But again that could apply to the other schemes…. I think maybe it's to do with the values he recognised in your approach to building. "Arts and Crafts" is a term he has used when describing some of your projects, including the Coates houses you did at the same time. It's not just that the buildings look a bit like Voysey or Baillie Scott, but they're built traditionally and honestly of natural materials, many of them won from the locality (like the specially quarried roof tiles for Bledisloe), there's an emphasis on craftsmanship and the way buildings are put together, and somehow they conjure up a flavour of Morris and his times. How do you react to this? Do you see yourself continuing the Arts and Crafts tradition?

The starting point for me was the vernacular way of building. That's what kicked off this particular architectural language, especially in the Cotswolds, and also at Churt where we were building in the grounds of a medieval barn. Perhaps one could say that some of the results were superficially similar to those of the Arts and Crafts architects. I was certainly conscious of the Arts and Crafts movement at Cambridge; we had lectures on the English Free School and we looked at buildings by Norman Shaw and so on. But I didn't set out to do things in the Arts and Crafts style. You referred to local materials, but actually there were very few materials which were from the locality. The stone tiles were, but generally the timber came from elsewhere and the sands and aggregates for the roughcast came from Dorset and the Thames valley. The Coates houses were built of aerated concrete blocks, rendered, and had Glulam beams. I was searching for a simple way of building, in single-skin rather than cavity construction with all its ties, damp-proof courses and problems of filling up with mortar. The timber for the structural frame to the veranda and for all the joinery was pitch-pine from demolitions, supplied by Jeremy Nelson. It had already had one existence in the forests of North America and another in the mills of the Industrial Revolution. I suppose that the pitched roofs could be seen as a reference to Arts and Crafts, but then there's the Japanese influence with the big windows facing the gardens. There's quite a complex mixture of influences there.

Say something more about the Coates walled garden scheme, which I think is one of your best (pp 88–91).

There was a continuity between it and the scheme I did for Christopher Bailey at Takeley before he became bursar at the college (pp 76–77). Both schemes comprised three- or four-bedroom houses, all of which had rather generous south-facing windows onto gardens, a lower single-storey block at right-angles to the main two-storey block, and clay tiled roofs. The Takeley houses, with their double-height south-facing loggias were certainly influenced by Japanese buildings but also by the farmhouses of the Feltrino in northern Italy although they were to be built with English-looking materials, brick with

1: Tea-house, Katsura Palace, Kyoto **2:** Interior (Baillie Scott) **3:** House near Feltri, north Italy **4:** Plan of Usonian house (Frank Lloyd Wright) **5:** Magdalen College, Oxford

pantiled roofs and quite large areas of glazing. The Coates houses took on a similar typology. I was studying Frank Lloyd Wright's Usonian house plans at the time, where the house is backed up against the north wall of the plot, closed to the north and open to the south, looking out onto the largest possible garden. Each of my houses was different but had identical details and identical sections, a two-storey section and a single-storey section. The single-storey section could be used in various ways, as a granny flat or an extra bedroom or a playroom. The south was fully glazed; a veranda that could be opened up to the garden when the weather was good. The relationship of the spaces downstairs was similar to the archetypal arrangement of the Usonian house where the kitchen backs onto the fireplace and the dining table is in a kind of spiral relationship between the kitchen, the dining and the sitting area around the hearth. Arts and Crafts houses were often planned as a series of rooms off a gallery so that all the major rooms could open to a garden or the sun. Wright must have been aware of this through his own friends in the movement, but his planning and use of grids was always much more sophisticated.

I guess you might be thinking of Baillie Scott's houses.

I became aware of his plans sometime later. He liked to cluster spaces for various activities around a 'great hall' where the family could meet and eat, and this was the first space into which the visitor was welcomed. My little timber-framed Gwynedd House was an exploration of that theme with its tiny private spaces surrounding a relatively large, top-lit hall for the family (pp 92–93). But to return to the Arts and Crafts at a general level, even though I enjoyed all these strands of thought and design, the most enduring influence was certainly the political stance of William Morris. You can't read his analysis of the inevitability of the destruction of craftwork by global capitalism and still think that a general return to Arts and Crafts methods is anything but a delusion. And of course this calls into question the whole matter of appropriate architectural language. This political/aesthetic question also propelled me to look for the essence of things, an essence which is different from minimalism.

How would you explain to a layman the subtle difference in architectural language between your Bledisloe building and, say, Porphyrios's work at Magdalen College, Oxford or even Quinlan Terry's at Downing College, Cambridge?

Those buildings take on all the trappings of the past style they are building in. For instance, the Porphyrios building (which incidentally is incredibly well built, with beautiful stonework I'm very envious of) has medieval profiles for the wall copings, string courses and windows, quite complex ones. The Terry buildings are neoclassical. My approach was completely opposite to theirs. It was to strip away all the details, to arrive at an essential building form.

But you could argue that drip mouldings are there for a functional reason.

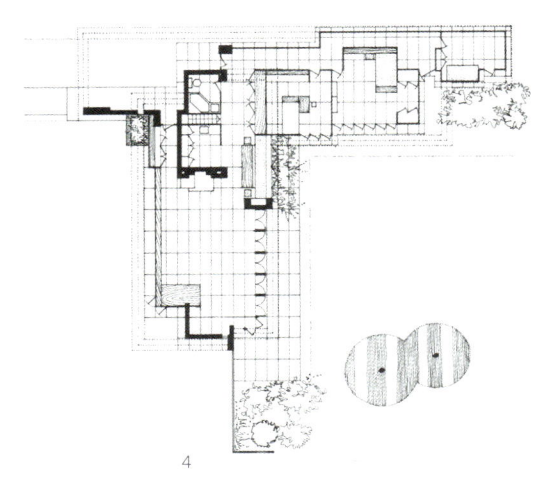

My own buildings, I wanted to have the basic qualities of the best old houses of their locality, built in the local traditional way in the local materials, but not copying the details which properly belong to the period in which they were built. By working on these lines I hoped that my buildings would at least have good manners and be able to take their natural place in their surrounds without offence.
Norman Jewson

I see simplicity not so much as a disregard for complexity, but as the clarification of the significant.
Glenn Murcutt

Yes, that's so, but the way it's done has come to be a stylistic trigger. The mouldings may be there for a functional reason but they're done in a certain way which takes on a style, neo-Gothic or neoclassical or whatever. My intention was always the opposite, to get back to the essential components while using vernacular forms and proportions. There are two main aspects to this. One is the roof, the other the holes in the walls, which signal whether they are medieval or classical or modern. If they're generally vertical but separated by mullions, they give a medieval feel. If they're vertical, single openings in a wall, they suggest neoclassicism. If they're horizontal windows, which require a big lintel above, maybe steel or concrete, then they look more modernist. Those are basic associations you make when you see a hole in a wall, to my mind anyway. All the many 1:50 elevations I drew for Bledisloe were my attempt to understand the implications of this, and also to meditate on the proportions of the openings.

This is interesting because one of the chief differences between the Bledisloe building and Coad Court [the later phase of student housing at the college] was the treatment of the windows. At Bledisloe each window was a series of narrow openings in the masonry which is what made them look a bit medieval, but when you moved on to the Coad building, the windows became big rectangular openings with a framework of oak mullions within, which still divided the window into opening and fixed panes but gave a more modern effect. By then you were already moving forward in your architectural language. You were beginning to get bored, may I suggest, with pitched roofs and dormers.

The basic idea for Coad Court came out of the Pembroke College competition—a very narrow block with a straight staircase serving two bedrooms on the ground floor and two upstairs, and with very economical circulation. The intention was to have no rooms in the roof, which I had come to dislike because they were awkward and had to have dormers. But we were forced by the client to have some rooms up there because he wanted to increase the number of bedrooms. But basically it was a very simple block with a clear, uninterrupted roof. That was the underlying geometry of the scheme. I did know I was walking on a knife-edge in terms of architectural language, but by going back to traditional forms, I thought I was clearing the decks for a new sort of integration of the past, because in many ways modernist forms didn't seem to me to be appropriate for those situations I was building in. I suppose I've come to think of the farming community as being an unseen critic of what I was doing. As I got to know more about living in the countryside, things had to work in a really practical way. Why not continue to build using tried and tested forms of building, but to develop them so that their real essence comes out? It's nothing to do with this or that style.

Let's talk about competitions now. Pembroke was the first competition you entered, followed by many more over the next 15 years. What is striking is that not one of them got built, though a few came near. Is there one common cause for this, or were there different circumstances attached to each?

1: Harvey Court, Cambridge (Leslie Martin and Colin St John Wilson)

They were all competitions by invitation, so we were always part of a small group of competing architects. They were not always design competitions; sometimes they were competitive interviews. There were different reasons for them going ahead or not. I won the ones for King's and Robinson Colleges and for the Hillier Gardens visitor's centre, also for Slaidburn Community Centre, and was runner-up in the one for Gonville and Caius College. In the case of King's we reached detailed planning stage but the college dropped it. They decided not to go ahead with my development on the site at that time. They had a history of doing this. Richard MacCormac had already done a project for a library, and for housing on the same site, and before him somebody else had done a similar project. In the case of Robinson there was a change of bursar mid-stream and the new bursar decided they didn't want graduate housing, at least not of that type at that time, so they also dropped it (pp 110–111). In the case of Caius, nothing was built on the main site and a different building was built on an adjacent site.

Which of the college schemes is your favourite?

I was pleased with an early one for Darwin (p 94). It was a little library, with a flat for a tutor. I thought it could have been a very engaging building in the way it addressed the river. I liked the relationship of the spaces within it, the library and the study spaces, and the access into the library from the riverside walk with its long window seat and low, sheltering eaves. I also liked the Caius scheme (pp 104–105). The proposed site was in the gardens behind Harvey Court. I used a similar section to the Pembroke scheme but strung the rooms out in long terraces threading around the existing gardens and between the magnificent houses on the site. The starting point was the way it addressed Harvey Court.

There's something rather nice about you designing what was almost an extension of Harvey Court and linking back to Leslie Martin, Sandy Wilson and your Cambridge student days.

I've always had a great admiration for Harvey Court—for its consistency, its very simple geometry, the access pattern to the rooms and also its nobility. It was really a privilege to design within that context. I went to see Leslie before submitting the proposal and he showed me the original intention for expanding Harvey Court into a number of courtyards which would grow out of the free-standing block on the south side of it, and presumably proliferate all over the site….

… and Cambridge too!

Yes, but my scheme was rather different. It was lower-key, a two-storey construction with a colonnade which referred back to the brick piers of Harvey Court and provided a covered way linking all parts of the site. There were people who pushed for our scheme quite strongly but unfortunately the bursar had decided that Arup Associates should get the job, and as so often happens with College committees which lack the determination to drive through a properly considered long-term programme, apart from the relatively small and somewhat bizarre Hawking building by Donald Insall Associates on West Road, they have yet to build anything there!

Can we talk about the last competition scheme you did at Cambridge, for Magdalene College? (pp 128–129) I felt it was the least good of your schemes for a number of reasons. One was to do with the rather rigid planning, very much based on Harvey Court, a tight courtyard with a blank exterior even blanker than Harvey Court's. I know that there was a difficult brief which included fitting a large sports hall somewhere on the site, and you sunk this beneath your courtyard, but I felt that things like the entrance lobby were not as well considered as in your other schemes, nor was the lower circulation passage, which didn't have windows because you wanted a blank exterior [the upper passage had roof-lighting]. Are these fair comments?

Yes, maybe—some details would certainly have been developed if we'd got the job. But the essence of the scheme I did actually like very much, partly because of its parallel with Harvey Court, as you point out. Also the brick elevations of Magdalene College towards the river and the First Court have always been one of my favourite set pieces in Cambridge. It's extremely simple brickwork and I saw my scheme as a kind of modernist equivalent and a continuation of the new brick language started by Leslie and Sandy. The key question was the relationship between the new court and the fellows' garden across the road, which involved finding some way to cross the road [this was a requirement of the brief]. It's a very busy road, so the obvious thing was to go underneath it. The way you would come out of the garden, go under the road and then up the steps within a portico which looked back to the fellows' garden from a higher level… and the transition between the world of the road and the quiet of the courtyard which could have been disguised by the sound of water falling from a pool in the courtyard… I liked all that, and the fact that the courtyard was the distributor, which seemed to me to work better than at Harvey Court. The courtyard would be lively as a result of this.

Sandy Wilson said, "The notion of a closed room, open to the sky, as a unit of both composition and way of life in the community's development over time is one of the great archetypes of civilization." This embodiment of a community of people, monastic cloisters, a simple restrained, even Spartan, lifestyle—these are things that have always attracted you. Could you have been a monk in another life?

Possibly—but I would miss the companionship of women.

More seriously, say something about the attraction that courtyards have for you.

I started thinking about them in the Churt scheme, when I explored the history of gardens—enclosed gardens, gardens in the desert, Islamic gardens, where you're enclosing a bit of the world which then becomes a paradise, particularly in a harsh climate. The development of courtyards in monasteries also came out of the defensive need against a potentially hostile world outside. Certainly nowadays, when so much of the public world is invaded by roads and cars, to find a sort of oasis of calm in a

1: First Court, Magdalene College, Cambridge **2:** Clare Hall, Cambridge (Ralph Erskine)

courtyard is a rather nice thing. I was very struck by this when I lived in London and used to go out at weekends and explore gardens like Sissinghurst. They're basically courtyard gardens with externally enclosed rooms open to the sky, and they are wonderful places. Even coming down to the present, and doing the courtyard of rooms at CAT, which is both enclosed and open to the landscape beyond…. The courtyard becomes a very lively place when those rooms are inhabited, particularly on fine days when all the windows are open and the students can talk to each other from various levels and get out into the courtyard. It's a lively representation of the community.

Whenever I go back to Cambridge and see all the new buildings, I feel it's a bit like a zoo exhibiting an example of each well-known architect's work. Had one of your schemes gone ahead, do you think it would have been a new and different species?

I hope that it would have represented continuity with the past, but in an architectural language appropriate for the times we live in, times which require us to build responsibly, to use as little energy and produce as little carbon as we can. I am very unimpressed by claims that a building made entirely of concrete, metals and glass can be a genuinely low carbon building, however little energy input it needs. You use the image of the zoo—haven't all these 'animals' evolved to fill a niche in the ecology of styles? They represent a kind of cultural fragmentation and they seldom relate to the environment they are placed in. This kind of approach quickly degenerates into the production of 'icons' and the pre-existing context is treated with contempt, with everyone trying to do something different.

So what do you think about Ralph Erskine's Clare Hall, say, which *is* different yet is a very civilized place.

I like it very much. I remember that the social spaces in particular have a civilized and democratic atmosphere, which reminds me of the Scandinavian buildings I visited in the 1950s–1960s. It is not over-bearing in any way, or formally rigid.

What about the competition system as a whole? I wonder what you feel about working up a scheme without the close involvement of a client that you get once a job becomes real.

Basically I feel it's a lousy system, but it has some advantages if it's run properly and allows young practices to break into more complex work. I think this happens in other countries more than in Britain. Maybe if it was run according to the RIBA competition rules it would be a good, or at least a better, system. There are a number of issues here. First, it encourages clients to avoid doing a lot of homework because they can just summon a group of people to present ideas to them and then they can pick and choose. If they were going to do it properly, they would select a number of architects and visit their projects. They would decide which one they wanted on a rational basis, and then work up the scheme with them from the beginning. That would be the ideal arrangement. Competitions are a way of exploiting architects. On the part of architects

We need an architecture that rejects momentariness, speed and fashion; instead of accelerating change and a sense of uncertainty architecture must slow down our experience of reality in order to create an experiential background for grasping and understanding change. Instead of current obsession with novelty, architecture must acknowledge and respond to the bio-cultural and archaic dimensions of the human psyche.
Juhani Pallasmaa

The beginning of any work must start from Belief… I distrust competitions because the design is unlikely to stem from Belief which is of religious essence out of a commonness sensed from other men.
Louis Kahn

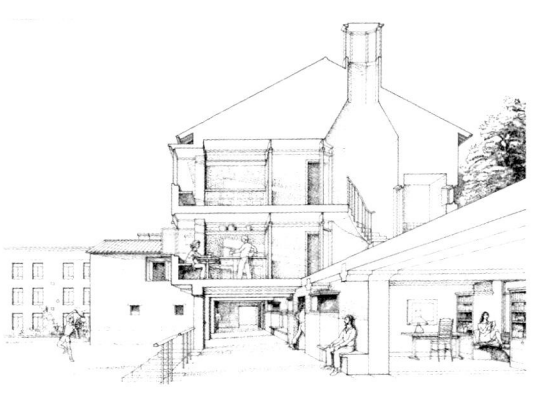

it's prostituting our talents. In the hope of getting work, we are prepared to do all this stuff, often for nothing and always for much less than it costs us. A further issue is that you never know what the basis for the decision is. In one case, a committee member told me that after the last person had done their presentation the chairman said, "Okay, which one do we like? Let's go round the room." They made the decision on that basis, with very little discussion so there was no way that they could summarise the reasons for their selection. This should be part of the feedback to the architects so they can learn from it for the next competition.

I'd like to return to two of your Cambridge schemes, for King's and Caius. There's a hint of Italy in both, as indeed there is in your proposals for a visitor centre at Wakehurst Place and the house at Stourton in Wiltshire. Is this hint engendered by an interest in the formal qualities of Roman and Greek architecture, or is it more to do with the sunny climate you hanker after?

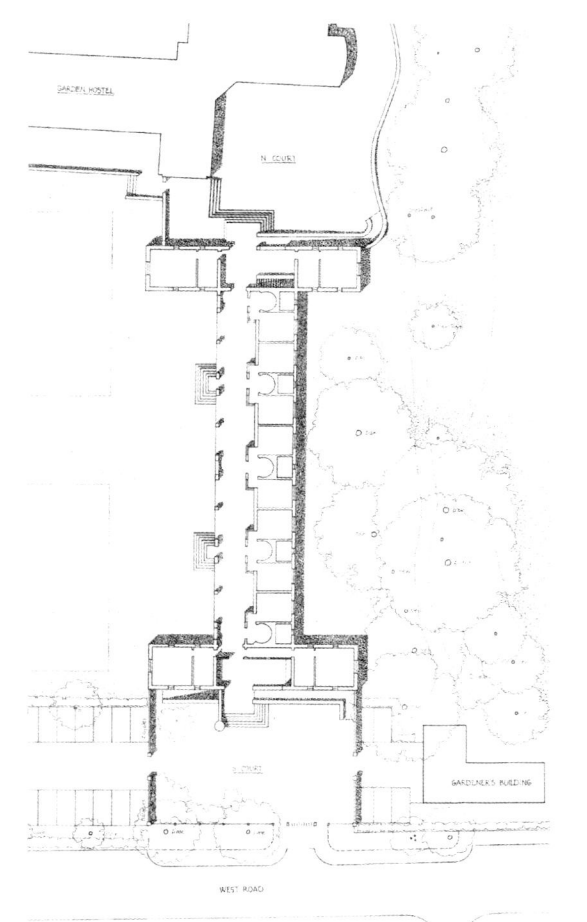

To start with King's, I think the driving force there was the fact that the college was my first client who had an environmental agenda actually written into the brief. I've always been more interested in the effect that's going to have on planning, materials and construction than on the energy cost of running a building because it will directly affect the form. Of course, as buildings get more and more efficient from the point of view of energy use, a higher proportion of the energy involved in buildings goes into the construction and materials. I took the King's brief to mean that one should use materials with low embodied energy as far as possible. I thought it'd be interesting to push that by not using concrete and steel, and so I attempted to design a building entirely in compression. To begin with it just had brick cross-walls and low-pitched brick vaults over the rooms on each floor, and that produced a force at the two ends of the building which had to be buttressed in some way and led me towards having those cross wings at each end. Then of course we were building in the grounds of the Garden Hostel which was a stripped-down classical building, and across the road was Harvey Court, so the context also pushed me in the direction of using brick. Then I thought about the roof. At that time I was turning to low-pitched roofs, partly because if you pitched a roof rather high there was the question of whether you had rooms in it or not, and that always got rather complicated.

There was also Giles Gilbert Scott's University Library nearby, with its pantiles and the slightly Italian flavour to its detailing. Your elevations make the scheme the most Mannerist you've ever done. They're almost Schinkelesque. Surely it's much more than just expressing brick in compression, which Kahn does very simply, after all. There seems to be something more going on.

I'm trying to think back now… I was very taken with Schinkel's Gardener's House at Charlottenhof, and his wonderful drawings. It seemed to me we could do a stripped-down equivalent, though Schinkel's is pretty stripped down itself. You know the way it opens at the end of the gable of the Gardener's House, and the roof's propped on very simple piers. Although we didn't do that for our final design, there were versions which

1: King's College: entrance elevation
2: Cross-sectional perspective
3: Plan **4:** Gardener's House, Potsdam (Karl Friedrich Schinkel)

explored that possibility. Actually, it wasn't a very satisfactory building and it's not one that I have ever liked very much. It was a kind of transitional building between the more vernacular-orientated ones and those that came after.

What about your proposal for the visitor building at Wakehurst Place? There's certainly a Roman influence here and you actually called part of the building a propylaeum. Did the site suggest this? (pp 106–107)

It's quite a drive to get there. There's lots of noise and the busyness of the road, and then you go from there into Wakehurst Place grounds and arboretum. I felt that one needed to make a long transition space between the car arrival and the quiet woodland. That inspired the rather grandiose entrance building, which doesn't have any function other than to make you pause and move slowly across the transition. That kind of linear portico is interesting; it's very strong axially along its length, but at right angles to it you get very generous openings. I also thought of it as a bridge over a stream, which did exist as far as I remember. As you crossed this space you looked down the valley to your left and on the other side the space was held by the semicircular shop. The roof structure of the entrance building was in the form of a bridge, two bow-string trusses leaning together to give a pitched roof above. The natural form for the semicircular shop was a mono-pitch roof facing the centre of the amphitheatre. As the forms developed, I felt they had these classical precedents.

Your project for a house at Stourton in Wiltshire was near Stourhead (pp 108–109). Was that in your mind?

It's a very classical landscape there, of course, and I was certainly thinking more 'southwards' at that time. The form of the house was basically a big wall made of a warm, pinky-orange brick, looking as if it had been there for ever. A kind of loggia leant against it, which was quite Tuscan in feeling. Its mono-pitch roof gave me a lot of trouble; I had always preferred rooms with dual-pitch ceilings as they feel centred. If you were going to take the space up into the roof, you'd see the pitch running down the centre of the room and it would feel balanced and calm. Whereas a mono-pitch, if you're moving down its length, is unbalanced and shoves you off to the low side. So it's most important that you approach the room at right-angles to its long axis, and then the descending roof concentrates your attention on the view.

Talking of sunny climates, do you think the wet Welsh weather has had an effect on your designing?

It has made me go first for pitched roofs rather than flat ones. As Walter Segal used to say, with a pitched roof you'd never have any trouble, and there's always this kind of response from clients, that flat roofs leak. And daylight and sunshine are absolutely essential to architecture, of course. In a gloomy climate like North Wales, it's very important to have good top light because you get two to three times as much light from the open sky as you do from a window (depending on what you're looking out onto, of course).

1
2

So I've always tried to get top light into my buildings since doing the library extension at the Royal Agricultural College where we had those strips of skylights along the top of the walls. You get a wonderful quality of light off a wall, which has a window directly above it without any space between the window and the wall. You get a glare-free light and it's surprising how much quite small openings can illuminate a room. We used that principle a lot in the WISE building at the Centre for Alternative Technology.

From the late 1990s your projects seem to become more modernist. Double-pitch sloping roofs become mono-pitch roofs, perhaps leaning against a wall as at Wakehurst, the Stourton house and your Robinson College scheme, and then these in turn become flat roofs with thin, overhanging eaves. I'm thinking here of one of my favourite schemes, your visitor centre for the Sir Harold Hillier Gardens in Hampshire (pp 118–121). It's almost as if you are returning to your early Cambridge days. Did you rediscover something in Modernism which you had forgotten in the intervening years?

I did, but it was a step-by-step process. The first scheme for the Hillier's visitor centre competition had a series of parallel pitched and vaulted roofs directly inspired by Kahn's magnificent Kimbell Art Museum which I have studied carefully though I have never been there. Also it seemed to have echoes of industrial ways of covering very wide spaces with a series of parallel roofs. The programme forced us to have quite wide spaces, which wouldn't have been easily covered with single roofs, so it ended up as a series of parallel bays. But even that was constricting. So one day I wondered what would happen if we had a flat roof. That was a tremendously liberating moment, and it was really a rediscovery of what I'd been through earlier on in my career. I had ignored up to that point how much a pitched roof defines the plan and how very difficult it is to escape from that.

I think it was you rather than Richard MacCormac who talked about the "tyranny of the pitched roof".

Yes, I'm sure it was me. With a flat roof, you can push the plan out in all directions and the building can be quite discursive. This was also coupled with my rediscovery of the Barcelona Pavilion and the wonderfully free placement of walls in relation to the column grid. This grid is a sort of field of measurement which could in theory be extended infinitely and you just select part of that field to enclose with walls. I started replanning the building on that basis and did a very simple model which seemed to encapsulate the freedom that I'd re-discovered. Then came the question of how the roof was made. Flat roofs do not give a very good fifth elevation if you look down from above. Normally this doesn't matter because you'd only see this from an aeroplane. But if you think of a city of flat-roof buildings and compare it with a medieval or Renaissance city with its dynamic roofscape, the fifth elevation, the roof, is generally awful unless you can walk out onto gardens and terraces. At Hillier's it wasn't really an issue as the building was on top of a rise and you couldn't overlook the roof from anywhere, but all the same… well, you know, they say God sees these things. It was very important that the roof would be as beautiful as the rest of the building so, with Tom Miller who was working with me at that time, I devised a

1: Library extension, the Royal Agricultural College, Cirencester **2:** Kimbell Art Museum, Texas (Louis Kahn) **3:** Barragán House, Calle Ramírez 14, Mexico City, 1947–1948, (Luis Barragán) Photo: Armando Salas Portugal

kind of ridge and valley system of stainless steel roofing, with 1.2m wide ridges draining into valleys or perimeter gutters. Phil Cooper, the structural engineer who'd worked on the Cambridge projects, rose to the challenge of designing this roof with its timber cantilevers. This involved beams, which had to thread through each other and devices for post-tensioning the cantilevers to get them just right. Maybe this was an example of a steel building form, which we were trying to do in timber — a theme we can return to.

Ekkehard Weisner worked with you on this scheme. When I chatted with him, he said he thought his job had been rather marginal. But what he did remember was supplying you with lots of nice pictures of gardens and courtyards. He also mentioned Luis Barragán's own house in Mexico, where there's this amazing wall that goes from inside to outside with a very minimal glazed junction between the two.

Yes, Ekkehard is a wonderful person to bounce ideas off, and he is a very good critic. As you say, he had an apparently bottomless fund of beautiful books and pictures. It was he who introduced me to Barragán and that wonderful picture of his house, which I now always use in lectures to illustrate the idea of connection between inside and outside space.

… which is harder and harder to achieve nowadays, what with thermal insulation, cold-bridging and so on….

… even at the simple level of a 4mm thick piece of glass going into a wall when it is just a line, but if it's double-glazed you get the spacer bar and everything, and it starts looking much cruder, and the essential clarity disappears.

Did Ekkehard have a hand in the design of the Hillier's project, or was his job more just commenting and feeding you with ideas?

Ekkehard certainly had a hand in it. He insisted on imagining what the space would be really like, what it'd be like to sit there or to look out of the window, or what sort of corner one would feel most comfortable in. He was very sensitive to those things and if my proposal was becoming too abstract, he'd want to know exactly what that space would feel like.

Perhaps Modernism comes at a price, though, particularly when it's adopted as an architectural language in a rural, conservative context. Your scheme for a community centre in rural Lancashire ran into problems because of its modernity — the locals simply didn't like its appearance. Had it been rural Switzerland or Scandinavia, I doubt this would have been an issue but Britain is more conservative. Do you think you were needlessly uncompromising at Slaidburn? (pp 130–131)

That was a very sad story. We had a wonderful client who apparently had complete faith in us (I did this project with Pat Borer). He was a benefactor to the village, had lots of money and wanted to put it at the service of the village as long as we did what

1

the village wanted. We went through exhaustive Planning for Real sessions with all the various groups, the school, the church, everybody in fact, over two or three days, and, as usually happens with the Planning for Real process, they changed our initial ideas and greatly helped us to plan the project. We intended to use their fine local sandstone in the form of ashlar blocks for the external walls. It was quite a wide building, on a tight site, so its plan was basically a block cut away in places. Because it's so wide it wasn't appropriate to give it a pitched roof. When we presented the design, it split the village in two. There were the people who were going to use it as a home for their various groups, the school, the doctor, and all the rest of the professional side of the village, who were for it, and then there were various tenants who were under the thumb of the local landowner who had taken against it in a big way and blocked it. Two points were at stake, both non-negotiable as far as the opposition was concerned—the building had to have a slate pitched roof and walls of random rubble. It became impossible for the client to go to the local pub because he'd be the focus of these two opposing groups. So I asked him what he thought about it, and whether he was happy with the project. He said it didn't matter whether he was happy; he was only concerned that I'd be happy, because he didn't want me saying afterwards that we should have done things differently. It was a remarkable response. Eventually he said he couldn't go ahead as it was getting too uncomfortable; he would do it another way and just get the existing building repaired.

What about the shop in Llanfrothen, where there were quite a lot of disgruntled feelings—perhaps this was a similar situation?

I don't know which disgruntled feelings you're referring to, but it was a complex situation. It had to go from sketch design to working drawings without any development period in order to get the grants, so the whole thing was very speedy, which is not an excuse but a reason for it being very difficult. There was also the question of cost. The building was designed for a particular tenant and we designed it quite closely with her. But she went bankrupt soon after the shop opened, and it was taken over by two people who were very negative towards it.

Some of the comments I heard were to do with the amount of roof glazing, and chocolate melting and vegetables wilting as a result.

That certainly happened and it's the only time I've had recourse to my insurers to help pay for ventilators to be put in. No, we didn't calculate that properly. But on the other hand it very seldom needs electric light. It has a very nice open atmosphere, and they put the lights on only because people think the shop's not open if they don't. It's a super-insulated building so it keeps very warm and it doesn't cost much to heat. The other thing about the over-heating was that I hadn't realised how much heat the fridges put out, so on a summer morning before people come in, you may have a lot of solar gain plus the fridges giving out a lot of heat. We also had problems on site, with the contractor and with site management, and also with leaking stainless steel gutters, but that's another story—lots of awkward things happening on my own doorstep, then. But

1: Llanfrothen shop
2: Blaen Camel, Ceredigion

I think it's far nicer now, although the previous tenants have done crazy things like cover the entire timber frame with melamine….

We've talked about two of the less successful schemes, so let's turn to the happier ones. I'm thinking of the house extension at Blaen Camel in mid-Wales (pp 122–125), where the clients, Peter Segger and Anne Evans, got from you much more than they ever dreamed they could get from an architect. They had had an architect involved before you, who'd come up with a scheme they weren't too happy with. They said to me that by the time you had built them this extension, the added value you gave them was priceless.

Well, that's very nice to hear. They were ideal clients. We shared the same values about the environment and many other things too. They wanted to use as many of their own materials as possible. We had some of their large oak trees cut down, and opened a little quarry on their land, which only needed a digger to get out the stones, which were usable as they were. We used their wool for the insulation, as well as cellulose fibre, and lime mortar and render. Again, it was a kind of Kimbell-inspired arrangement of parallel roofs, which covered rooms of different sizes, with top light coming down between them. So although it's got a deep plan, it's very well day-lit in the centre of the house. I remember Peter saying he got up one night and wandered around the house, enjoying the moon and the stars, which he could see through the roof glazing. The job was a wonderful experience, though we did have a few differences of opinion with the builder.

Yes, let's talk about the building process of this job and of another one, the Oasis of Peace in Porthmadog, which was rather similar (pp 112–115). I gather your experience with small builders was very different at each of these two jobs.

I've worked with some very good small builders. Tim Strang, who worked on a little cottage the Seggers have, was an excellent builder and we had a very good relationship. It was the same with Richard Fox, who built the Oasis of Peace in Porthmadog and Bridge Pottery in the Gower (pp 126–127). With the builder at Blaen Camel there was a problem. He was a fairly experienced oak timber-framer and he knew how oak would behave and how much it might move and he became very unhappy about it. I knew that too but I was prepared to accept quite a lot of movement. I discussed this with the clients and they also were aware of it. They wanted to use their own timber, so once we were on that course we couldn't turn back even if we had wanted to. The spans are actually quite short, 3.2m maximum between columns, I recall, which helps to control the twist, but you can certainly see the twist in the beams and in some of the columns. They've gone very free.

When I visited the house, it seemed to me that on one hand here were these clients who were incredibly happy with what they had, and on the other hand, staring you in the face, were twisted columns, timber doors that didn't close because they were warped, sliding doors they couldn't move any more and a Kahn-inspired roofscape of parallel strips of gutters, glazing and slate roofs no longer straight and true, and also leaking. Peter said he'd probably have to re-do the glazed gutters in due course because it's such a problem.

1

We have had problems with the welds between the lengths of stainless steel gutters, just as we had at the village shop. Although the material is durable the site workmanship appears to be unreliable. In fact we have now lined the gutters with EPDM membrane in continuous lengths.

I think I could see what you were after and assumed you had in mind the straight lines and regularity of Mies, Kahn and Glenn Murcutt, and yet because you wanted to use natural materials, you were trying to get more than was possible. There was a mismatch between what you were after and the means by which you got there.

No, not really. If I'd used Jeremy Nelson's pitch-pine, there wouldn't have been any of that twisting. It would have worked perfectly well with a straight-grained timber but home-grown Welsh oak, with all its stresses and strains, does move and I think I completely accept that. Actually all the timber for the doors and the internal joinery came from the Welsh borders. It was a different timber, straighter grained. It wasn't Peter's, but it still moved. You know, it depends what you're trying to do. I certainly wasn't thinking I'd build with the precision of Glenn Murcutt or Mies. I've always stressed the quality of naturalness in the way materials behave, the patina of ageing, natural movement and so on. Green oak for the structural frame is bound to have shakes and splits as it dries out.

I've been to only two Kahn buildings so I can't really judge but I have heard it said that Kahn's detailing sometimes lets him down. I gather there are some rather sad sights at the Kimbell Museum. Have you seen these?

No, I haven't but you can certainly see them in the photos, places where the concrete has stained quite badly. I think it's important to remember what the intention is in these matters. I think you present it as almost a surprise that things have gone that way, but I'm not really surprised. But something that does surprise me is the way lime can be so difficult. Whenever I have used lime putty, there seemed to be no consistent way that it behaved. Sometimes it worked, sometimes it didn't. I specify exactly the same thing for one condition and it won't work for another. I find that very difficult, which is why I don't use it anymore. I find hydraulic lime is safer.

I was talking with someone in connection with this book about you and he said "Oh yes, is David Lea that architect who works in Wales and designs Steiner schools?" He was muddling you with Christopher Day, I realised. That got me looking back at some of Day's books and photos of his buildings, and I came across a passage in *Places of the Soul* which I'll read to you: "I try to make buildings which belong in the place they are, which are rooted in the earth, which give one the feeling that they've always been and always will be. Places which have this eternal feeling can convey stable yet life-filled tranquility in a way that those bound to a transient moment of style never can." This could be you writing, and yet the buildings that you and Chris Day have produced are very different. Maybe we can bring in here the thatched studio you built in Somerset (pp 95–99) because on the face of it, it looks rather different to your other work, its organic-ness and so on, yet I can see that comes

1: Magney House, New South Wales (Glenn Murcutt) **2:** Goetheanum, Dornach (Rudolf Steiner) **3:** Nant-y-cwm School (Chris Day) **4:** Tea-house waiting-place, Katsura Palace, Kyoto

precisely from the construction, the bent saplings you used, making it a very functional building rather than something Chris Day might build. I know you dislike his buildings, yet your philosophy is similar, isn't it?

I met Chris Day when I worked at John Seymour's farm. He had established his smallholding and ecohouse quite close-by. We were on friendly terms. I like him very much as a person but I wish he could escape Steiner's influence on his architecture. I probably told you that the only building I've ever visited that has made me feel physically sick is Steiner's Goetneanum at Dornach. I think Steiner leads him into what one might call eco-formalism, which can develop in opposition to the idea of truth to materials. This seems wilful to me. Chris's ideas are lovely and I share a lot of them, but as far as his architecture goes, I don't see any similarity. You talk about the little studio in Somerset and, as you rightly point out, the form was derived directly from the materials we decided to use at the last minute. The original design was post-and-beam construction with straight lengths of timber, like a little Japanese tea-house. When we went to look for the trees to make it, we stumbled upon a glade of rowan saplings we thought we could use instead. The client had been camping at Greenham Common in a bender, so we thought maybe we could make a bigger and more permanent bender. That is how that form was born, not out of a desire to make a curvy building!

You spent a lot of time building it with the client.

Yes, to me it was an opportunity to show how you can go out into the natural world, harvest your building materials and bring them back to make yourself a shelter. We thought it would last 15–20 years, but it's still going strong 30 years later.

Has it been listed?

No. It has a great sense of solidity even though it's built of lightweight materials. Thatch was the obvious material to use for the roof as it would go round curves. Everything was grown except for a little chicken-wire and a few miles of bailer twine.

Would you like to be involved in the actual building work of more of your projects?

Not now, but I would have done in the past. It's a question of scale, isn't it—that's the problem. If we were to put our finger on the main problem of getting things built, the way we want, it is that we spend so little time on site, and that really the split of architects from the construction industry has been a disaster. We should be on site as in medieval times. Whenever I've come close to that, better buildings have resulted—most recently at the WISE building at CAT, where Pat and I went on site about three times each week and went through every detail with the builder. That's much the best way to do it.

Say something about Bridge Pottery (pp 126–127).

The Japanese does not accord his house much importance as a necessity of life; for him it is only a 'temporary' home. Indeed he thinks it is a superficial, even a sinful attitude, to live a materialistic and princely life in a splendid house. He derives deep joy from a contented life in a simple, natural house and an ethical and artistic manner of life.
Tetsuro Yoshida

The real architect of a building … must be his own clerk of works, his own carver, his own director, he must be the familiar spirit of the structure as it rises from the ground… to make the most of the site and the building as applied to it.
J D Sedding

This was done at the same time as Hillier's and Blaen Camel, in the late 1990s. It was one in a series of designs for small single-storey buildings that have walls that wrap around at a constant height and can be built of anything. In this case, timber frame with boarding. The windows are generally full-height and above the external envelope there's a roof that appears to be floating, as the gables are glazed. It has a very tent-like feeling inside. It also has a wall-washing rooflight which is combined with the gutter and made of glass sections manufactured by Regulit, so a soft light comes through the gutters, which need cleaning occasionally as leaves collect and make patterns. It's a wonderful site by a river and the main opening was onto the river, so you get lovely dappled light reflecting off the water and onto the ceiling. It was a very simple building, as cheap as we could make it, so it's a kind of successor to the studio.

Weren't the planners difficult because it was so near to the water?

No, I don't remember this. At one point it was to have a flat roof but the planners wanted a pitched roof so I gave it a pitched roof as it would be equally nice either way, maybe even nicer inside with the pitched roof. The building stands on oak piles pressed into the soft mud of the river bank by the careful operator of a JCB with a front bucket.

You've had quite a lot of run-ins with planners in your jobs, starting with the Eddystone housing at Churt.

Yes, that was my first experience and we had huge problems with the planners. They held the first phase up for 14 months, which I suppose isn't that long as these things go now. They said that in this area they thought Lutyens would have built differently, using stone and brick and timber. The situation became locked and we tried various devices to resolve it. In the end Walter Segal came to the rescue and dictated one of his crafty letters. As a result they suggested I changed the elevations a bit and added some timber to them. So I drew some timber in place of the white panels, and it went through. And when we put in the next phase, the planners said, "Ah, yes, we actually quite liked it after all." So the next phase went through without any problems at all… I believe that we should never start with the idea that we have to satisfy the planners' personal aesthetic judgements; very few of them have any visual training at all.

One place the planners were never really concerned about was the Centre for Alternative Technology at Machynlleth in mid-Wales [although in an area of outstanding natural beauty bordering the Snowdonia National Park, the site is largely hidden in a former slate quarry]. The centre was established in 1973, just a few years before you moved to Wales. When did your involvement begin there?

I called in at the National Centre for Alternative Technology, as it was known then, very early on, probably the first year I arrived here in Wales, because I'd read about it in the newspapers. It was raining and I spent a happy couple of hours helping to re-point one of the cottages at the back of the site. I kept in touch over the years and used to go to parties there. That's where I met Pat Borer. He was drumming in one of their bands.

1: Lower station, Centre for Alternative Technology
2: AtEIC building, Centre for Alternative Technology

Pat didn't live on the site but he did help them with all their buildings. At that time Rod James was the director. He was also an architect and had studied with Pat at Kingston. They did the buildings together but when they had what they called their first gear change, going up a big rung in public visitor numbers, it became more of a visitor centre than a research establishment. They had to get visitors up to the site from the car-park so they decided to invest in a water-balanced railway as the most economic and efficient mode of transport up the slate tip. That meant designing two stations. Pat asked me to help him at that stage. We both worked on all the details; I took responsibility for the design and planning of the lower station, Pat did the upper one. After that we designed the AtEIC [Autonomous Environmental Information Centre] building, which included a shop. CAT also asked me to do a master-plan for the site but they didn't like my solution. I felt that the site needed to be organised in a clear way for visitors. It's always been an anarchic jumble of exhibits, reflecting the social structure of CAT and directors have made various attempts to co-ordinate it in different ways. My plan for the place was very axial and took the theme of water falling on the surrounding hills, filling the reservoir and from there driving the turbines and so on, and it would finally flow into a long straight waterway linking the back of the site to the railway station. But it was developed in a different way in the end, much freer….

Did they not like your idea, or was it more the idea of being regimented that they didn't like?

Peter Harper who was the landscape gardening guru there at the time, declared that it was a fascist imposition on the naturalness of CAT. Couldn't the edges be bent a little so it appeared to be more flowing? I thought there was already quite enough naturalness at CAT, what it needed was a little humane order to link everything together and to make the site legible to the visitors. Then Pat involved me in the AtEIC building, but they felt the scheme was becoming too architect-heavy so they asked Pat if he could do it on his own and I was shunted out before it got on site—a pity as it had all sorts of nice things which I would like to have been involved with, particularly the very high quality rammed earth walls.

One of the great advantages of working with the clients at CAT was that experimentation was always encouraged and was indeed a fundamental part of the way they operated generally. Say something about the experiments you carried out, particularly with rammed earth.

CAT was a fantastic client from that point of view because they always wanted buildings to innovate in some way but also to bring low embodied energy methods of construction into the mainstream. I suppose the main innovation in the AtEIC building was the rammed earth structure. CAT wanted to demonstrate this as possibly the lowest embodied energy construction method of all. Ideally you'd dig the earth out of the site but because CAT was on a slate tip we had to get the earth from a nearby quarry—but then that closed and we found a quarry near Shrewsbury. The WISE [Welsh Institute for Sustainable Education] building demonstrates rammed earth construction in the lecture theatre but on a much bigger scale. We also introduced the use of hemp-lime for the external walls. We were looking for a permanent version of straw-bale construction which wouldn't be eaten by mice and wouldn't rot. Pat had been doing experiments on his own account, mixing various wood fibres with lime, particularly woodwool which was produced near Welshpool. There seemed to be a problem with this because we couldn't get any of the 150mm thick test blocks to dry out in the centre. We needed walls at least 500mm thick to achieve enough insulation. So we cast around for a solution, and tried to get various bodies like Bath University to help us. In the end we used a proprietary product marketed by Ian Pritchett of Lime Technology Ltd, a French material Tradical which was actually lime with cement (but he was cagey about how much cement). That did carbonate, or probably the cement gave the initial set and carbonation took place over a longer time. That was a brilliant material as you could just spray it on in whatever thickness you wanted.

Returning to the rammed earth, wouldn't it have been the obvious thing to use slate waste rather than earth?

How? Do you mean crushed up and used like earth?

That's a possibility. But when you look at the slate working sheds in the old quarries, they have huge thick slate rubble walls.

CAT had used slate waste a lot in the other buildings. They are always keen to demonstrate different methods of construction, and wanted to move on.

The latest building, WISE, I see as a culmination of your career (pp 138–145). I can recognise many themes re-used from your other projects, plus some new ones, and your management of daylight reaches new heights here. What do you feel you have achieved in this project that goes beyond your others?

It's interesting to think how the building started. CAT had a very short brief, not quite one side of A4, just a list of possible rooms. We did Planning for Real sessions over a few days with all the different user groups and we got them to plan the building shoving around bits of card with the names of spaces on. This indicated to them how difficult it is to get everything in the right relationship. After that process we started with a plan they had virtually reached themselves, but it was a very compact plan with the lecture theatre in the middle. We were unhappy with this as many of the rooms were landlocked without a view so we took the lecture theatre out of the middle of the scheme and created a courtyard instead, giving all the rooms an outside view. All the major spaces have a view, they are all naturally lit and they're all naturally ventilated. The next move took the bedrooms, which were originally planned for a different site (pp 144–145) and incorporated them into the scheme. As this was going on, the scheme developed in a rather discursive way and as the building grew I felt at first that it was a pity it wasn't more of an object in the landscape. Somehow it had got too loose. But then as the spaces began to form I started to enjoy the feeling of a hill village. It had lots of different sorts of spaces, lots of different views and the clear routes around the scheme became very important. In a way the things I most like about it grew during the process of designing it, in a rather freer way than I felt had happened with any of the other buildings I'd been involved with.

It's interesting you say you had wanted it to be more an object as I thought your buildings are generally not objects but containers of space or arms flinging out to grab space — very few of them are blocky objects in the landscape.

I think at this time some architects were building objects in the landscape and I was intrigued by the minimalist idea of the block which was rather mute as far as use goes, and quite abstract — as in the Magdalene College scheme you said you didn't like. But it didn't go that way because other things are so much more important — giving views, and getting light and sound into the building. Sound is very important at CAT, from the water, the birds, the wind in the trees. The main aim was to make people feel an attachment to nature in those spaces.

There's something very pleasant about the big sliding windows to the bedrooms which can all open out to the courtyard and the landscape. On that point, it's interesting that you had designed something very similar for Coad Court at Cirencester, 30 years earlier.

Yes, we should have done it then! There is something wonderful about removing the window completely and turning the room into a balcony, like the famous corner window at Rietveld's Schroeder House.

You're joking, presumably. You're not really saying you feel what you did at Coad Court was not the right thing, are you?

I think this would have been better.

And acceptable to the planners and to the college governors?

Maybe not, because the vertical emphasis of the timber framed windows in that wall was probably more familiar to the Cotswold planners at that time, but this shouldn't be an issue. One of the problems of this kind of elevation — and I still haven't worked out my position on this — is if you have very large windows which are basically timber-framed, the frames become so massive that you lose the finer detail, so I want to turn them into something else, to find some other way in which the finer detail can be expressed. I don't think we quite managed that in the WISE building. You could go to much finer frames with aluminium, where there's hardly a frame at all, just an edging to the glass, but I've never had the opportunity to try that. The other way is to have big areas of fixed glazing with a timber vent beside it, as we had to do in a couple of the bedrooms at the WISE building, the ones for disabled people.

Prince Charles came up to visit the building in 2010. How did he react to it?

I don't know, he didn't say very much. He wasn't over the moon about it by any means. He had an advisor in the Princes Trust who had been responsible for the house he did at BRE [the Building Research Establishment], and he very much liked the building. He told us that Prince Charles had a problem with buildings that didn't have classical columns. I expected that he would at least notice that our columns had entasis, but I don't think he did.

When the RIBA gave the WISE building an award, Peter Clegg said in his presentation speech that sustainable architecture had come of age at last. That must have pleased you.

Of course. I like the fact that other people seem to enjoy it. I think the quality of the natural light is one of the most important reasons. They also appreciate that it is a modern building that doesn't refer back to the past except in the sense of those timeless things we spoke about earlier. Many people have commented that the lecture theatre feels like a sacred space.

Something we must talk about is your collaboration with Pat Borer, firstly because his input was just as much as yours, and secondly because this partnership raises interesting questions about how you work. What other projects did you work on with him?

We worked a lot together. One of the biggest projects was Holme Lacy Agricultural College, near Hereford. The clients had high aspirations for it. They wanted to turn it into the foremost organic agricultural college in Europe. We did a feasibility study for the site, a huge project for us, £25m in 2001. We also did the Rixton Claypits and Slaidburn Community Centre together. Pat did the structural calculations for a number of my buildings, and SAP calculations too. If it was a project I brought in, my name would come first on the letterhead, and if it was one of Pat's, his name would. I would do lots of sketches and quite detailed drawings, then we'd discuss them until we agreed everything. Sometimes he'd do a lot of the drawings. Before email, we'd send everything by fax. I was more interested in the formal aspects, the historical context of the buildings, he was more interested in the technology. We did share things more equally to begin with, but I gradually relinquished the more technical things to him because he was much more efficient at them than I was. He's an incredibly efficient person, unbelievably productive—the drawings he did for the WISE building are astonishing, the number and the detail….

… but you are too….

I used to be like that, but I can't do it by hand any more. I can't do those drawings because of my eyesight—and my natural resistance to it.

You have never run a conventional practice, and you have never had any partners, chiefly I think because you prefer to work on your own and find it hard to delegate

1: Holme Lacy Agricultural College, Hereford

and let others have free rein (perhaps you learned this at Sandy Wilson's office!). And yet your partnership with Pat, albeit an informal one, seems to be very successful. Do you know why this should be?

Actually it's not quite true that I have never run a conventional practice. Many wonderful people have worked here and I have almost always enjoyed our working relationships. I like the companionship and I like discussion about design issues. If this is not to hand I often send drawings to people whose opinions I respect, and ask for a crit. Sometimes I teamed up for particular jobs with various contemporaries like Ekkehard Weisner and Nick Alexander, and at other times I had younger assistants working for longer spells. Letting others have free rein is another matter; after all I have to take responsibility.

As to working with Pat I think we really respect each other's roles and abilities. I certainly respect his. He's a good-natured person, and easy to work with. I've been very lucky, but I don't know how long it'll go on after this point. We have very little work.

I have read Walter Segal's account of his way of working and I see lots of parallels, though some interesting differences. For instance he tried to keep drawings to a minimum (which you don't) and I don't think he made models (which I know you consider essential). Have you consciously followed Segal's example or is it just that you are rather similar in character?

I loved his description of how he should run his practice: basically freeing himself from virtually everything! He was a past master at doing things in the most minimal way possible. I remember him showing me his job files and each had just five or six bits of paper. That was the whole job! He was uncompromising in what he was prepared to do. He wasn't going to do anything outside the system he had developed. He made this quite clear to his clients, and there was no question of him taking on board clients' whims. I don't think I am like that. Also I always want to explore different ways of doing things. I prefer Sandy's statement that if the solution is too simple, it gets very uninteresting and one should add formal problems to solve in order to create tension in the design. This would make it more human because it'd be more like the tensions in life, when you can't resolve everything. You want this kind of dialectic in a building. I suppose it depends what you think a work of art is. In a way it's the struggle to integrate things that don't want to be integrated. I don't think Walter was the least bit interested in that. He wanted a system that would just fall into place naturally and there wouldn't be any moment when you'd scratch your head and think how the hell do you resolve that?

Working as a one-man band can restrict the scale of work you can manage. What would happen if you won a very large job — I'm thinking of the Holme Lacy project?

We always realised we couldn't do that sort of thing. Pat has a good relationship with Jonathan Hines of Architype, as I do. We involved them at an early stage, and in fact they did the whole submission with us for Holme Lacy, an enormous amount of work.

For me there is more joy in seeing a smaller building through from beginning to end than playing a limited part in the construction of a larger design.... The most typical aspect of my practice is the firm desire to exercise complete one-man control. This involves the continued effort of extending such control over as many fields as possible, by acquiring more and more knowledge and by taking more and more responsibility.
Walter Segal

[Lea] is a man of firm determination albeit grounded wholly in legitimate architectural philosophy. That philosophy I found profoundly stimulating and agreeable.... Whereas in others his obduracy could have been thought to be obstinacy, with him and his persuasive charm borne of conviction, it was a resolution which, in the end, I always found entirely legitimate.
Sir Richard Storey

*"I cannot see, Mr Lethaby, that you have done a single thing that I asked you to do."
"Well, you see, my first duty as an artist is to please myself."*
Andrew Saint quoting from notes left by Norman Shaw's son

When you go for these OJEC things, you have to supply the entire documentation of a similar project, it's completely ridiculous and resulted in one man from Holme Lacy, the Project Manager, having to go through a roomful of boxes of projects from all the competitors. I don't know how it would have worked out... temperamentally I prefer to work at a much smaller scale.

You are choosy about the clients you work with and have never been involved in jobs where you are not in sympathy with the client or at least with the client's ethos. But it's not a perfect world we live in and not all your clients have been easy. This can lead to a clash of wills, a situation I know you prefer to avoid. Do you feel your personality has got in the way sometimes?

My determination to do the best I can has got in the way sometimes, when other people don't share my view of the route to get there. People don't foresee the implications of certain moves they think they want to make. That happened very forcefully on the Dorset house project (pp 137–137). The clients were determined to get a lot of accommodation into the basement and it resulted in all kinds of problems which I foresaw but couldn't persuade them to avoid. Particularly with private house clients, you think it's going to work but as time goes on, you realise that they have quite different ideas about what houses should be like. That can be quite demanding. I don't think I have ever chosen clients. I haven't had enough work to choose clients, but on the other hand I've never found advertising fruitful. The few occasions I have tried to advertise, it hasn't brought anything. It's word of mouth, really.

When MJ Long was interviewed for the back page of *Building Design* and was asked which architect she had learnt most from, she said you for your principles. What principles do you think she was referring to?

I think you have to ask her! That was very nice of her, but I really don't know — determination to do the best possible, or something like that?

Aren't you just being modest? You worked on a scheme in Cornwall with MJ (pp 132–133). Might this collaboration suggest some clues about what she had in mind?

That's interesting, I hadn't thought of that. In retrospect I think MJ was quite willing to draw something initially to please the clients. She was very skilful and accustomed to working for these sorts of people, and knew what they wanted. I wanted to work out what it was I was drawing first. That was an amazing scheme, or it could have been had it got built. It involved turning an old stone quarry close to the sea at Penlee into the last safe yacht haven before Land's End. They were going to blast through the thin neck of land which separated an amphitheatre of rock from the sea, so you'd sail into the heart of it. The scale was heroic. There'd be terraces all around with a hotel, housing of various kinds, workshops and chandleries. MJ took the northern side of the site with the hotel, the marina and associated buildings, and I took the southern side with the housing. MJ is very good at doing atmospheric pencil sketches showing indicative massing of buildings; I always

1: Keith Jones and Harri Puw
2: Penlee masonry **3:** Hemplime project, The Welsh School of Architecture

wanted to work out the plans of the houses first and then develop what they looked like from there, but at the same time having an idea of the total effect I wanted to produce.

That's the difference, perhaps—she was working like most architects do, with an eye to what their clients want, whereas with you it is more what you believe the client should have.

I want the client to tell me what they want, but I don't want them to design the building. That's my job. They can send me pictures of things they like. The Cornwall client did actually send pictures but I thought they were completely inappropriate! I always hope I can win such clients round, when they see how wonderful it could be.

Wasn't Penlee another job where you got involved in a hands-on way, although it didn't actually turn into a proper job?

The scheme would have required some rather massive terracing, an opportunity to build out of Cyclopean blocks of stone. I went down there with two stonemasons from Gwynedd, Keith Jones and Harri Puw, and we built a sample section of walling out of blocks weighing up to seven tons.

You have always enjoyed teaching students and you are currently teaching on the diploma course at CAT, which must be a gratifying experience as the course is run in your new building. What do you enjoy about teaching?

Actually I hadn't done that much teaching as a visiting lecturer or tutor until the CAT course. In the early days I always tried to turn teaching into a live project, for example I had a group of students up at Ogoronwy, investigating local conditions and the potential for local material production etc. More recently I ran a studio with Sylvia Harris at the Welsh School of Architecture. We built a section of a vaulted room using only hemp-lime to form structure, insulation and vapour control. There was no timber frame required. I want to build a house to demonstrate this technique if I can find a suitable site. All that early work here at Ogoronwy was done with students, some like Nick Smith staying quite a long time. I have gradually grown into the course at CAT by going to give talks and studio tutorials, and I keep it to that. Discussing students' ideas with them is a very good way to clarify one's own. I always find something to interest me, even in the most unpromising schemes. And I like to try to help them to draw out what they're aiming at. I usually find I want to design the building for them and it's quite difficult to restrain myself from doing that but I think that kind of interest is encouraging for them and it's certainly very enjoyable for me.

But there is a step lacking in architectural education which I don't think many are aware of, that is the connection between architectural form and language, and emotion and feeling. I first realised this when I sat in on a masterclass for lieder-singing held by Peter Pears in Aldeburgh. A friend of mine had gone to study there. The entire class was devoted to precise analyses of the techniques by which feelings are transmitted in song.

Materials and surfaces have a language of their own. Stone speaks of its distant geological origins, its durability and inherent symbolism of permanence; brick makes one think of earth and fire, gravity and the ageless traditions of construction; bronze evokes the extreme heat of its manufacture, the ancient processes of casting and the passage of time as measured in its patina. Wood speaks of its two existences and time scales; its first life as a growing tree and the second as a human artefact made by the caring hand of a carpenter or cabinetmaker. These are all materials and surfaces that speak pleasurably of time.
Juhani Pallasmaa

The atmosphere was serious, intense and respectful and there appeared to be a language in which such subtleties could be conveyed with reasonable accuracy. All this seemed a very long way from my own architectural education. I felt we had missed out an essential, perhaps *the* essential thing which makes architecture an art. It is one thing to point to a lack. It's quite another to work out what to do about it in the absence of a shared set of values, though Peter Zumthor's 2013 RIBA Gold Medal talk about the quality of 'presence' seemed to suggest a way of thinking about this.

What do you think is the purpose of architectural education today, when there are already too many architects chasing too few jobs?

The purpose is to turn out good architects. By good architects I mean people with a flair and ability for design who think in terms of space and form. It's very noticeable when you're teaching that some have it and some don't. Those that don't often get stuck in social engineering while those that do tend to start with an image which may contain poetic spaces before they have considered the brief. That sometimes works. In fact it may result in the best schemes in the end, which rather stands the whole thing on its head. We were always taught to analyse the brief first and develop the scheme from that. But this can result in ploddy schemes that don't actually lift the spirits very much. The question is how can we teach students to see what they are doing and to strike the right balance between investigation and inspiration? Also, placing their work in a historical context is very important, so that they realise that other people have been through similar problems and come to certain archetypal solutions. It's important to make the students aware of the archetypes of what they're doing, as Colin Rowe did for us. That was one of the main things Cambridge taught me.

There must be an element of leaving a legacy when you engage with students. How do you view your achievements and successes of over 40 years' work? What legacy would you like to leave to the world?

I think that's a bit grand. It's another of those questions where it's not up to me to answer. But if people could see there's a connection between the natural world, how we use the land and what we produce from it, and the buildings we build, that would be good—if I could help people to see that. How people use the land and our attitude to nature are really crucial for our survival now. And it always has been. You need only read Jared Diamond's *Collapse* and you see how misuse of nature leads to the collapse of societies. Now the destruction is world-wide rather than just limited to one particular ecological niche. It matters very much to me what buildings are built of, and whether they remind us of these fundamental things. Is that fair?

Yes, and it begins to answer my next question. How do you rate the state of architecture today and the quality of modern buildings? I guess you don't see much hope….

One of the big problems is the complexity of architecture and building today, and that's grown out of our misuse of the land. If we used the land properly our buildings could be

1: Barcelona Pavilion (Ludwig Mies van der Rohe) **2:** Säynätsalo town-hall (Alvar Aalto) **3:** Katsura Palace, Kyoto

very simple and they wouldn't need to rise much above three or four storeys as a general rule. Because of this increasing complexity, it has become impossible for architects to manage the business of building. We have given away much of our uniquely integrating role as architects to project managers, engineers, and surveyors of various kinds, and so we are often left with basically decorating a structure. I was reminded very forcefully of this when I went to the new library in Birmingham, a filigree-covered box with one fairly interesting spatial move inside. The structure and the materials are just dire. I could talk about the cruelly oppressive nature of Rem Koolhaas's CCTV building in Beijing, imposed on a city which used to be beautifully laid out in one or two storeys of courtyard houses which have been swept away, along with the culture of which they were a most beautiful expression. The architects of these so-called iconic buildings seem to be as blind to their meaning as they are to their effects on the fragile frameworks of existing communities.

You've just mentioned two bad buildings. If you were to pick just three of your favourite buildings, which would they be?

Well, let's take two modern buildings for a start: the Barcelona Pavilion, firstly, which I visited over three days. It is interesting that the original one was demolished very soon after the fair in 1929 but it lingered on as an idea in people's minds rather like a musical score until there was a new performance of it. I thought it was one of the most moving buildings I'd ever been in. It affects a lot of people that way. We have talked a bit about the tensions between different aspects of architecture and I thought this building integrates Eastern and Western ideas in a very profound way. It's a classical temple on a podium, with columns and entablature, very regular, and it's also very free in plan. I don't know how much Mies knew about Zen and gardens and Japanese architecture— presumably quite a lot as he would have known Bruno Taut's book (though he denied any knowledge of Japan in an informal talk with students at the AA in 1959). It's amazingly free, and there are surprising views which look out onto beautifully integrated half-inside and half-outside spaces, and onto that enigmatic sculpture at the back. And it's all done with such attention to detail and precision. It's certainly a timeless building if we're going to talk about timelessness, but it also looks as if it could have been built today.

My second choice is the little town hall at Säynätsalo in Finland. I like Aalto's attitude to the community there. think it was Göran Schildt who described a meeting when the clients said they thought the council chamber was a bit high. Aalto replied that it was the same height as the council chamber in Siena and they deserved nothing less. It has a fine nobility starting with that great flight of steps up to the courtyard, and then the intriguing route that gradually winds up to the chamber—a real journey. But it's all done with a low-key humanity. It's noble and humane at the same time. I like the details too, for example the upper part of the wall outside the courtyard where those vertical recesses in the brickwork catch snow. It's quite high, so it gives the impression of a kind of entablature over the windows, suggesting classical proportions. There's a grille of fine wooden slats which projects out from the wall of the staircase leading to the council chamber; Richard MacCormac said it was there to suggest that the members should hush their voices as they approached the big central space.

Architecture, that grandest of sciences, is fallen to a mere trade, and conducted not by artists but by men of business.
A W N Pugin

59

A house of men or of priests is at home in natural surroundings; it adjusts itself to the lie of the land whether it be forest, plain or valley.... It is made in the image of the law established thousands of years ago, namely, that a man comes to a place, tills the land and builds a shelter for himself, his wife, his children, his men and his domestic animals.... This is where it shall be. We will enclose a portion of this space between walls, organize our lives inside them and, confining ourselves to this area, we will spend each day cultivating and maintaining this little space that we have taken from nature.
Fernand Pouillon

It's enough to play just one note beautifully.
Arvo Pärt

He's completely out of step with the zeitgeist, and yet he's enormously popular, which is inspiring. His music fulfils a deep human need that has nothing to do with fashion.
Steve Reich, about Arvo Pärt

1

My third is Le Thoronet. I knew nothing about the monastery when I went there except that Corb had produced a beautiful book of photographs of it, so he evidently approved. On route I visited La Tourette. I thought that Corb's destruction of the idea of the cloister in favour of crossing routes high above the ground violated the fundamental monastic arrangement of rooms around a protected garden for no apparent reason. There are two other Cistercian monasteries near Le Thoronet and I saw them first. They are both lovely but Le Thoronet is of a different order. The handling of the levels, the arrangement of the spaces in plan and section, the minimal but powerful detailing and, essentially, the cutting and laying of the hard and splintery stone in rough courses, give the building tremendous vigour and life. Fernand Pouillon in his book *The Stones of Le Thoronet* imagines the trials, doubts and unswerving commitment, which such a work demands of the architect. It is the best book on architecture I have ever read.

Still on the favourites format of Desert Island Discs, I imagine that one of your musical selections might be a work by Arvo Pärt.

Yes, it would be. His music is of today and it's got a modern tension yet it has a great sense of history. It's part of the struggle to get to the essence of things. He starts with his theory of tintinnabulation and tries to get to the purest sound. He said it's the waiting before the first sound to begin which fascinates him. He gave a master-class on this, and said that the upbeat of the conductor, before his hand drops, that's the essence. I like that sort of idea, that one should always look for what's really crucial and important. I think you feel that in his music. I went to an early performance of his Fourth Symphony in Cardiff; he was there, and it was a very powerful occasion. People find his music reassuring but at the same time it's got an obvious tension in it. There are lots of disharmonies that don't resolve themselves, which I think reminds us of how we feel in this period of the world's existence. Silence has a special presence in his music, the space between blocks of sound. The equivalence of silence and space suggests architecture. Pärt's purity of expression recalls the music of Bach, particularly the unaccompanied sonatas and partitas, though Bach's music is far more complex of course. Bach demands an intense engagement. You wonder where on earth this tune is going to go next? And in that next moment the progression there seems inevitable. Bach's music reminds me about the acceptance of life as it is, and offers re-assurance about our place in the universe.

But my musical world is not limited to the meditative side of life. I also love the exuberance and energy of rhythm, drums and dance pouring out of Africa into the blues, jazz, rock and reggae — the rhythm of the earth. So I would want Oscar Peterson and Charlie Parker alongside Bob Marley's glimpses into human situations, sometimes extremely intense — listen to the acoustic version of the "Happiness" song. Taken together they are a tremendous affirmation that there is a better way, that we can work together, and I would want a Dylan song, maybe "Blind Willie McTell", a eulogy, but also an entire history of black slavery in the Southern States, snapshots of scenes drawn with incredible economy and precision. Or maybe "Highlands", a beautifully deadpan, extended meditation on growing old. It is full of moments which I feel in myself: "I've got new eyes, everything seems far away."

1: Le Thoronet, France

I came across a quote by Lethaby, which I know you'll like as he lists seamanship, farming and housekeeping as three of the great forms of life activity. We have discussed farming already and can perhaps skip the housekeeping, but sailing and your boat are immensely important to you, aren't they?

Well, why would we skip the housekeeping? Surely it's fundamental for architecture, the spaces, colours objects which form the setting for our lives, the food we eat and its preparation, all the necessary daily tasks, these are all part of an integrated life. My enjoyment of sailing goes back a long way. When my father returned from the war, the first thing he did was to take us on holiday in Aldeburgh and hire a sailing boat. I think I was eight when I first started sailing and I've sailed all my life in various ways, first with dinghies, then crewing for people, then crewing on that extended voyage to America. But it wasn't until 2000 that I bought my own boat, Schnapps (which I've just sold) (pp 146–147). It was a wonderful boat, a Tumlare designed in the 1930s by a Dane called Knud Reimers, and it was probably the most advanced boat of its kind at that time. It was a small wooden cruising/racing boat and sleeps two. I sailed to Ireland a couple of times, round the coast here, and down to Cornwall. The thing about sailing is the sense of freedom, but at the same time you've got to work with nature, with winds and tides, and you've got to understand these things. The sea—people call it the trackless sea, you can go anywhere once you're on the sea. That's a huge sense of freedom.

One of the reasons I have asked you about this now is I imagine there's something to do with minimalism, what is minimal and essential to life, when you're in a little boat.

Everything on a sailing boat has a function. All the rigging is doing its job and you don't have anything on it which is superfluous. There's always a balance between working with natural forces on a boat and actually going where you want to go. Sometimes you have to judge that and work against what the natural forces want you to do. This raises the fundamental question of how to sail into the wind rather than away from it. People have been doing this for a very long time. I've just got a book, *Man and the Sea* by Philip Banbury, which explores the history of sailing from the earliest times The dust jacket shows a Viking ship sailing into the wind. So there's that sense of being part of a very long tradition, particularly on the west coast of Britain, the main transport route for this part of the world. You can see the most wonderful things when you're sailing which you can't possibly see any other way because you don't have the infinite combinations of light and movement. Just the weather effects can be astonishing.

I haven't asked you any questions of a personal nature, but there is one I'd like to ask because it intrigues me—are you a religious person?

I'm not religious in the sense of outward forms, going to church and so on. I do think going to church is important as a sharing of community-held beliefs but I don't find that I can go there anymore as I get irritated with its apparent lack of focus on today's conditions.

Have nothing in your houses that you do not know to be useful, or believe to be beautiful.
William Morris

But I should say I have a spiritual view of life. I feel the life of the spirit is the essence of things. I feel more drawn to Daoism and some versions of Buddhism than to Christianity because they see us humans in the context of the natural world; Christianity doesn't seem to be particularly interested in that. It's more like a dramatic story, although it does have a warmth, a humanity which can sometimes seem a bit lacking in the oriental religions, though perhaps this is a Eurocentric view.

What is the relationship between these matters and architecture?

Our buildings are the home of our present and future existence, so we have to ask: what future do we wish for, and what do we want our buildings to say about it? How do we want to live? What kind of society do we want? What relationship should we have with our environment? Buildings never lie, either about our intentions or our abilities, so architects can't avoid these questions; and maybe to answer them is the basic task of architecture. When we look at pictures of our world from space we can see that the atmosphere is extremely thin and fragile in the surrounding vastness. When we build we wrap walls around a tiny bit of it, and when we dig for the foundations we find that there is only 150mm where plants grow. This is the depth on which the lives of all land-based creatures depend. So we need to remember the vulnerability of the biosphere, and our responsibility to guard its integrity for future generations.

Architects can intensify perception of our place in the universe by manipulating space and light. Views out to surrounding landscapes can change and unfold in surprising ways as we follow the route from room to room. Daylight and sunlight tell us of time and weather. We can open every space to the sun and to the sounds of wind, water and birdsong. And at night we can look up and see the stars. I want people to experience the beauty of nature, the amazing complexity and harmony of its patterns and its ever-changing effects. And I want my buildings to contain these complex, life-enhancing relationships within simple forms constructed mainly of low-energy materials put together in a natural way for the times in which we live.

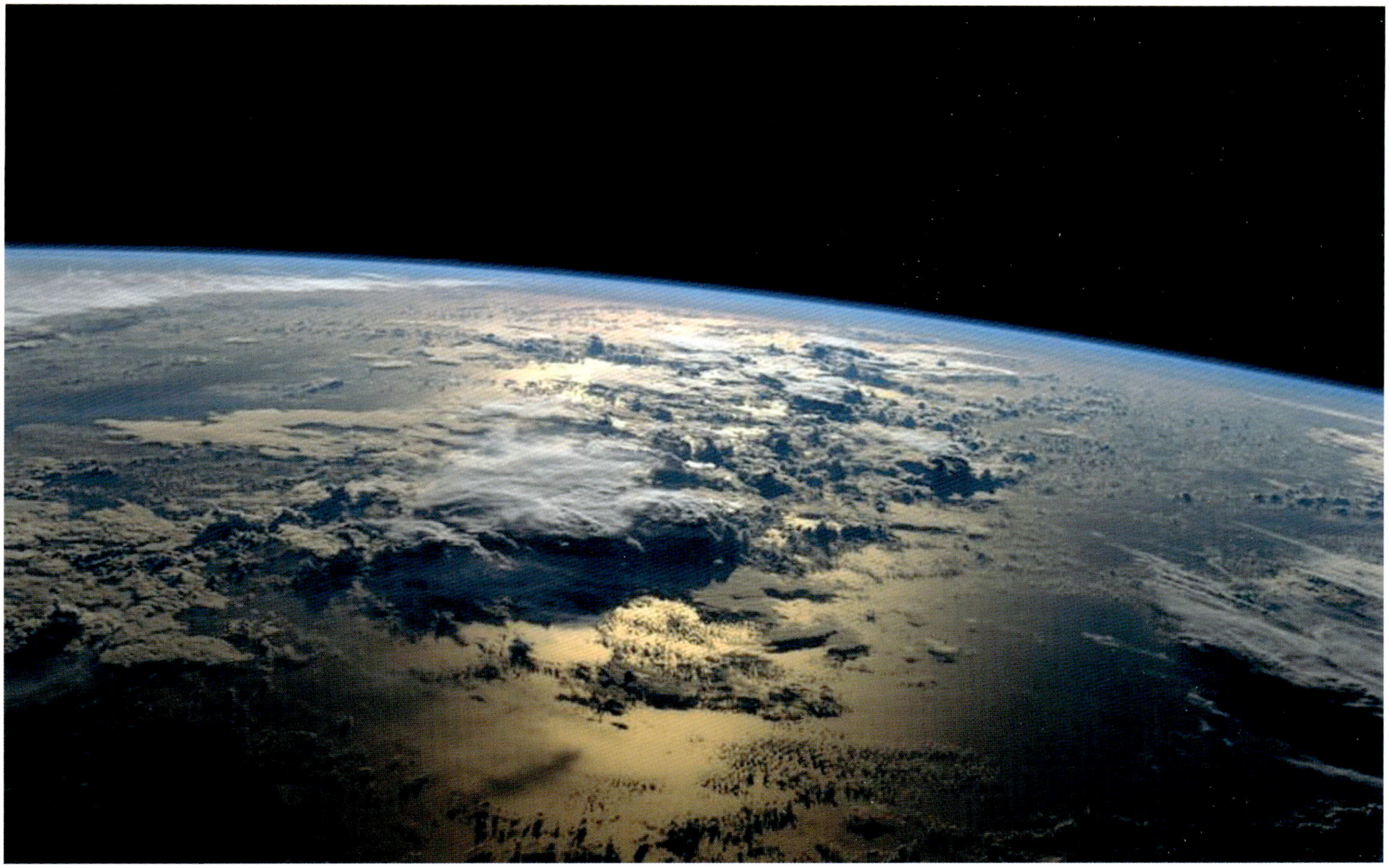

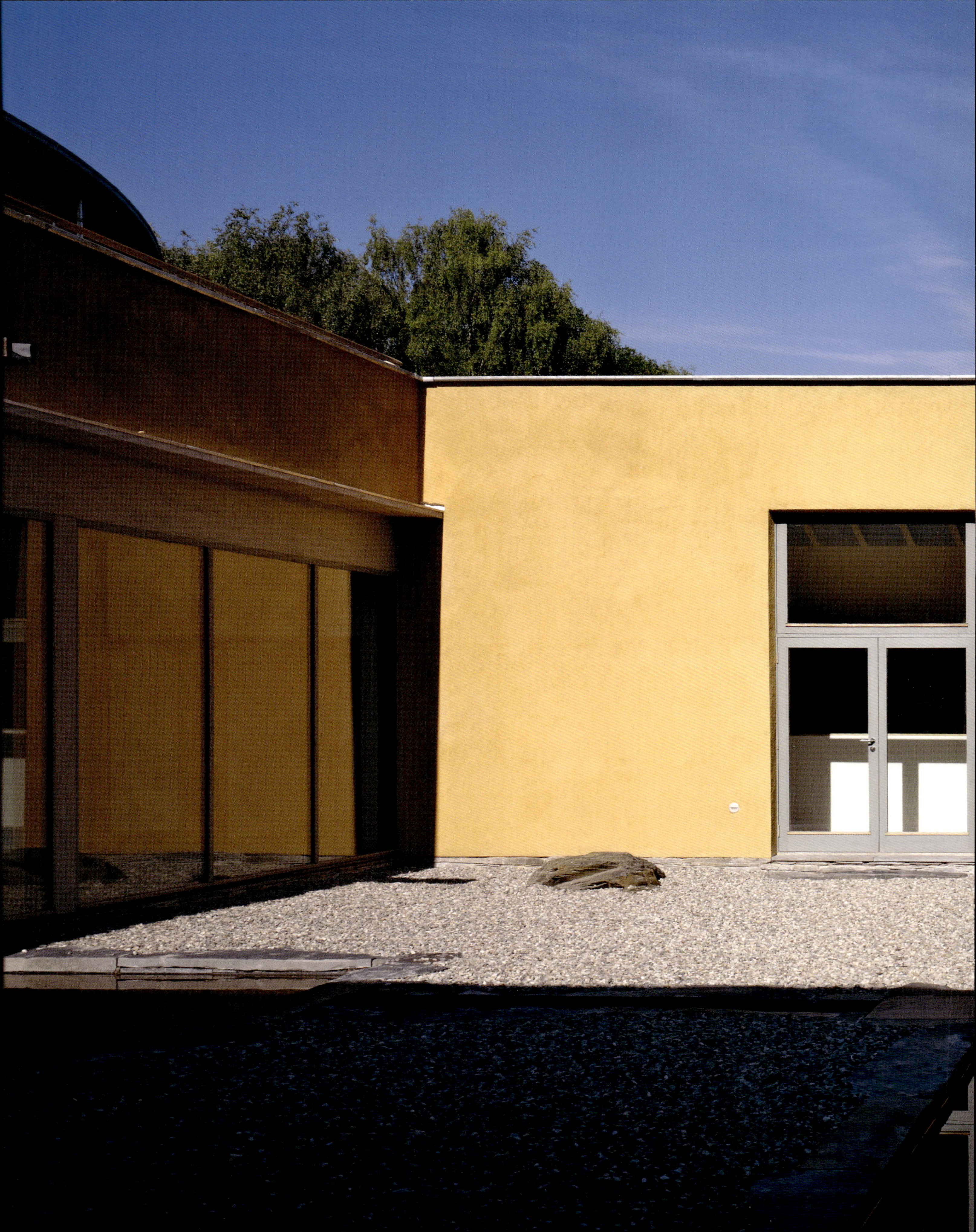

Projects

Housing,
London Borough of Merton
1967–1968

Pains Fireworks Factory Site
The site had been used as a testing ground for Pains Fireworks; it was a wilderness when the Borough took it over for housing. The proposed five-storey walk-up blocks, laid out around the perimeter like a Georgian square, preserved the wilderness as an 8 acre playground for children, and provided a rural outlook from the housing.

The accommodation was arranged on half levels around each stair with the main access level one floor up from the ground forming a wide cloister looking out to the wilderness. Shallow ramps at regular intervals connected the cloister to the ground. Two maisonettes were placed above this cloister, and one flat below it. Each flat had a garden and a balcony, and each maisonette had a balcony or a roof terrace. Cars were parked at the lowest level.

Eventually this scheme was abandoned in favour of the house type developed at Pollards Hill. The site is now known as Eastfields.

480 dwellings. 28.75 dwellings per acre. 100 bedspaces per acre.

Pollards Hill
Both Pains and Pollards Hill were inspired by the perimeter development theories of Lionel March and Sir Leslie Martin at the Centre for Land Use and Built Form Studies in Cambridge. At Pollards it was found that densities of over 100 bedspaces per acre could also be achieved using houses on the ground with gardens and integral garages, giving better living conditions, particularly for families with young children. Apparent density could be reduced by expanding the available perimeter, both by increasing the public open space at the centre of the scheme and by folding the terraces of houses into a Greek key pattern which yielded protected green spaces for children's play, alternating with hard surfaced car courts. Each court in the key pattern steps up the hill.

The narrow frontage three-storey houses have kitchen/dining rooms on the ground floor opening onto private gardens. The garden gates lead to the generous, grassed and sheltered play areas which in turn open through a narrow gap to the park-like open space on the south side of the hill. The living rooms are on the first floor, either overlooking the gardens or opening onto a balcony over the garage depending on the orientation of the block.

Three key design moves help to maintain the density: maximise the perimeter, reduce car court dimensions by including the garage partly in the house, and fill the corners with accommodation, in this case three floors of flats.

850 dwellings. 28 dwellings per acre. 116 bedspaces per acre.

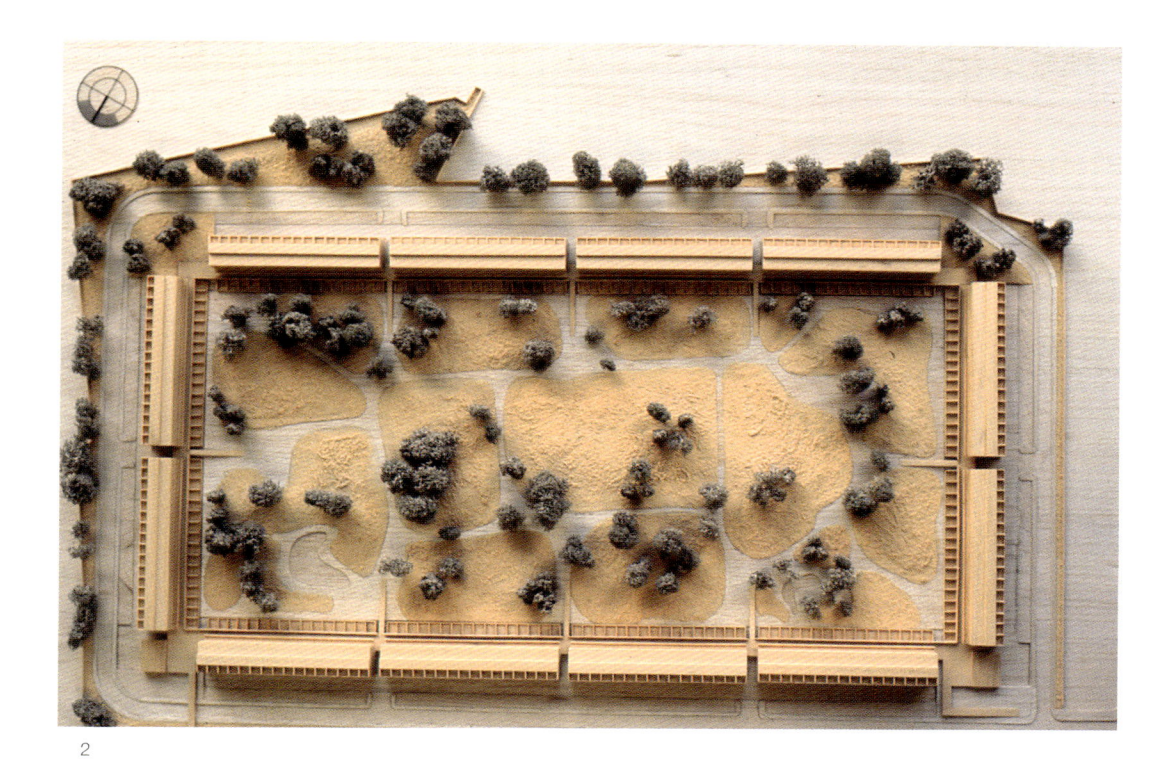

1: Pollards Hill
2: Pains factory site (first scheme)
3: Pollards Hill site plan

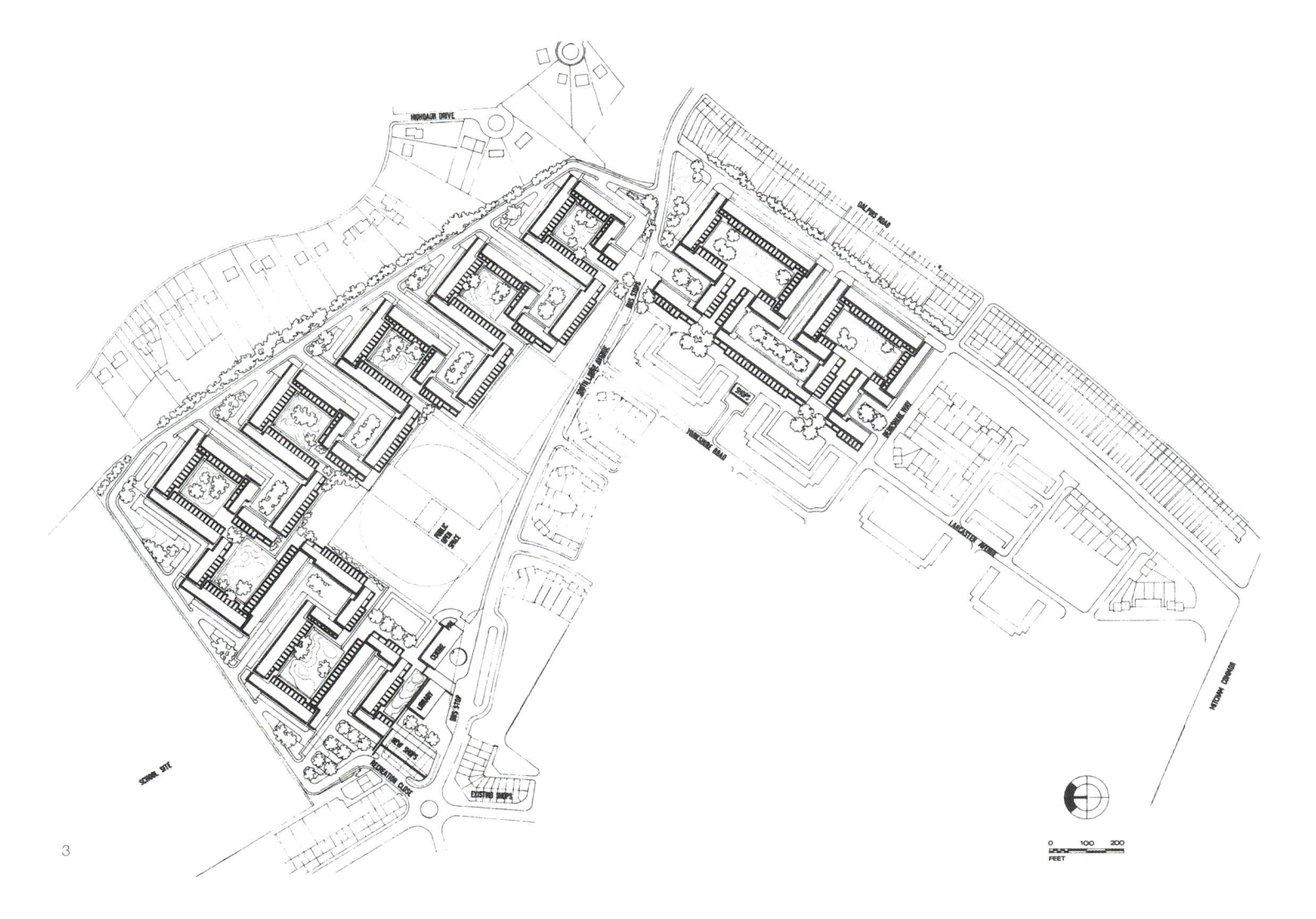

2

3

67

Land Use Studies, Edgbaston, Birmingham
mid-1970s

1: Urban farming in Birmingham **2:** Barrett Homes plan for Edgbaston site **3:** Perimeter development of same site

In the nineteenth century wealthy industrialists and financiers built some very large houses in Edgbaston set in spacious gardens. The City Council wanted to double the population of the area during the early 1970s and Barrett Homes were busy filling in the open spaces with their housing layouts. A group of residents invited Lea to look at some alternatives.

Taking for example the area bounded by Augustus, Norfolk, Harbourne and Westfield Roads, Barrett Homes' site plan showed the typical irrational meandering road system favoured by the volume house builders. No less than 3 hectares of tarmac, excluding hardstandings to houses, served 320 houses and 90 flats.

If these houses, with an average of 300 square-metre gardens had been deployed around the perimeter of the site, an area of 13.1 hectares would have remained as open space in the centre. This could have been developed as woodland, or as allotments for 500 families, one and a half times the number living around the site. Or at 1.5 cows per acre, a small dairy farm would produce 2.5 pints of milk a day for each family. Once land is built over, this productive potential is lost for the foreseeable future.

In Lea's proposals, the average plot width of the perimeter houses was 5.8m. This allowed considerable variation so that some of the houses could be in narrow frontage terraces while others could be more spacious, semi-detached or detached.

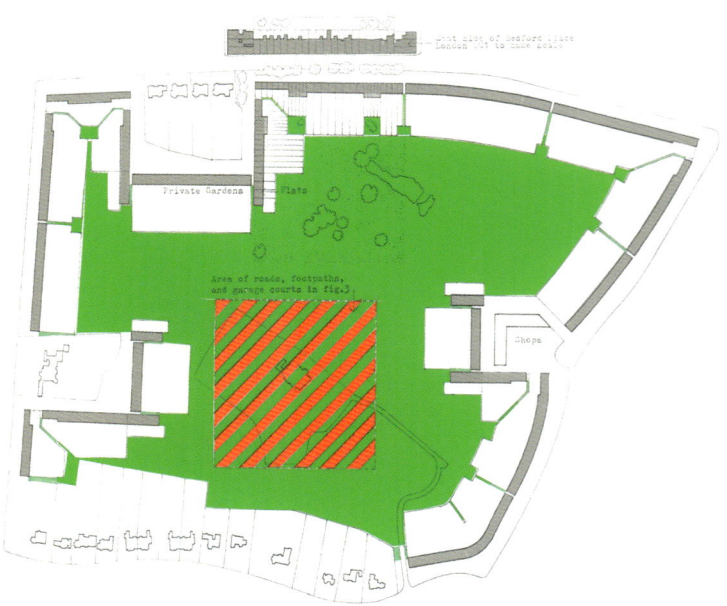

Sheltered Housing, Churt, Surrey
1968–1981

1: House plan (Phase 1) **2:** Aerial perspective of Phases 1 and 2

The Eddystone Housing Association was founded in 1966 by Ruth Douglass for single professional people retiring to Britain without a home to return to. After converting the old house at Quinnettes to flats, she asked Lea for ideas to develop the fine, large garden. She suggested a variety of accommodation, including a flat for a nurse and warden and some communal facilities, and she wanted the units to be easily adaptable and on one floor. Lea used his knowledge of perimeter planning as expounded by his Cambridge teachers and later put into practice by him and his colleagues at Merton. He also drew on Jørn Utzon's courtyard housing in Denmark, which he visited in 1967 just as he was embarking on the first stage of houses for the Association.

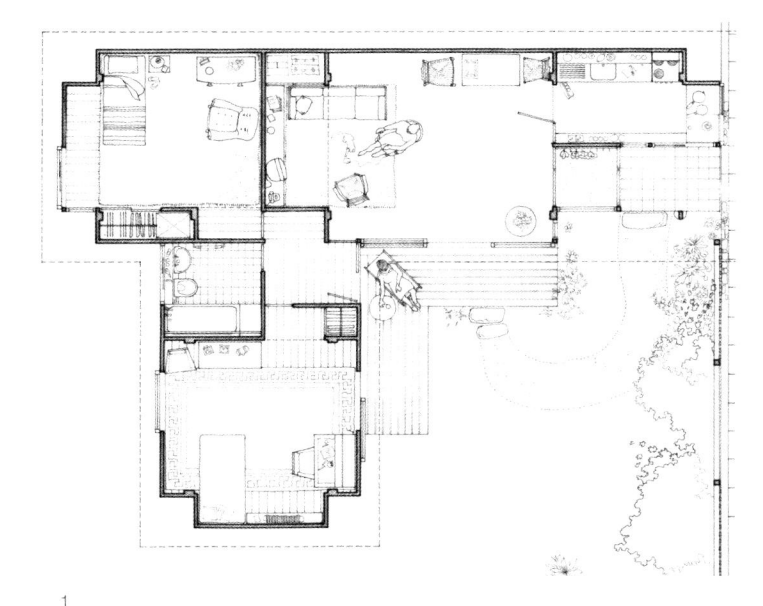

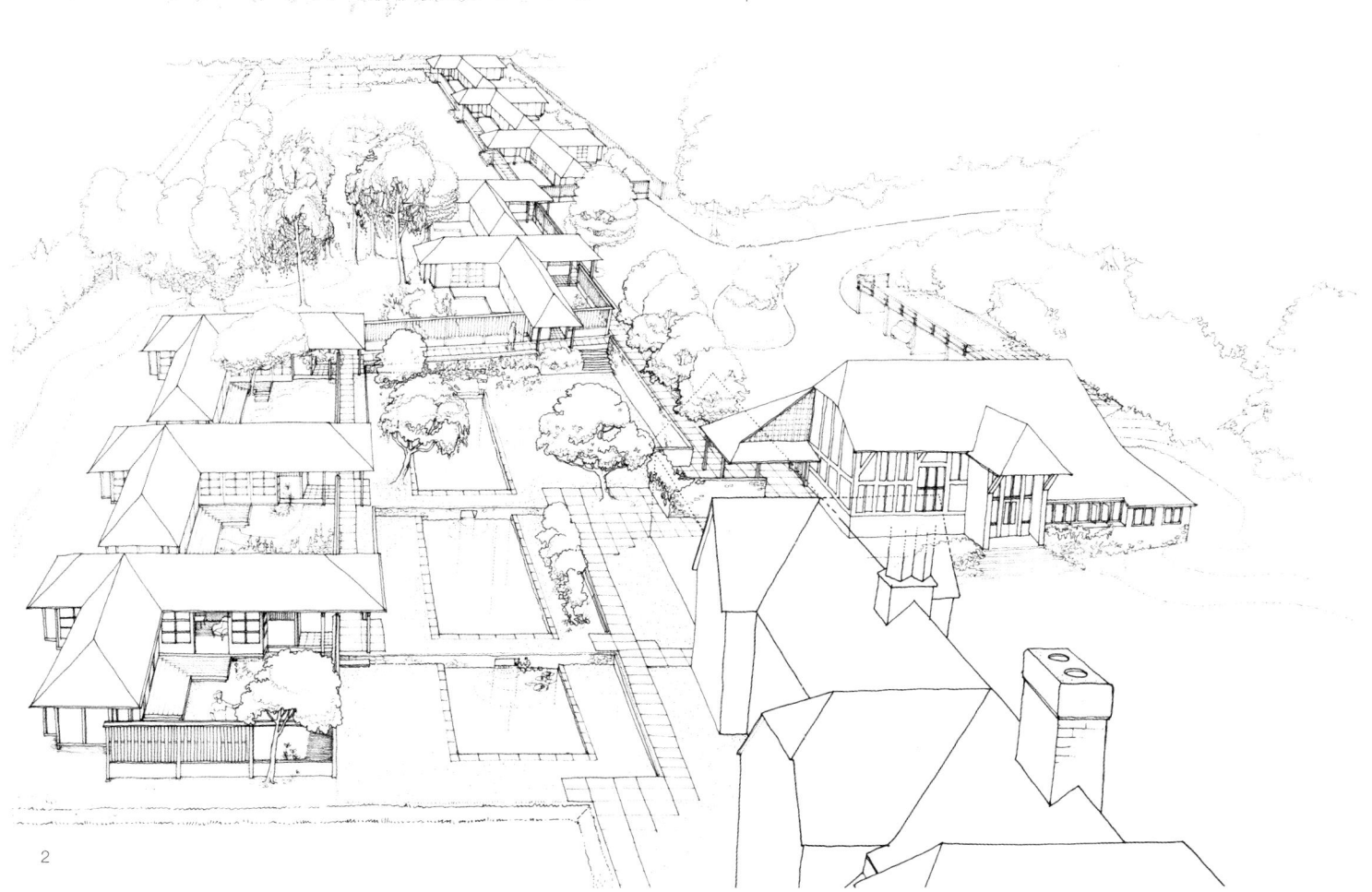

Houses 1–5 (1972)

The group of five houses forms two sides of an enclosed garden, the third side defined by the old house. Each house, in the form of a T, encloses its own private garden and is linked to the next by a path that passes through the covered porch of each house. Lea chose timber-frame for the construction as he felt less confident with his experience of brickwork. He also had in mind Japanese houses and their gardens, and Frank Lloyd Wright's Usonian houses which he had seen during his year in the US. Adapting the ideas of Walter Segal (whom he got to know at this time), he based the plan on a modular tartan grid of 2ft (610mm) with a 2in (50mm) structural/partition zone, enabling standard uncut boards to be used between intersections, their joints covered with timber battens. Partitions and external walls were of woodwool, faced with plasterboard internally and with 3mm Glasal externally, thus avoiding wet trades. The opening windows were unframed sheets of glass sliding in aluminium channels, like in Segal's system (more recently they were replaced with conventional windows). The biggest departure from Segal's system was the roof, however—Lea preferred pitched tiled roofs to flat ones. He also changed the spacing between the external battens as he felt Segal's spacing looked too busy.

Porch Walkway Walkway with porches View to south-west

Houses 6–10 (1974)

Initially to be a continuation of the T-plan houses, the second phase was changed to a terrace of square houses along the east edge of the site, facing a shared lawn to the west. Each house had a connecting living-bedroom space open to the ceiling of the sloping roof, and ancillary accommodation to each side, where the roof swept lower. Lea changed to a 900mm centre-line grid (still with a 'tramline' for the structure), mainly to resolve the problem of narrow doors in the 610mm grid. Other modifications included the thickness of walls (to keep in line with improved thermal insulation requirements), solid floors (Houses 1–5 have raised timber floors) and the use of 1,800mm-long woodwool slabs laid horizontally to maintain the 900mm grid without wastage.

1

2

1: Interior of House 6 **2:** North-west elevation **3:** Detail of external wall **4:** Section (Houses 6 and 10) **5:** Plan (House 6)

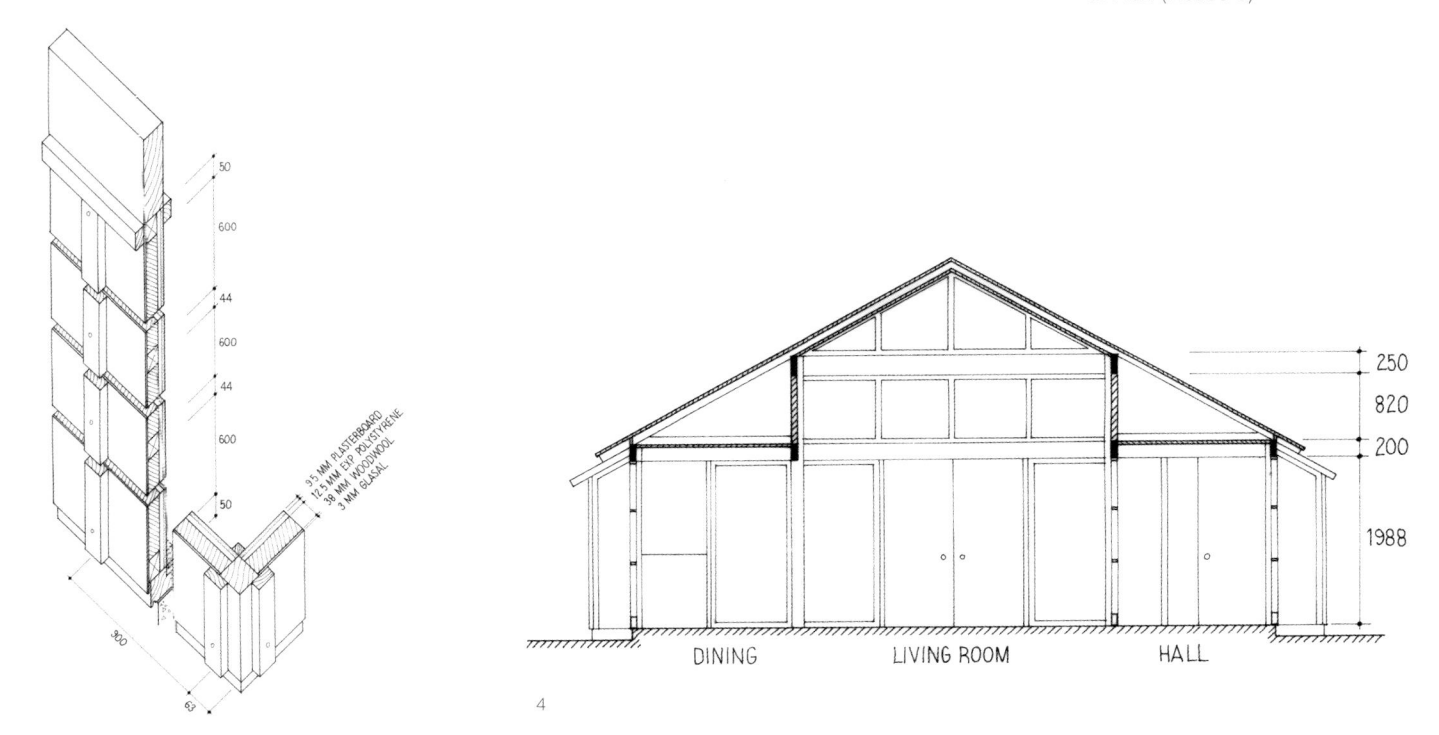

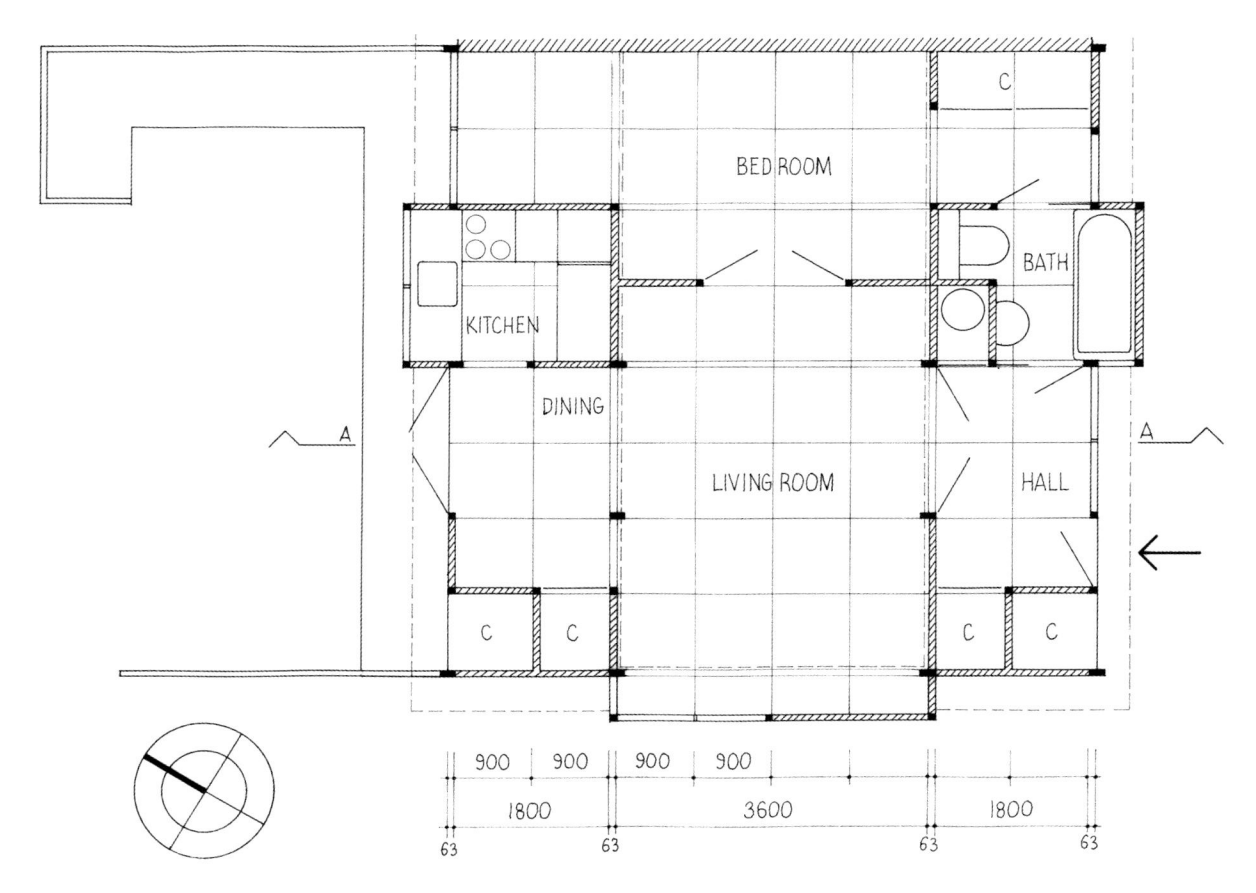

Houses 11 and 12, and the Warden's House (1981)

The third phase of accommodation completed the second enclosed garden implied by the two earlier phases. Lea visited Japan in 1975 and the trip influenced his approach to the latest houses, taking him even further away from Segal's system. Instead of uncut sheets held in place with timber battens, the walls were now plastered or rendered, and the construction relied on carpentry joints rather than lapped and bolted connections. The stained timber of the earlier houses was replaced with clear-finished British Columbian pine, its warm colour and grain exposed. Lea made these modifications to give clarity to the primary structure, which he thought was lacking in the earlier houses.

1: External doorway to bedroom (House 12) **2:** South-west elevation (Houses 11 and 12) **3:** Plan
4: Veranda **5:** Window detail

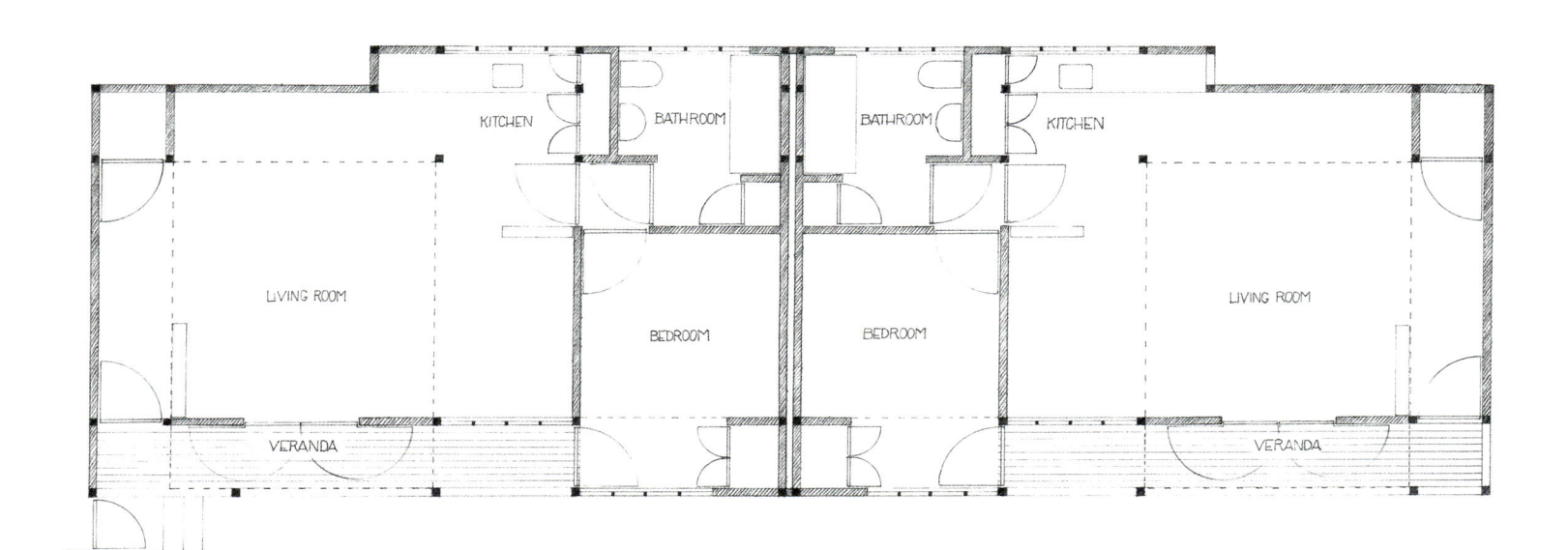

3

4

5

75

Housing, Takeley, Essex
1974

1: Perspective **2:** Ground floor plan **3:** Section **4:** East elevation

The client wished to make use of a piece of land adjacent to his market garden and proposed to build and sell these houses. They were the first of a family of wide frontage houses with their living rooms opening onto their gardens through lofty, south-facing loggias. This is an archetypical pattern observed from Japan to the Ticino in northern Italy and through to Frank Lloyd Wright's Usonian houses. Like the later houses built in The Walled Garden at Coates they have a two-storey main block flanked by a single-storey wing which in this case extends northwards to form a shared entrance courtyard. The entrance door leads directly into a large family dining room closely linked to the kitchen, a smaller sitting room lies round the back of the big fireplace.

The gardens are of adequate size to keep horticulturally-minded families in fruit and vegetables for most of the year.

2

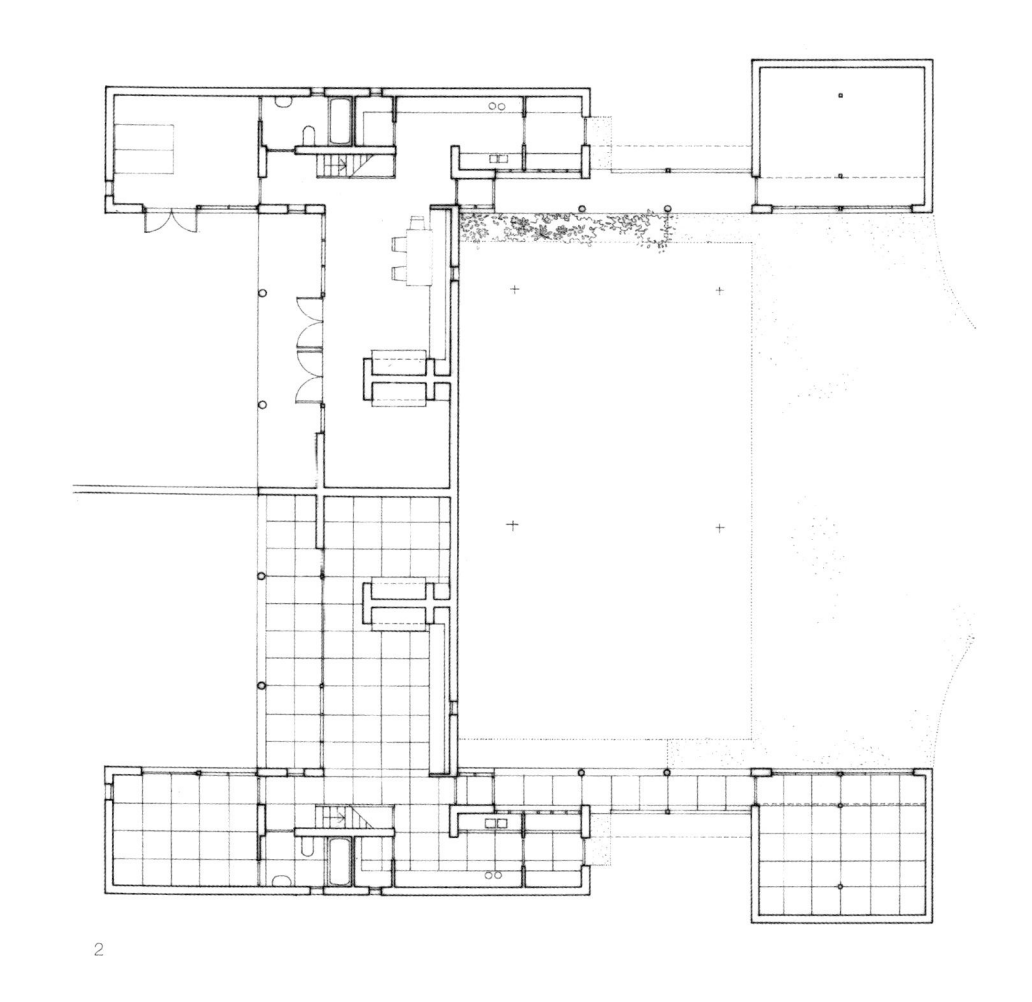

3

4

New Office, Ogoronwy
1981

1: Idealised view from new office
2: Ogoronwy in its setting
3: Cottage and new office from the east

Between the Moelwyn Mountains and the Irish Sea lies a magical land of small valleys, huge rocks, clear streams and ancient oak woods.

Ogoronwy stands on a level platform cut into the north side of one of these valleys, enjoying a distant view of the sea, gleaming through the trees.

When Lea bought Ogoronwy in 1976, the house, built in the early 1900s, was separated from the original cottage by a ruined barn and cowshed. The cottage, built of large, rough stones is a typical, probably seventeenth-century, small Gwynedd farm building. Rerooofing, repointing and rerendering were the first tasks, carried out with the help of architectural students on summer camps.

Reconstruction and alteration of the barn followed to provide an office space for up to four architects. This room is entirely glazed to the south. When the windows slide back on their slate runners, the room can be open during a deluge, protected by the oversailing eaves.

The random rubble walling stone lay on the site where it had fallen, the structural timber was supplied by a local reclaimed timber merchant, and the slates came from Blaenau Ffestiniog. The builders were Lea, Adam and Frances Voelcker, and two antipodeans who turned up looking for work, Phil and Julie Edney.

OGORONWY
VIEW FROM SOUTH EAST

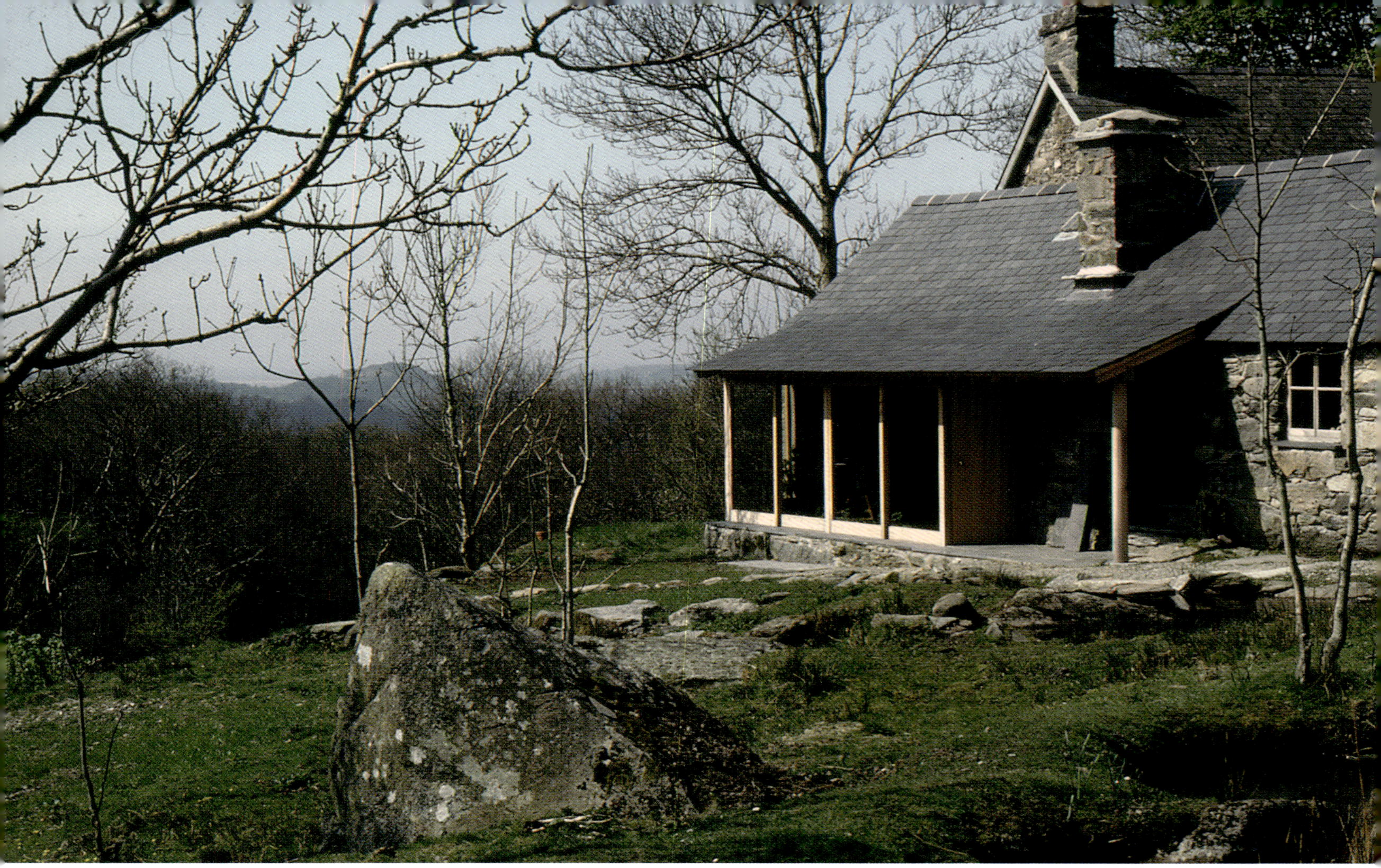

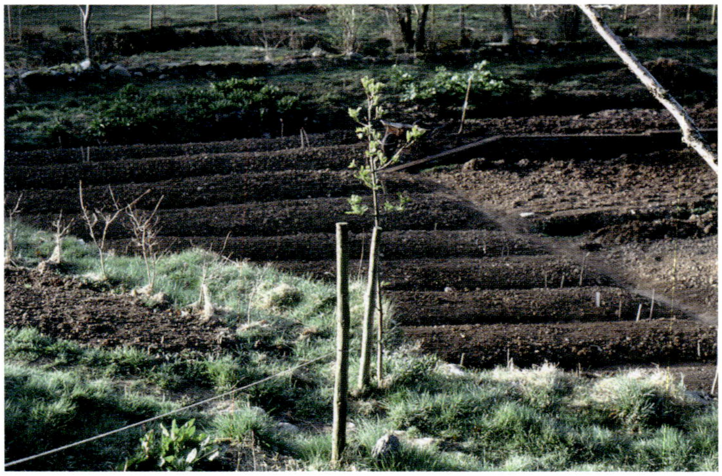

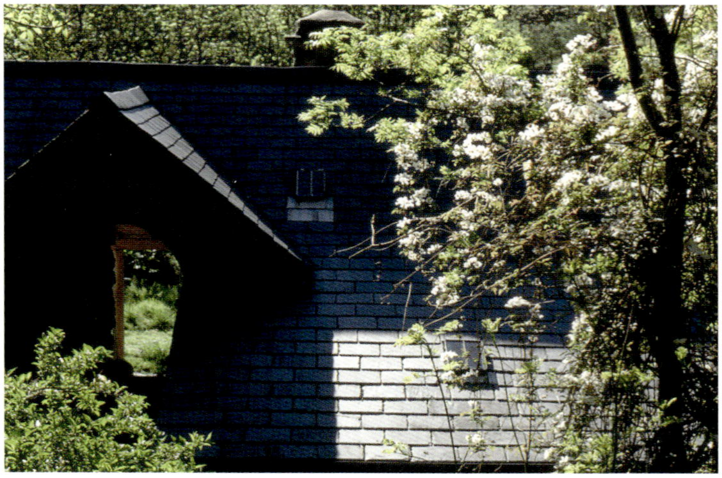

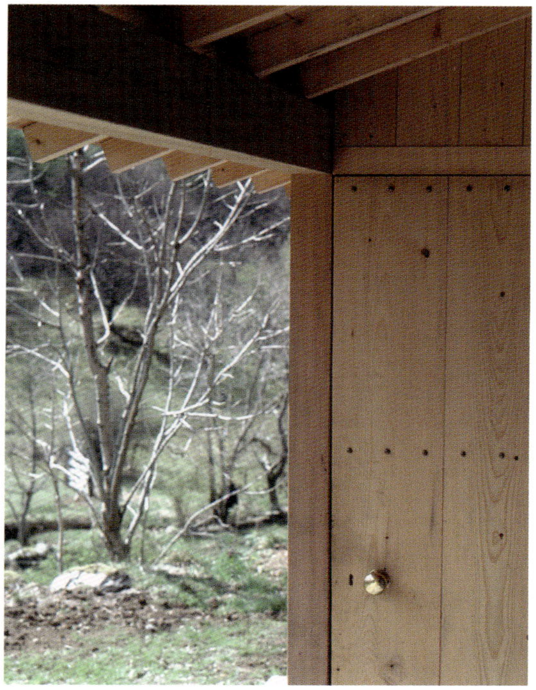

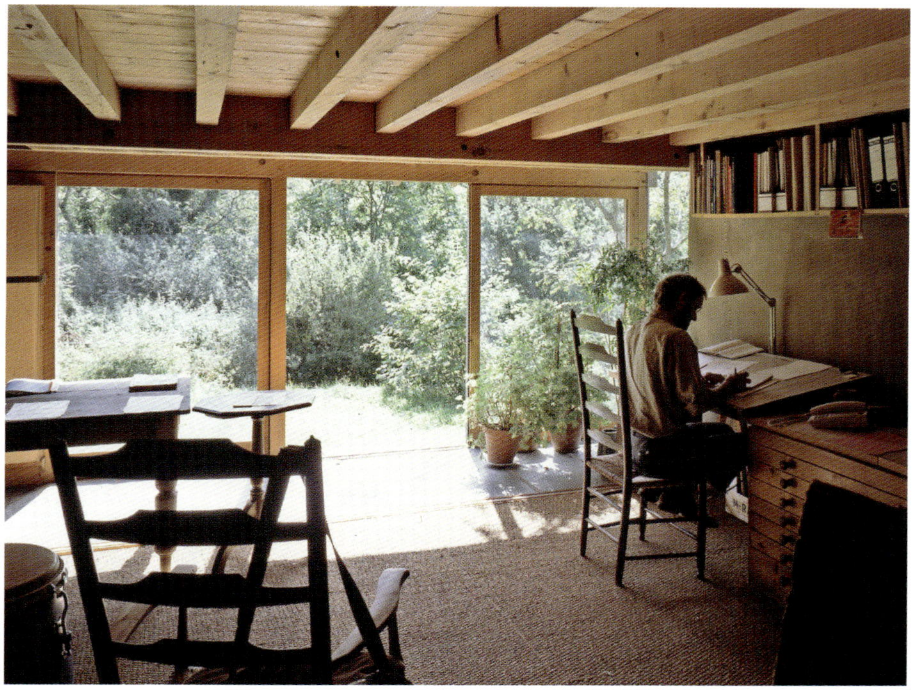

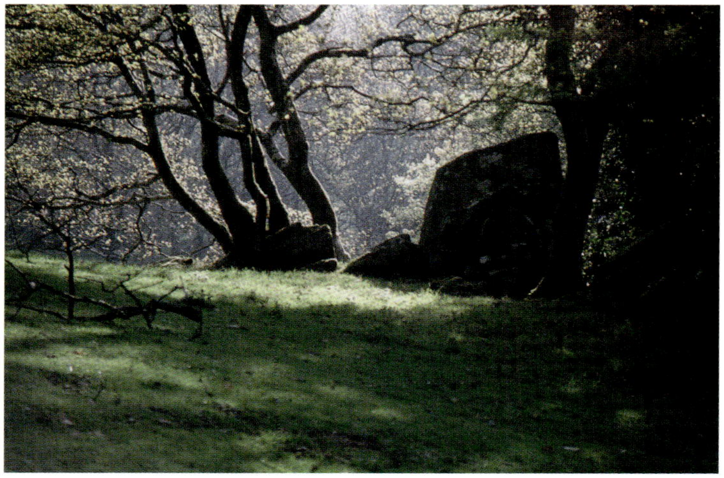

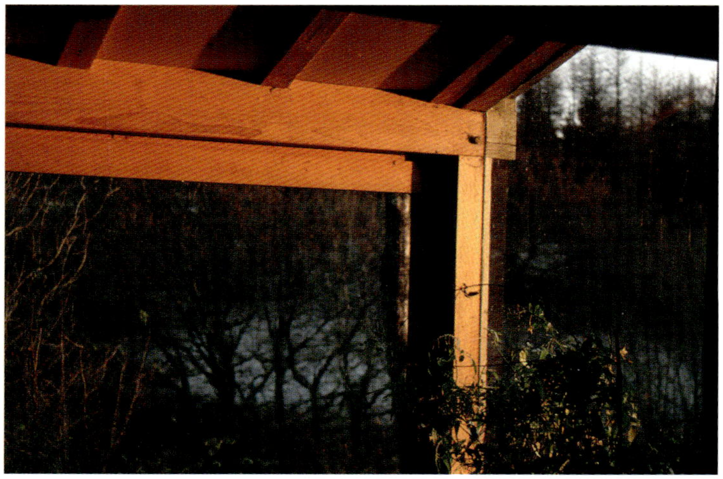

Bledisloe Court, The Royal Agricultural College, Cirencester
1981–1982

1: East elevation **2:** Cotswold stone roof **3:** View from corner of courtyard **4:** Ground floor plan

Bledisloe Court, consisting of 59 student rooms with shared bathrooms and 'gyp' (kitchenette) facilities, formed the first phase of the proposed expansion of the college in the 1980s in anticipation of establishing degree courses. The courtyard plan and the arrangement of rooms around a staircase were a direct result of Lea's Cambridge experience and also of a visit to Oxford made by the bursar and the governors, convincing them that the simplicity and serenity of traditional collegiate courtyards was far preferable to the student accommodation they saw elsewhere.

There are six houses of ten rooms, grouped either side of a staircase (four above four, plus two in the roof) and these share bathrooms and a small 'gyp' projecting out from the staircase landing like an oriel. Each room has a basin and its plan spirals like a snail-shell from the door to the desk aedicule, getting more enclosed and intimate as you go further in. The courtyard is three-sided, its open side facing away from the college in a westerly direction. It is entered on each of the three sides and gives access to three houses; the other three are entered from outside the courtyard. In this way it is not a dead space, nor is it so noisy that the ground-floor rooms are disturbed. A simple gravel path surrounds a lawn which, until playing fields were provided beyond, faced out over an expanse of cornfield across a ha-ha—like a quay-side, a sheltered harbour and the open sea beyond.

The construction is insulated cavity brick/block walls, in-situ and pre-cast concrete floors and a steep timber roof. The window and door surrounds are of limestone, the windows single-glazed directly into the stone or in metal frames where opening. The walls are finished with roughcast using local sands and aggregates, and the roofs with stone tiles specially quarried for the job and laid to diminishing courses in the traditional manner. The decision to use roughcast brick and genuine stone roof tiles was made (not without some client reserve) as a stand against conventional concrete 'look-alike' products, which consumed more energy in their production and were, in Lea's view, dishonest. The details are simple, minimal, and traditional without aping period details. To achieve a flat aesthetic for the elevations, projecting sills and hood-moulds were avoided and windows were designed as repeated holes punched in the wall, again much in the traditional manner. Internal details are plain and robust, strong enough to withstand misuse by rowdy students yet at the same time displaying an elegant, Shaker-like simplicity.

2

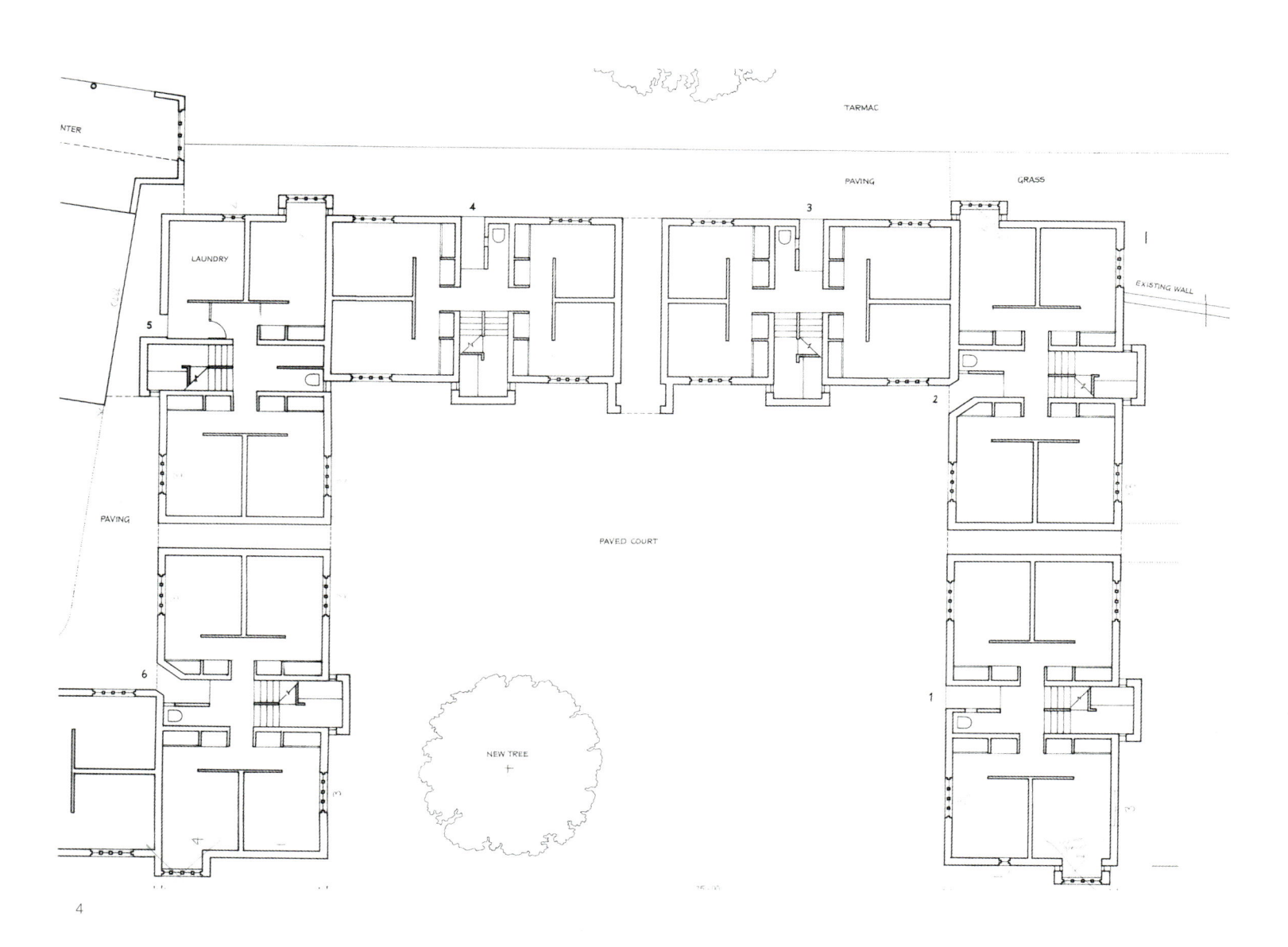

3

4

Library Extension,
The Royal Agricultural College,
Cirencester
1982

The first of Lea's new buildings at the college, this extended the Hosier Library (built in 1976) and provided a space for individual study and another for group study and project work. The underlying idea was the cool, shady space under a tree. The tree stands in the centre of the individual study room, supporting an umbrella of roof that descends gently to cover two arms of group study space placed protectively around the main room to the north and east.

Natural daylight enters at the centre of the main room (at the apex of the roof) and at its edges (through a continuous strip of skylights), washing with light the walls and the glazed bookcases below. A similar strip lights the group study spaces, again providing excellent lighting conditions for the books directly below, and a strip of timber windows lights the periphery.

The construction is conventional: insulated cavity brick/block walls finished with roughcast, a concrete floor slab and a timber-rafter roof finished with Welsh slates. Windows are purpose-made in iroko. Internal joinery and furniture are mostly in ash and inspired by Shaker design.

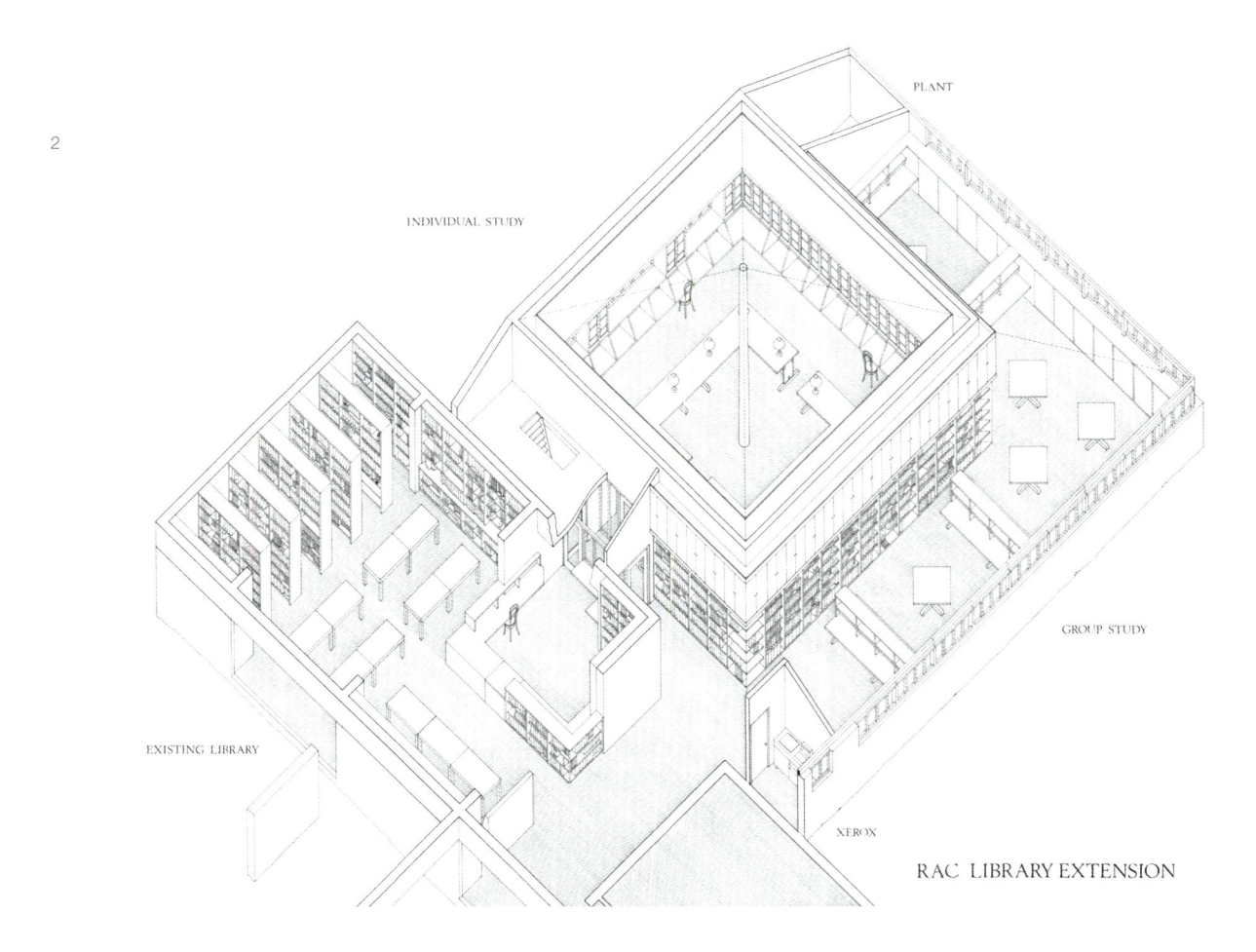

1: Individual study room, towards window 2: Axonometric
3: Section 4: Individual study room

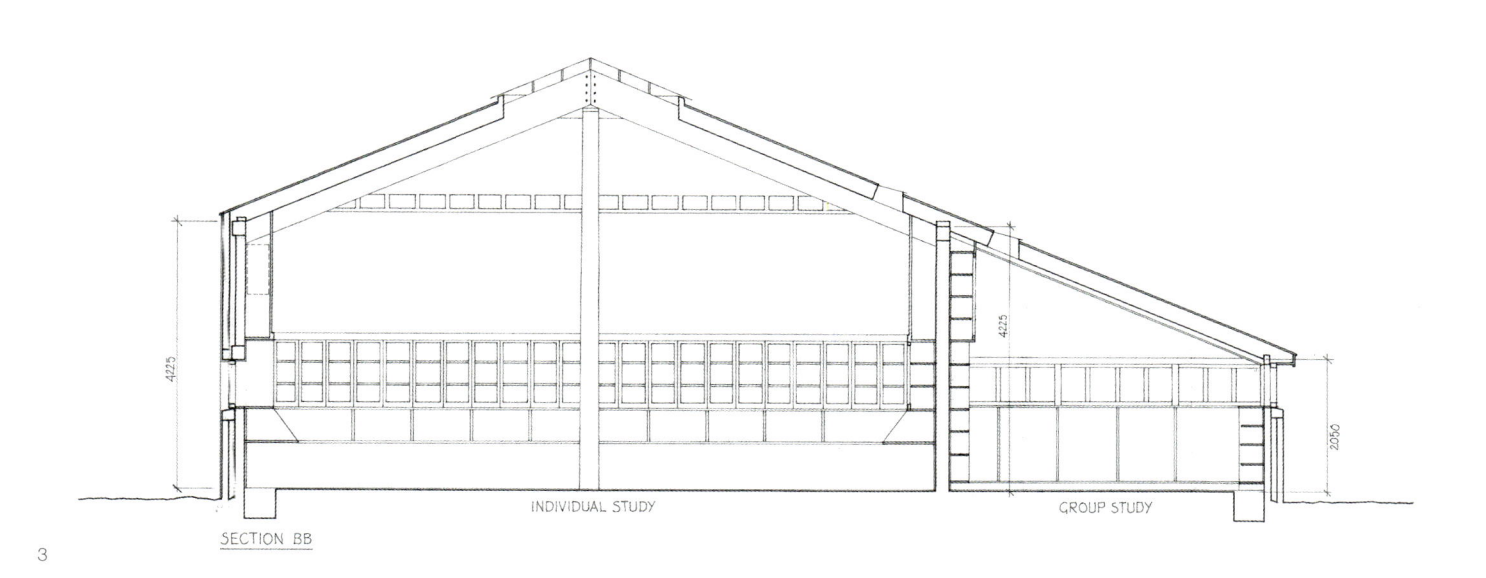

SECTION BB   INDIVIDUAL STUDY   GROUP STUDY

Pembroke College, Oxford
1986

1: Perspective (north-south)
2: House plans 3: Common room
4: Study bedroom 5: East-west section through courtyards
6: Block plan

This scheme was short-listed with three others, from an initial list of 16, for about 100 study bedrooms on a site overlooking the River Thames. As the development would be at some distance from the main college, one of the requirements was for it to engender its own spirit of community. Indeed, the brief went so far as to stipulate a collegiate layout. Because pedestrian and vehicular approaches to the site were from opposite directions, posing a potential security problem, just one point of entry was made a requirement.

Lea's design is an elaboration of Bledisloe Court. The layout is based on a sequence of collegiate courtyards. Two of them are open (one at the entrance, the other around a lagoon) and two are enclosed (the first on axis with the entrance and the communal building, formally paved and with a fountain; the second, grassed and more relaxed, with a large tree at its centre). The rooms are grouped in houses of six, and share bathrooms, a kitchen and a welcoming common room immediately adjacent to each entrance. As all the study bedrooms are dual aspect they can be placed on any side of a courtyard and will still receive some sunlight during the day.

A noble loggia of double-height timber columns leads to the common rooms which occupy a three-storey barn-like building with large fireplaces, an exposed-structure roof and a glazed gallery oversailing the river. With its brick and stone walls, the steep clay-tiled roofs and the oak windows, it is unselfconsciously traditional, yet in its simple detailing it is straightforward in a modern sense, using natural, local materials in an unfussy manner that brings out their qualities.

1

2

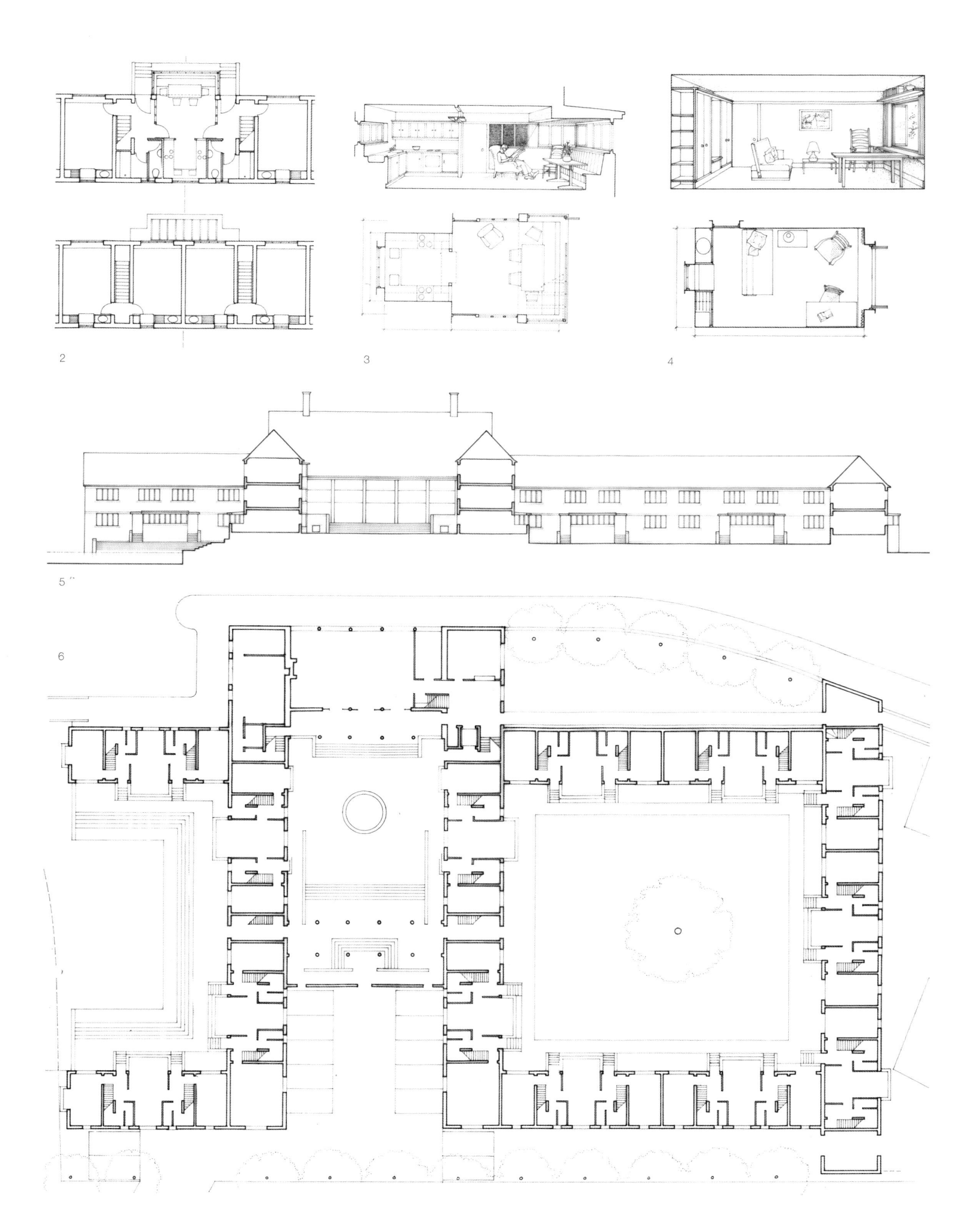

3

4

5

6

The Walled Garden, Coates, Gloucestershire
1986

The houses were built in the walled garden of Bledisloe Lodge, a mansion (formerly Coates Manor) owned by the college until sold to raise funds for their expansion programme. The plots were purchased separately, one by a self-builder, two by clients employing a contractor in the usual way and two by the same contractor acting as developer.

Each house has an L-plan and sits at the corner of its plot, facing south or south-west to its garden. Although each is different, they all share the same set of parts: a living/dining arm at right-angles to a bedroom/study arm, with a kitchen and entrance at the angle, near to the garage wing. The spiral relationship of kitchen, dining table and gathering around the fireplace is a version of Frank Lloyd Wright's Usonian house arrangement where the kitchen is placed in a little bay screened from, but part of, the living room. Upstairs, almost entirely in the roof, are more bedrooms and a bathroom. On the entrance side, windows are small and placed in a continuous strip; on the garden side, they become full height glazed sliding doors, neatly contained below the roof which projects down from the main eaves to define a threshold between the garden outside and the more protected living/dining area within the main body of the house, like the south-facing sheltered veranda often found in Japanese houses.

The houses feel rooted in their gardens and in the landscape as if they had always been there; they display a unity of design, with all their components and fittings specially designed to be consistent within the overall aesthetic concept; and they are beautifully crafted. The materials are natural and are used in a straightforward way (clay roof tiles, roughcast wall finish using local sands and aggregates) and traditional building methods are used side by side with new ones (solid aerated concrete block walls, Glulam ridge beams). The houses continue to please their owners, most of them still the original occupants. One is reminded of Morris's *News from Nowhere* when his narrator describes some "very pretty houses" along the River Thames: "they were mostly built of red brick and roofed with tiles, and looked above all comfortable, and as if they were, so to say, alive and sympathetic with the life of the dwellers in them."

1

1: Perspective (House 1) **2:** Living room (House 5) **3:** View from bedroom wing (House 5)

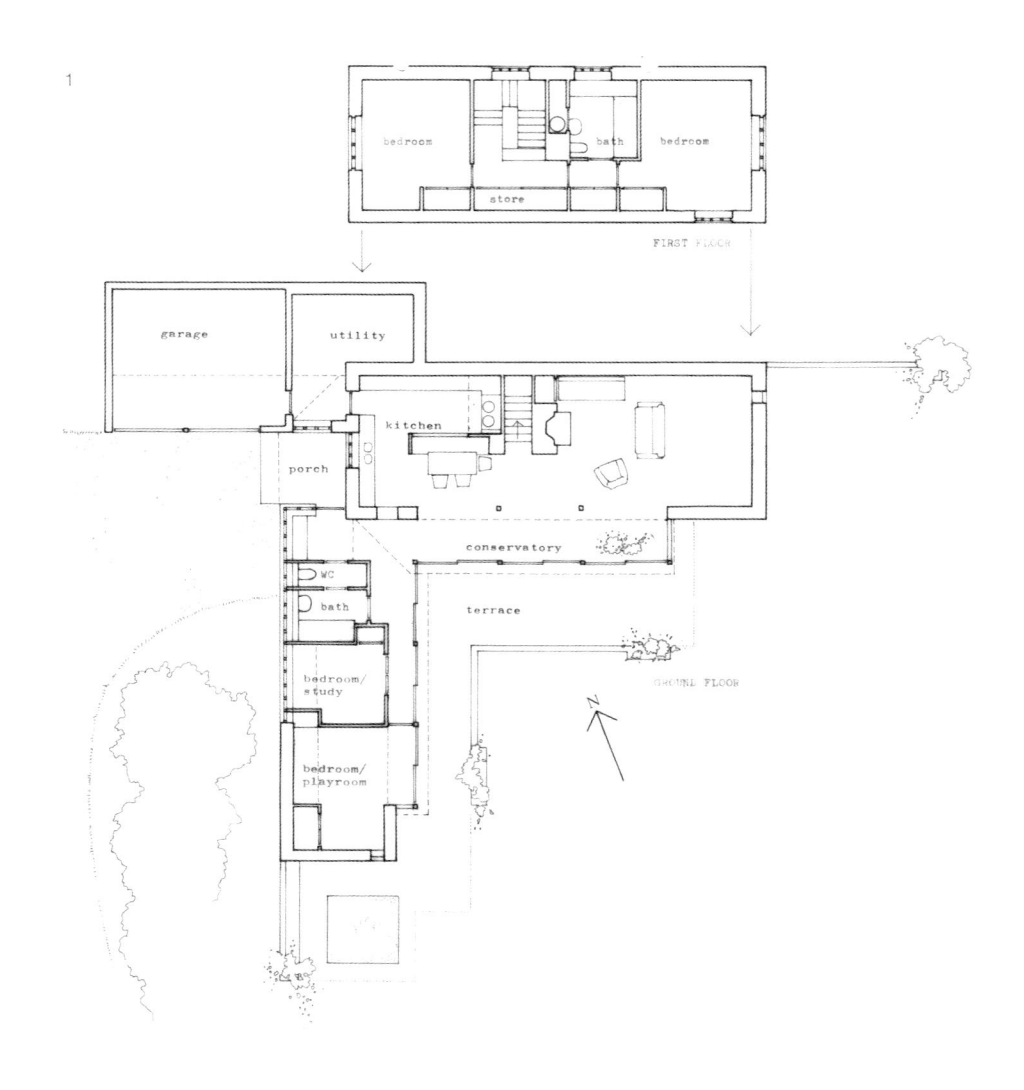

1: House plan (House 5)
2: Garden side (House 5) **3:** Living room (House 5) **4:** Site Plan **5:** View from south, garden of (House 4)

MANOR FARM

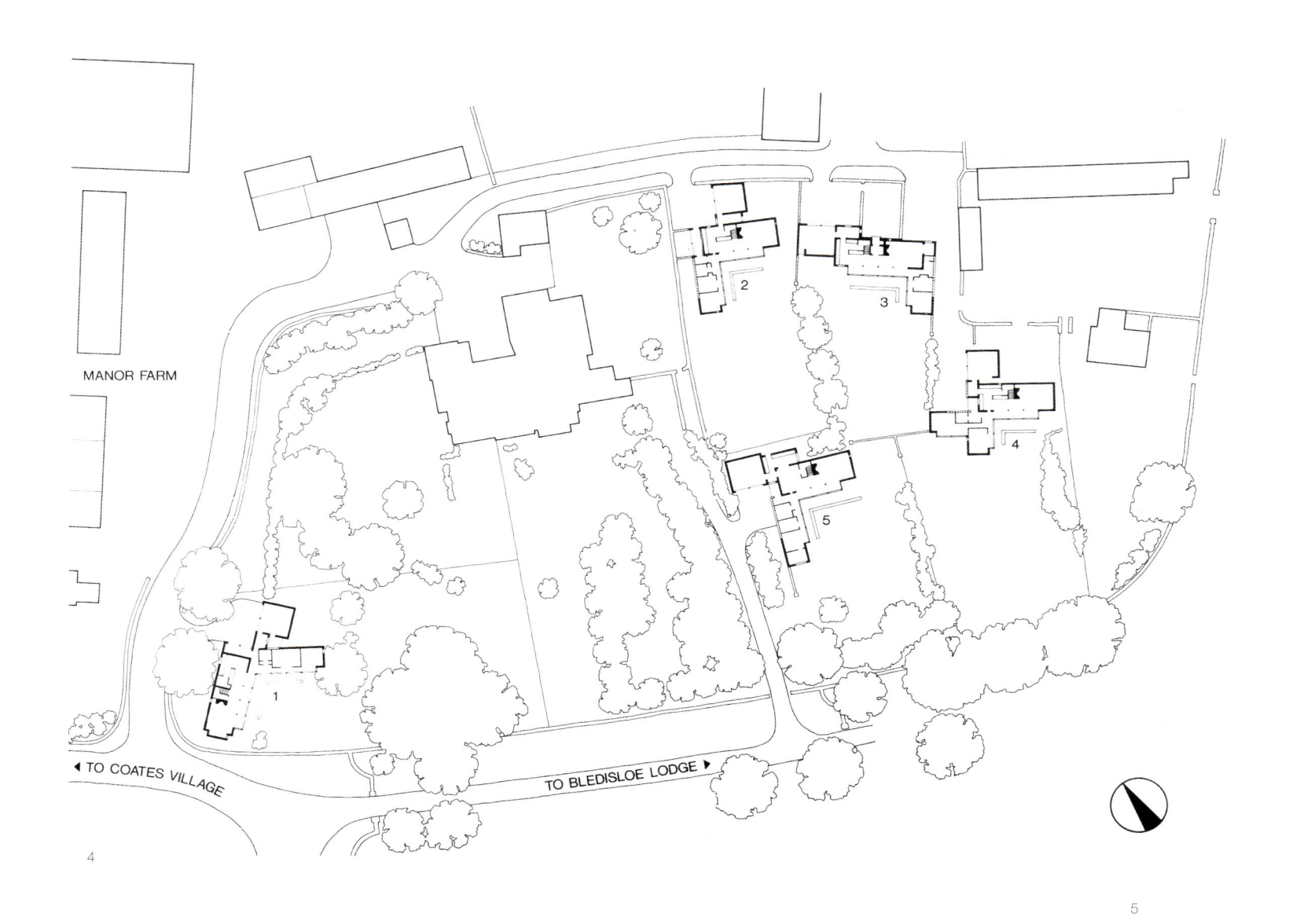

◀ TO COATES VILLAGE   TO BLEDISLOE LODGE ▶

4

5

91

Timber-Framed Gwynedd House Project
1988

1: Plan **2:** Interior **3:** Ideas for a timber-framed house

A fine stand of 60-year-old Western Red Cedar from the Glasfryn Estate on the the Lleyn Peninsular was felled to provide all the timber, structure, trim and ceiling boards, for a show house to demonstrate the use of local materials.

The house had a very economical plan based on a lofty top-lit living room surrounded by smaller spaces for cooking, eating, washing and sleeping. Sky light is particularly welcome in a cloudy climate when the days are often dark.

The living room was entered first, its open hearth extending a welcome to family and guest alike, a small version of the central halls of Baillie Scott's houses.

Despite the support of Antur Llanaelhaearn it proved impossible to find a site or finance for this house and so the timber gradually found its way into other projects.

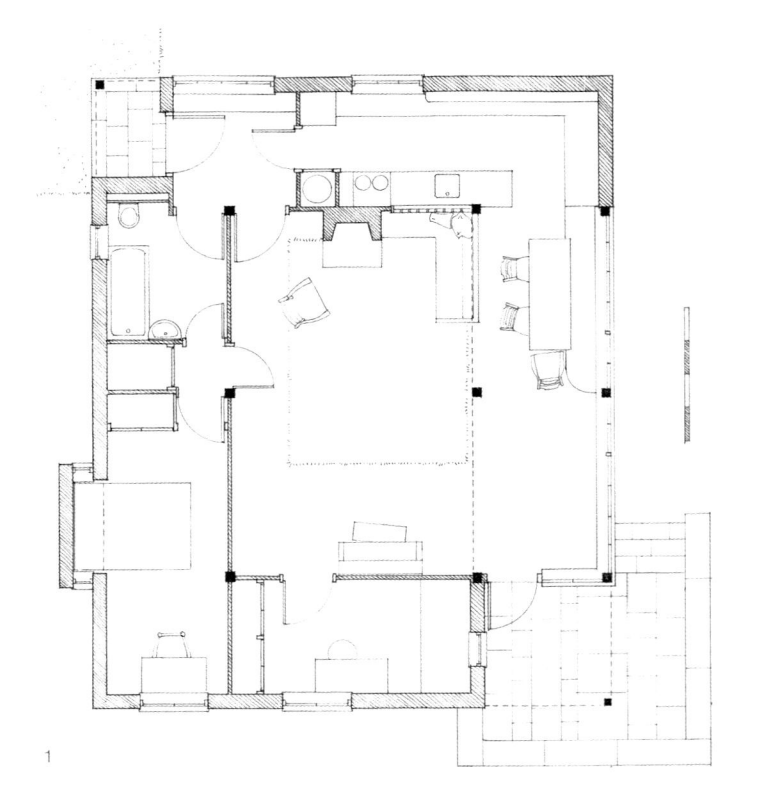

①

A fire in a woodland clearing

A big, top-lit living room — good for a wet climate

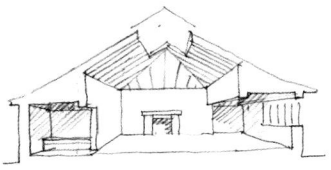

A big living room surrounded by little spaces, cabins for sleeping, cooking, bathing, eating — make a little house seem big.

②

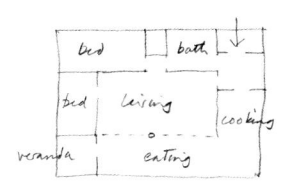

A compact plan without corridors — no waste space

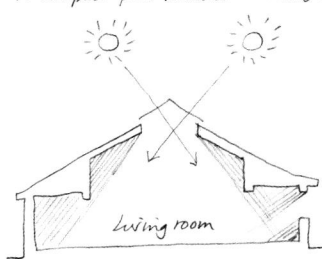

A house which can face in any direction and still receive sunlight into the living room.

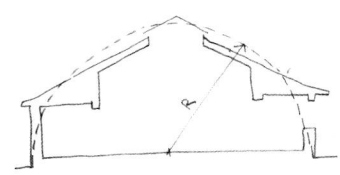

A shape as close as possible to a hemisphere — maximum volume for minimum surface area — least amount of material and most economic to heat.

③

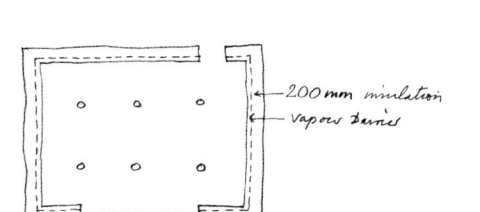

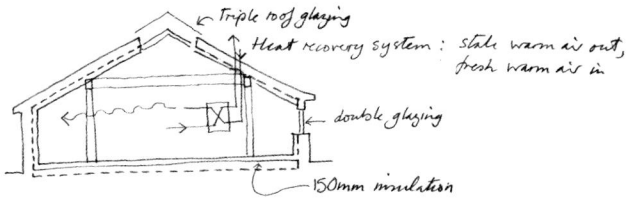

- 200 mm insulation
- vapour barrier
- Triple roof glazing
- Heat recovery system: stale warm air out, fresh warm air in
- double glazing
- 150 mm insulation

A house which is very cheap to heat

A house which can easily be extended

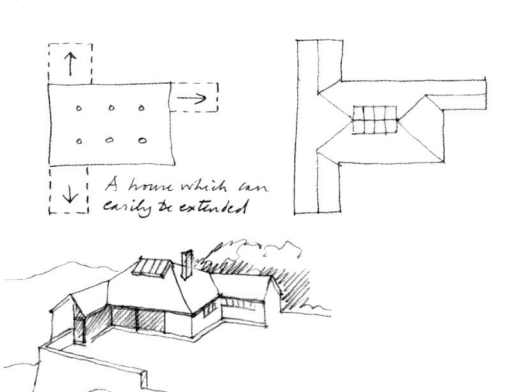

④

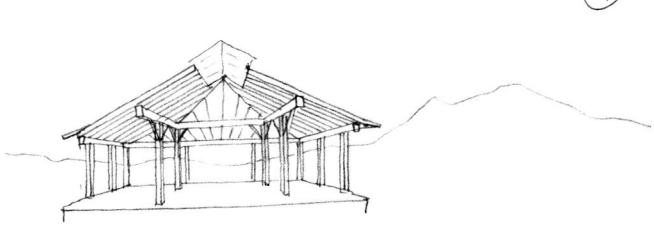

A house which is easy to construct in a wet climate because the roof goes up first — to make a site workshop.

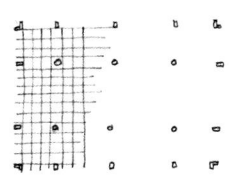

A house with a regular structural system to make pre-fabrication and use of standard materials easier.

A house built mainly of wood, so that most of the structure can be produced, converted and assembled locally, without large machines.

Darwin College, Cambridge
1989

1: Section through computer room **2:** Section through library and colonnade **3:** Riverside elevation **4:** Plan

Lea was one of four architects chosen to develop ideas for new rooms on a site owned by Newnham College and a library/study-centre on the main site on Silver Street. His first proposal was a circular library with a domed ceiling and circular lobes attached to the main space, but the college decided to change the site to a long, narrow sliver squeezed between Silver Street and the Mill Pond. In Lea's revised scheme, a vestige of the circular reading room survives in the round double-height entrance hall that acts as a hinge to the two wings of accommodation radiating from it. The short arm between the drum and the Old Granary contains WCs below a study bedroom; the longer arm contains the main double-height reading room, open to the barrel-vaulted roof and overlooked by a gallery at each end, leading to a computer room and staircase. The staircases are expressed as little towers on the river side, and between them the roof sweeps down over a glazed loggia that gives access to the reading room, its sill so low that one might touch the water, like the beautiful timber wash-houses along rivers in France. Windows are small on the road side (the main spaces are lit from a continuous skylight along the ridge), allowing the elevation to be read as a garden wall (which in fact it is). The materials are a warm brick for the walls, clay tiles for the roofs (including the conical roof over the drum) and oak for the windows, doors and loggia structure.

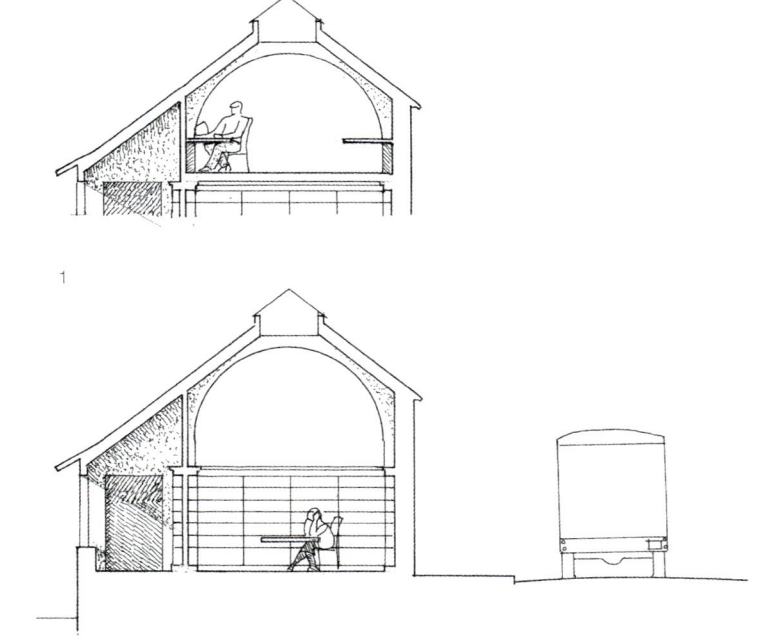

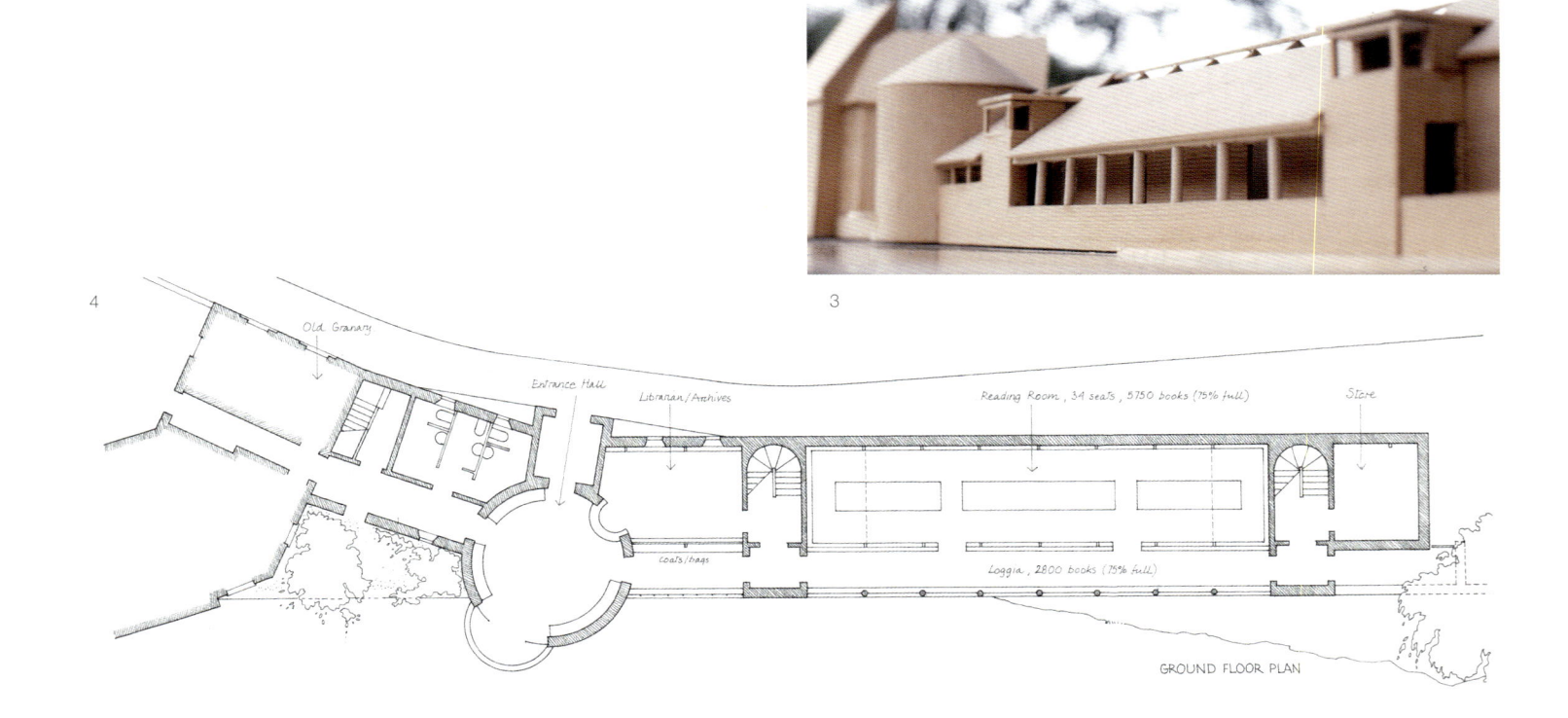

Artist's Studio, Somerset
1989

1: Preliminary sketches for first scheme **2:** Window/bed place

When the client, a painter, left London and returned to her childhood home in Somerset, she asked Lea to design her a studio. Initially the idea was to use timber from trees on the estate. To reach these, a dense undergrowth of saplings would have to be cleared but it occurred to Lea that he could put these to good use and spare the maturer trees. After experimenting with a pair of saplings bent and tied together to form an arch, he sketched out a small structure of oval plan, like an upturned boat, with glazing at both ends and a bay window (for the bed) at the centre. The sapling hoops, at 0.9m centres, were stuck in the ground and screwed to an edge board, and then held together by a lattice of thinner saplings. A lime render was applied to straw covered in chicken-wire, inside and out, and wheat straw thatch laid on the roof. Lea prepared only two A3 drawings for this structure and was permanently on site during the first few weeks of its construction, helping the client and her friends to build it.

The studio is a tiny project, but it embodies so much that Lea stands for in his search for an architecture appropriate to its place, one which sits lightly on the earth and does not waste the planet's resources. It also illustrates the way Lea constantly reduces everything to the essential: materials used as near as possible to their natural state, structure kept simple and functional, the paraphernalia of modern life dispensed with. All this so that the essence of life itself can be enjoyed to the full. The client spent the last five years of her life here. In its Zen-like simplicity one senses that Lea was also designing the perfect hermit's cell for himself.

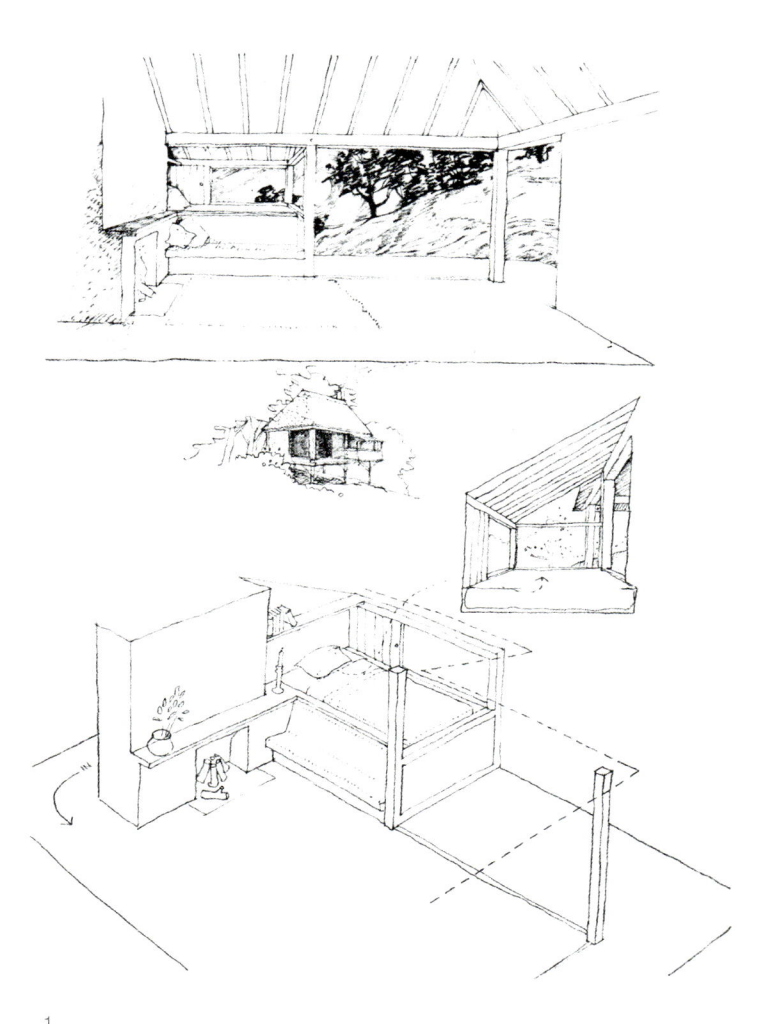

96

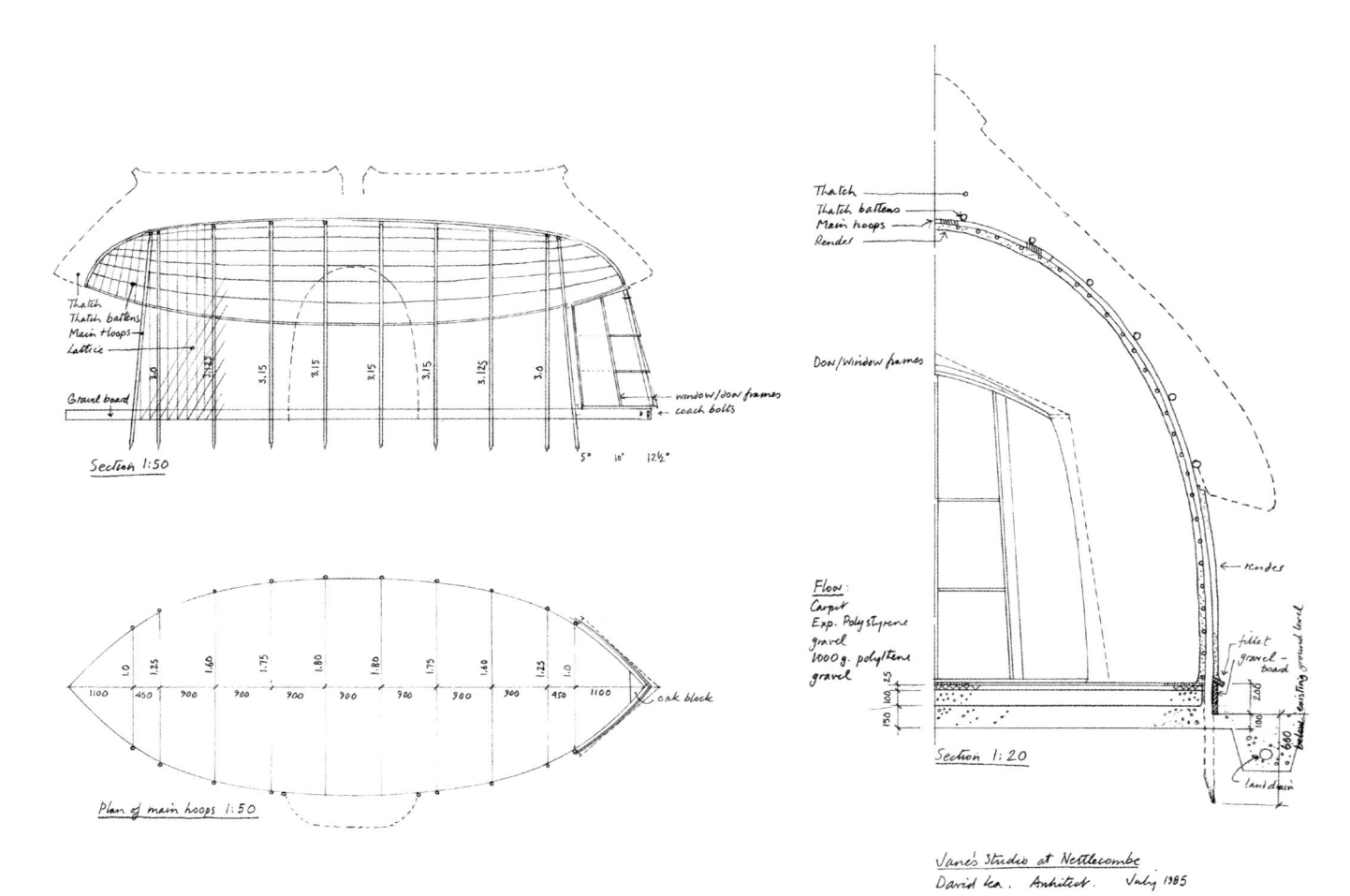

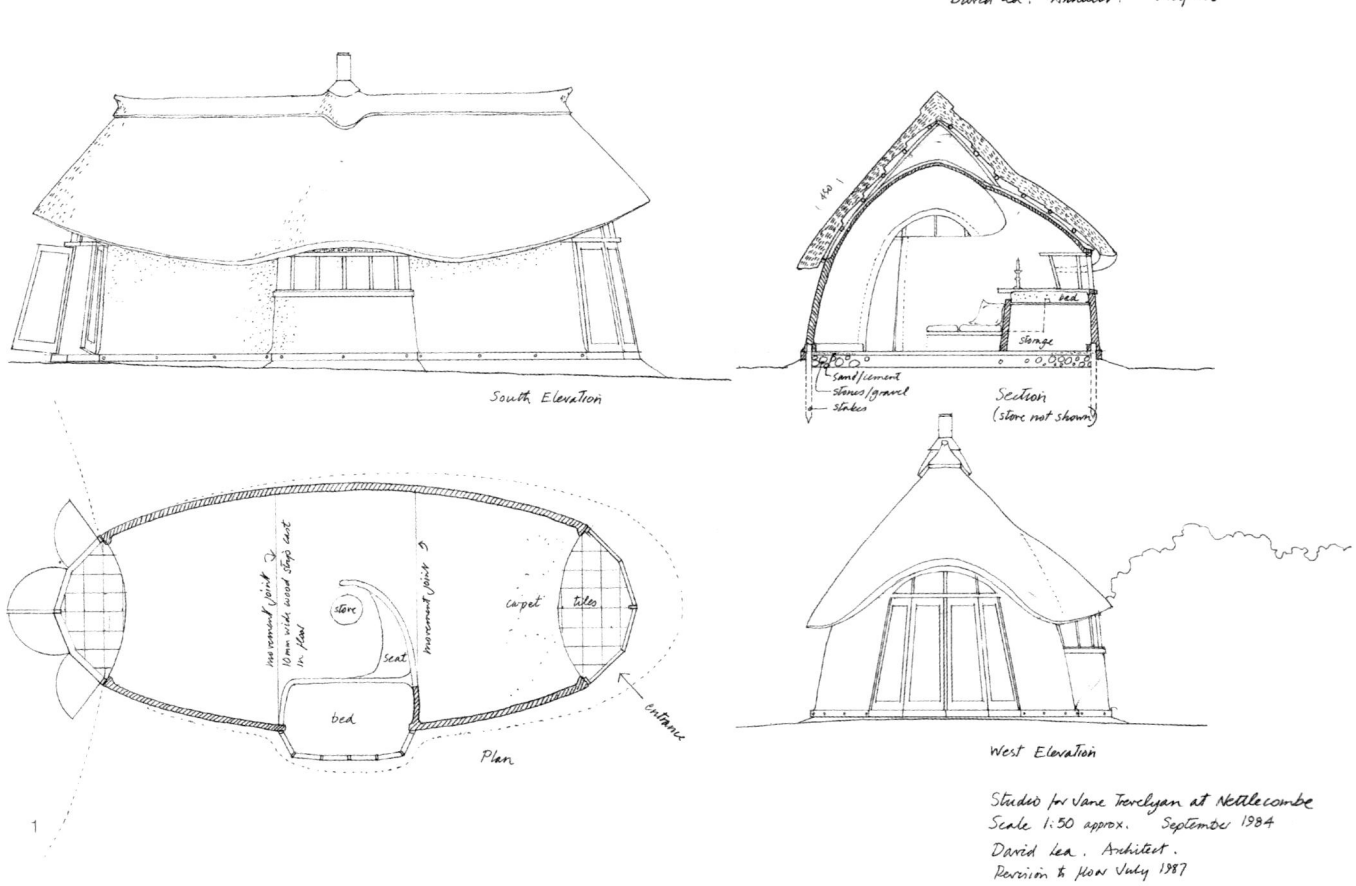

1: Working drawing
2: Construction sequence

2

97

It is not an ordinary sort of hut I live in. It measures only 10ft square, and is under 7ft in height. As I had no fancy for any particular place I did not fasten it to the ground. I prepared a foundation and on it raised a framework which I roofed over with thatch, cramping the parts with crooks so that I might remove it easily if ever the whim took me to dislike the locality. The labour of removing, how slight it would be!—a couple of carts would suffice to carry the whole of the materials, and the expense of their hire would be that of the whole building.
Kamo-no-Chomei (c 1154–1216)

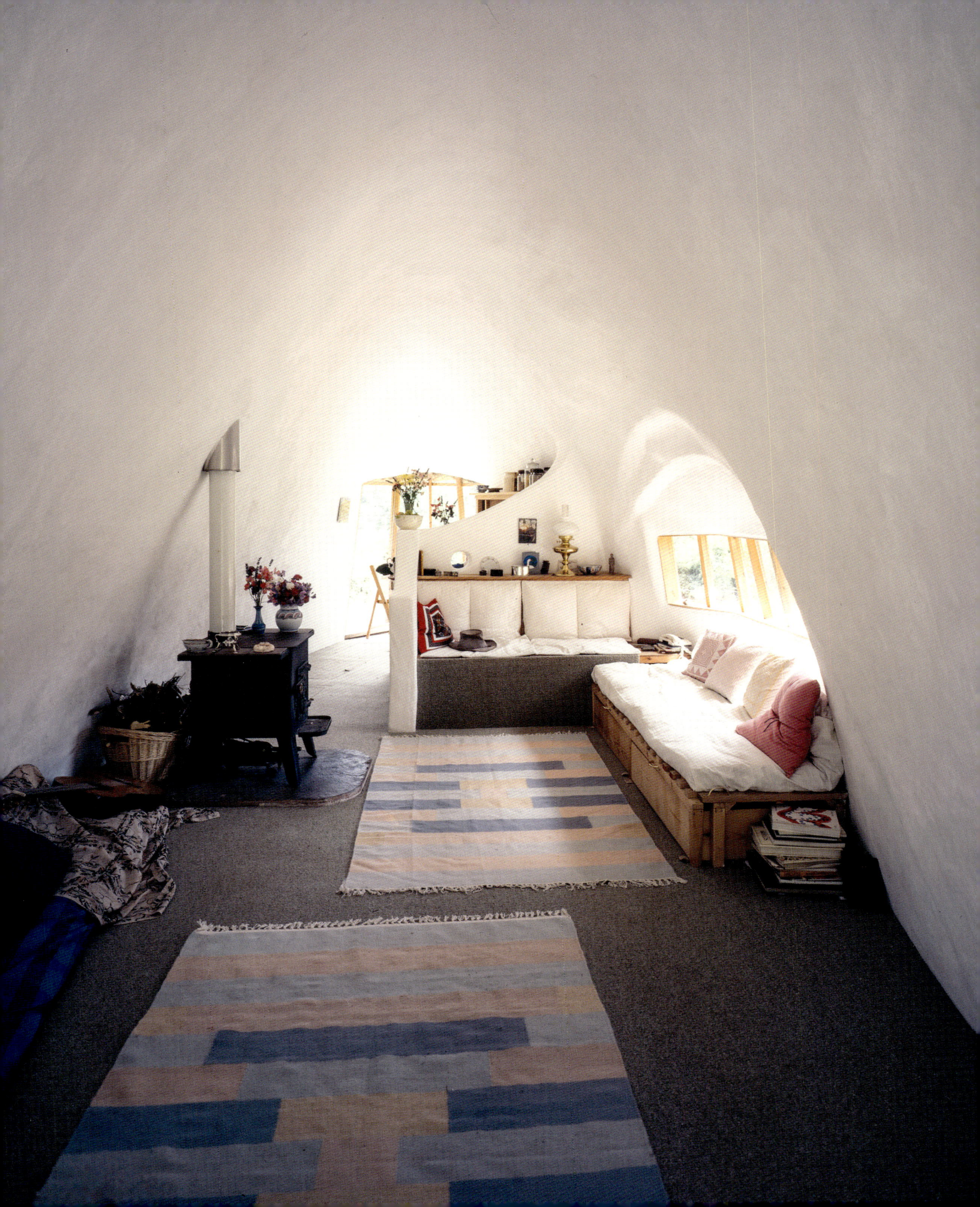

Coad Court, The Royal Agricultural College, Cirencester
1991

Almost a decade after Bledisloe Court was designed, a second phase of 53 student rooms was built to its north, forming the first of four proposed courtyards that would extend as far as the northern boundary of the college. By this time standards for students and holiday lettings had risen, so en-suite bathrooms became essential, and although the Bledisloe Court plan could have been adapted, a single-banked cloister arrangement proved a better way of integrating the bathrooms and avoiding north-facing rooms.

The rooms are deeper and narrower than the first-phase ones and, like the standard hotel room, are entered next to the bathroom, each with its little window. There are no shared 'gyp' rooms (to encourage students to eat in the central dining facilities) but each room has a kettle corner. The basic materials for walls and roofs are as at Bledisloe Court, but the windows are now single structural openings containing oak casements and with projecting sills (used continuously as a string course at upper-floor level)—lessons had been learnt in the first phase.

The detailing is plain and simple, and although the gabled dormers and the ogee soffit of an oriel window are perhaps surprising in their overt reference to traditional detailing, the formal language of the building derives less directly from the Cotswold vernacular than at Bledisloe Court. It is also richer spatially as the monastic-inspired cloisters provide not only an additional palette of materials but also a new dimension of 'threshold' space, that magical transition between outside and inside.

1 SOUTH-EAST ELEVATION

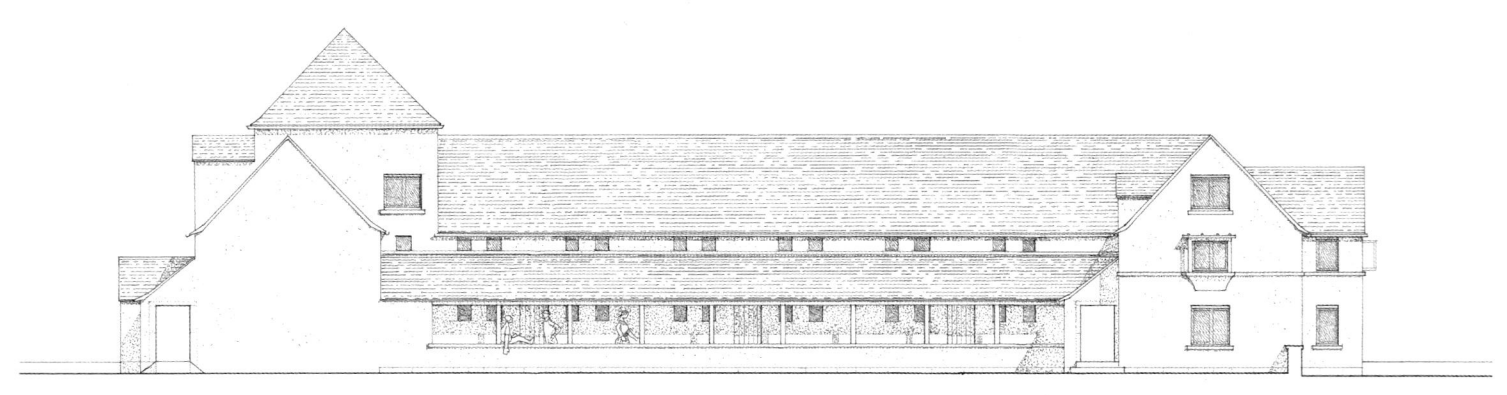

2 NORTH-WEST ELEVATION

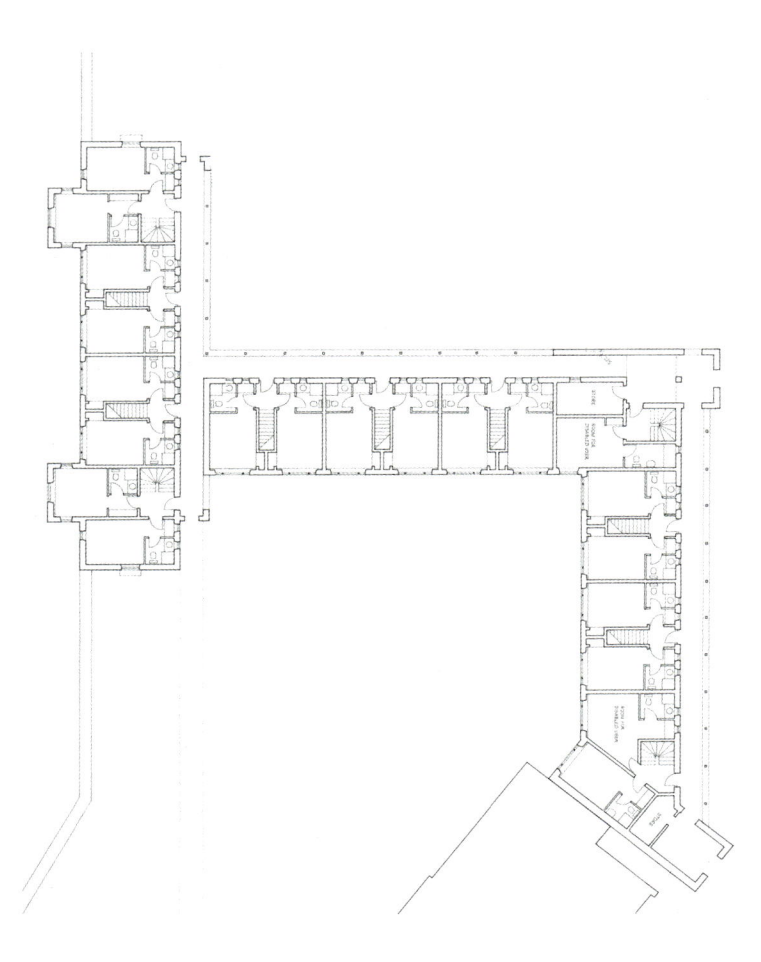

1: South-east elevation
2: North-west elevation **3:** Block plan **4:** North-west elevation

1

2

3

102

Perspective North-west elevation, with Bledisloe Court behind Detail of north-west elevation Window seat Cloister Masterplan

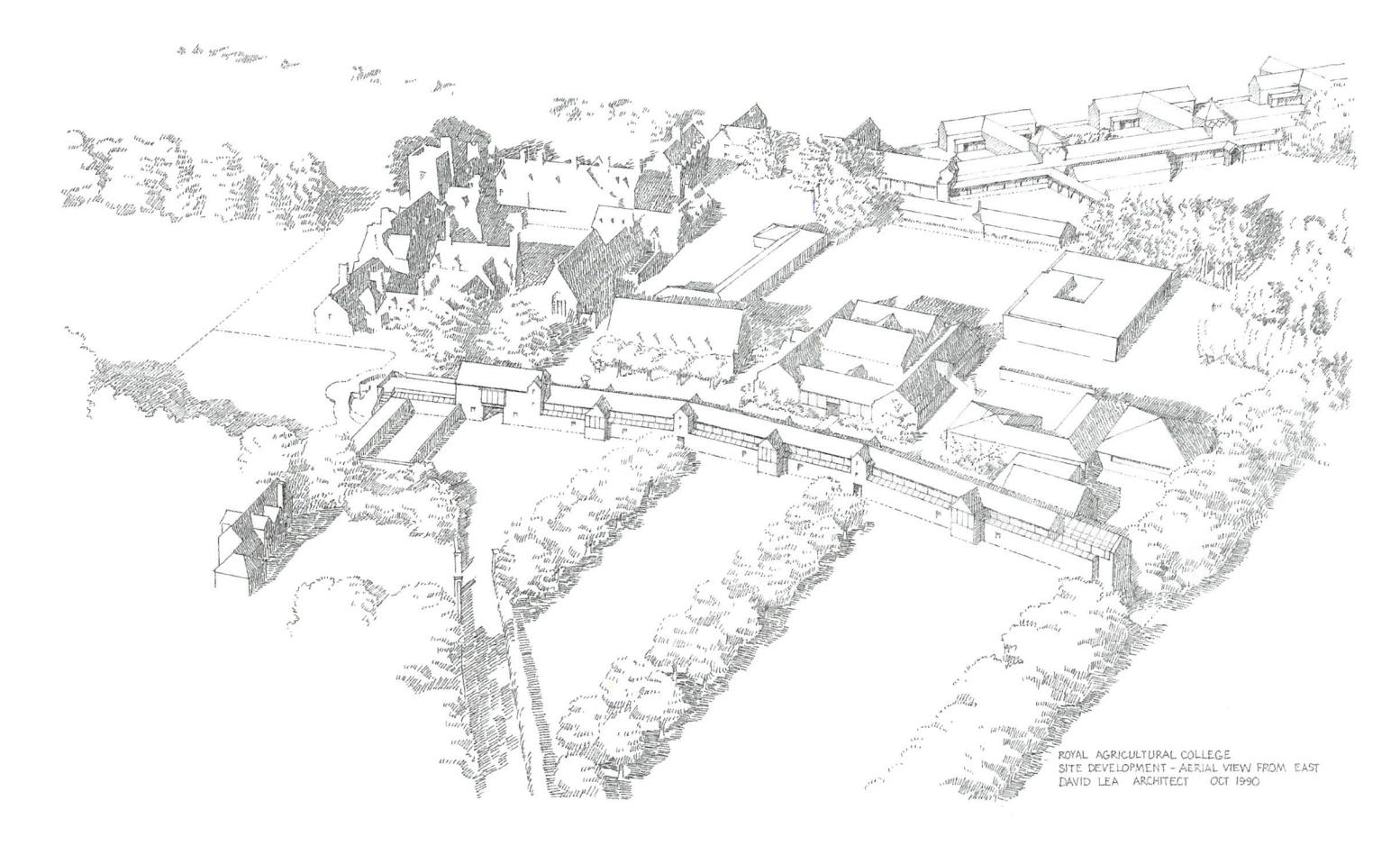

Gonville and Caius College, Cambridge
1992

It seems entirely appropriate that Lea should have found himself on a short-list to design a scheme for 150–200 new student rooms and associated accommodation in the gardens of Harvey Court and adjacent houses. Harvey Court was designed by Martin and Wilson in the early 1960s while Lea was at the Cambridge school of architecture. Lea's scheme was in effect the planned expansion of Harvey Court that never happened.

Lea's strategy was to enclose the gardens with a string of loosely-connected colonnaded blocks to provide covered pedestrian routes across the site. At the same time they would form new courtyards of a scale appropriate to Harvey Court (though, with the existing trees on the site, the character of the courts would be less formal and hard) and the perimeter arrangement would allow the buildings to be kept low. The main courtyard, South Court, is placed symmetrically to the south of Harvey Court. A strip of water divides the two, its bridge aligned with the steps up to the courtyard within the acropolis that Harvey Court has now become. The student rooms are grouped in houses very much like the Pembroke College competition scheme but the cloister of Coad Court at Cirencester is incorporated in addition, its oak posts now chunky brick columns more in keeping with the heroic fins of brickwork that support the stepped exterior elevations of Harvey Court.

1

1: Model **2:** New lecture theatre (left); route past Harvey Court (middle); East-west route past Harvey Court (right) **3:** New building with Harvey Court on right

105

Visitor Centre, Wakehurst Place, Sussex
1992

1: Topography of site **2:** Site plan
3: Entrance building colonnade
4: Framing the view to the west

A scheme for a visitors' reception building at an outpost in West Sussex of the Royal Botanical Gardens, Kew.

Visitors may have travelled a considerable distance and arrived feeling tense from the speed of the road. The colonnade of the entrance building, like a Greek propylaeum, offers a chance to unwind as they enter the quiet world of the garden. It spans the head of a shallow valley with a stream, and forms a bridge between two worlds, inviting the visitor to take a little time to cross it while enjoying the view to the south. A semi-circular building like an amphitheatre encloses the valley to the north containing the ticket office, shop, display area, offices, toilets etc and looking onto a courtyard with a water-pool.

Elements that begin to appear in this and later schemes are the mono-pitch roof leaning against a wall that looks as if it pre-dated the project, perhaps as a ruin; strips of skylight high up the roof, casting shadows down the wall and reminding visitors of the weather or the time of day; pools of water reflecting ripples of sun onto eaves soffits and ceilings. One feels everything is becoming simpler in these schemes, as if Lea is searching more and more for essence—the fundamental nature of the building as a whole (in Kahn's sense, what the building wants to be), the clarity of its structure, the essential characteristics of its materials.

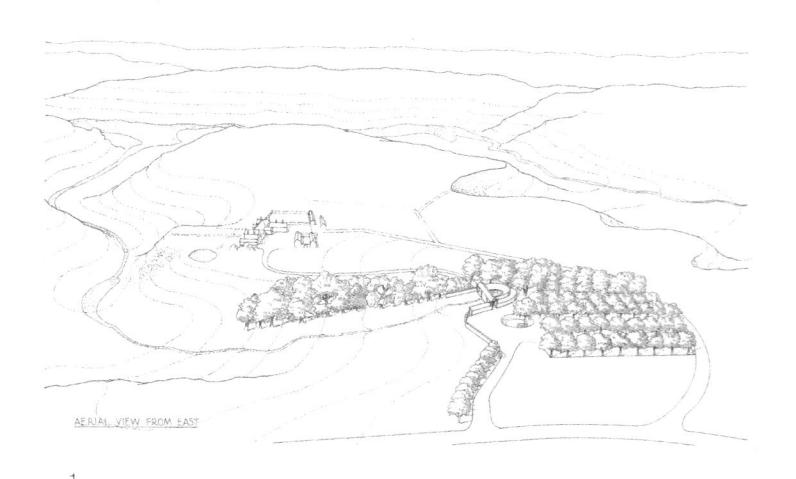

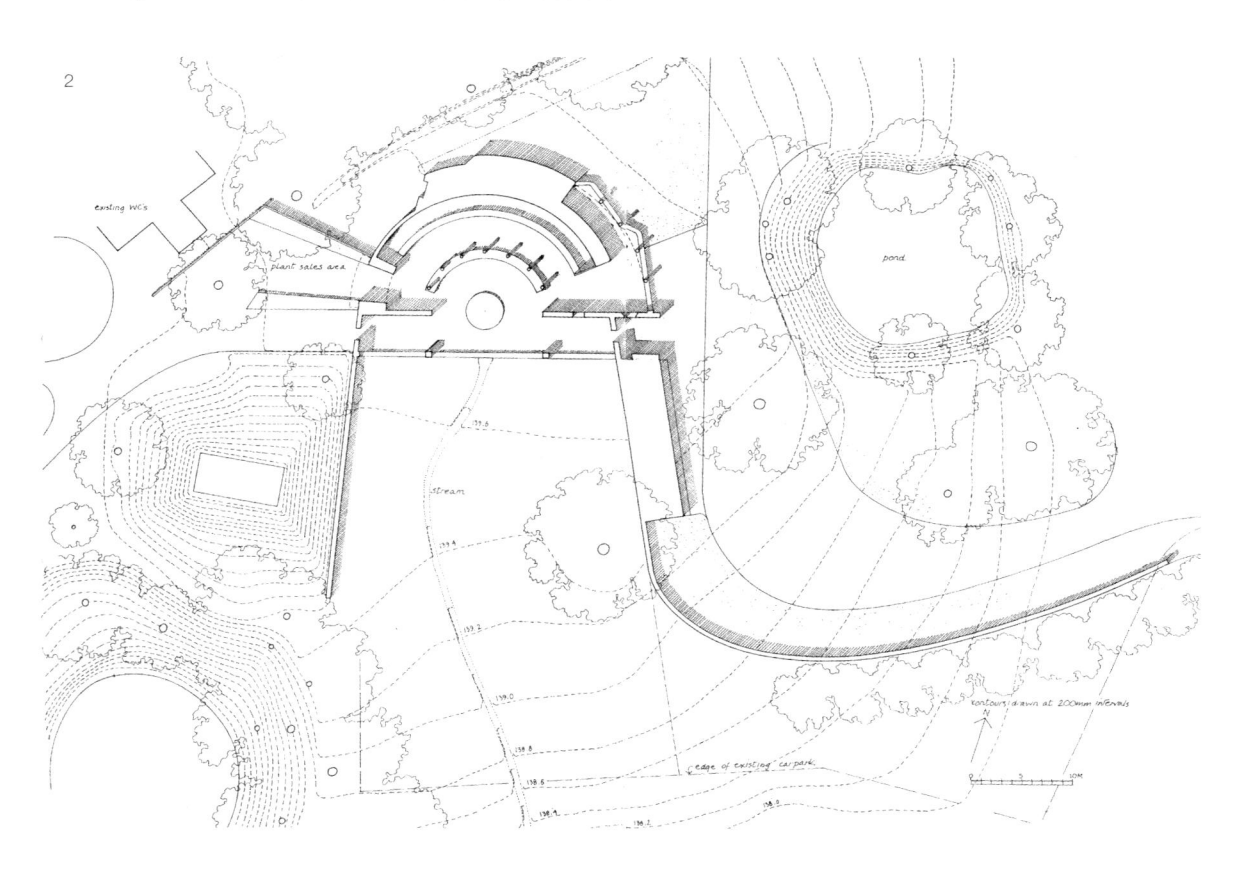

VIEW TO SOUTH FROM SHOP   David Lea Archite

House in Wiltshire
1994

1: South elevation of model
2: Orientation and views
3: Ground floor plan **4:** View from west **5:** Section through entrance and living room

The heat of Tuscany seems to radiate from this house, not inappropriate to its idyllic rural setting near Stourhead. Lea imagined an old garden wall lying in wait for a building, like a greenhouse in a walled garden. The living room leans against the wall on the sunny side, looking down south-west across a valley, hardly more than a pantiled roof supported on some posts (with large areas of glazing between). Behind are the service areas (arranged as an enfilade of services rooms in the traditional country house manner), the entrance hall and a snug drawing room for evening or winter use. Above these, on the rear side of the spine wall, are two bedrooms treated like the living room but facing north-east over the entrance court and walled garden to woods on the hill. A guest room occupies the corner between the porch and drawing room. If the house has a traditional, even vernacular, flavour, it is not one of cosy, rural England. As in the Wakehurst project, Lea looks further afield for inspiration, in time as well as place.

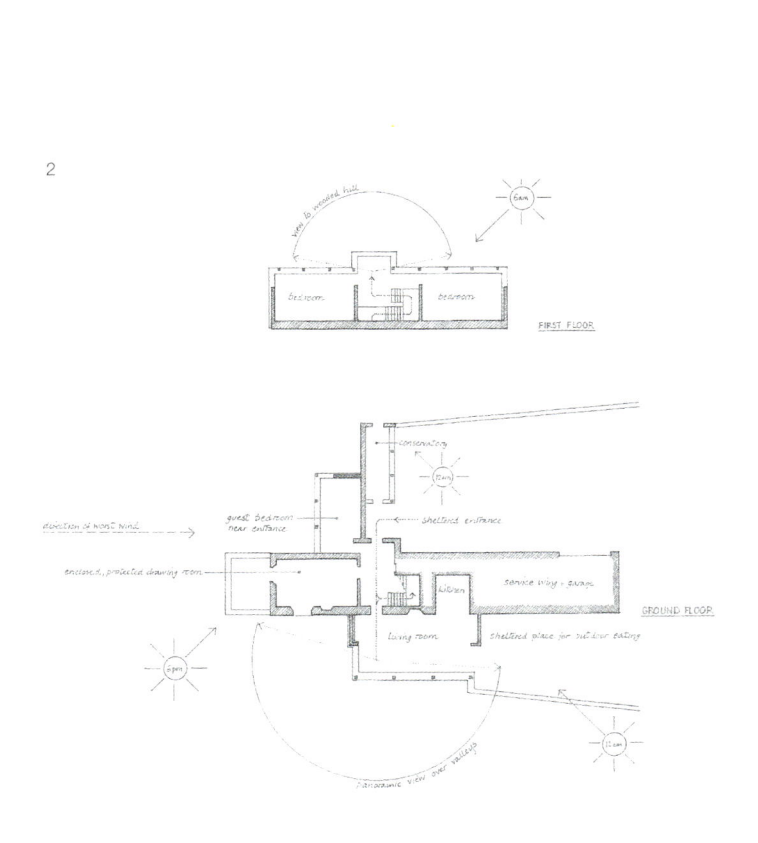

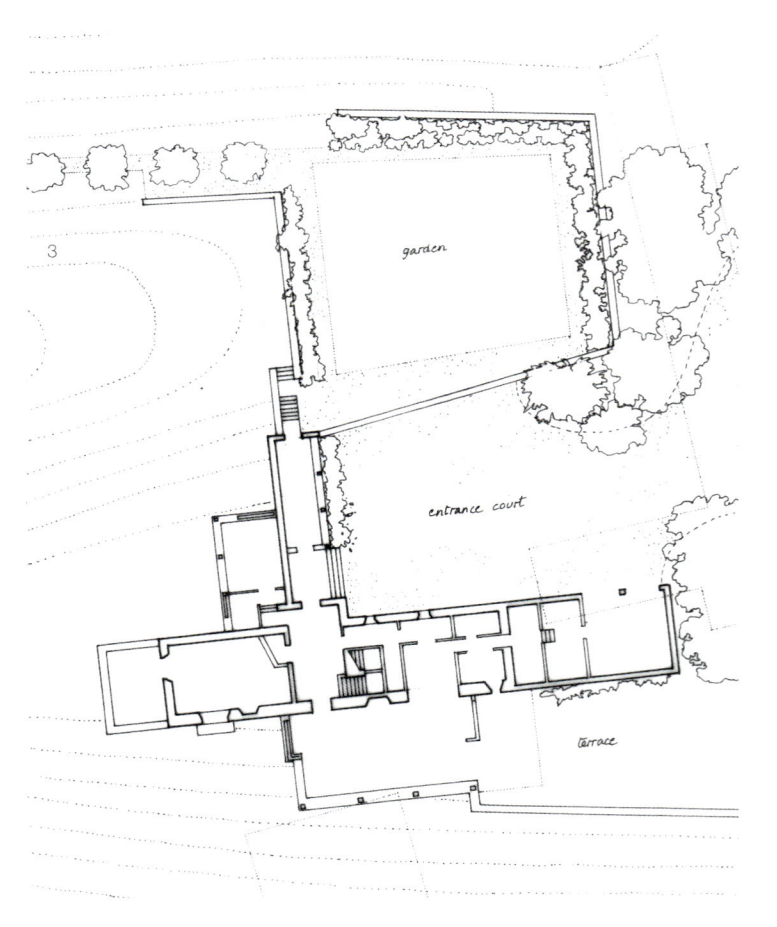

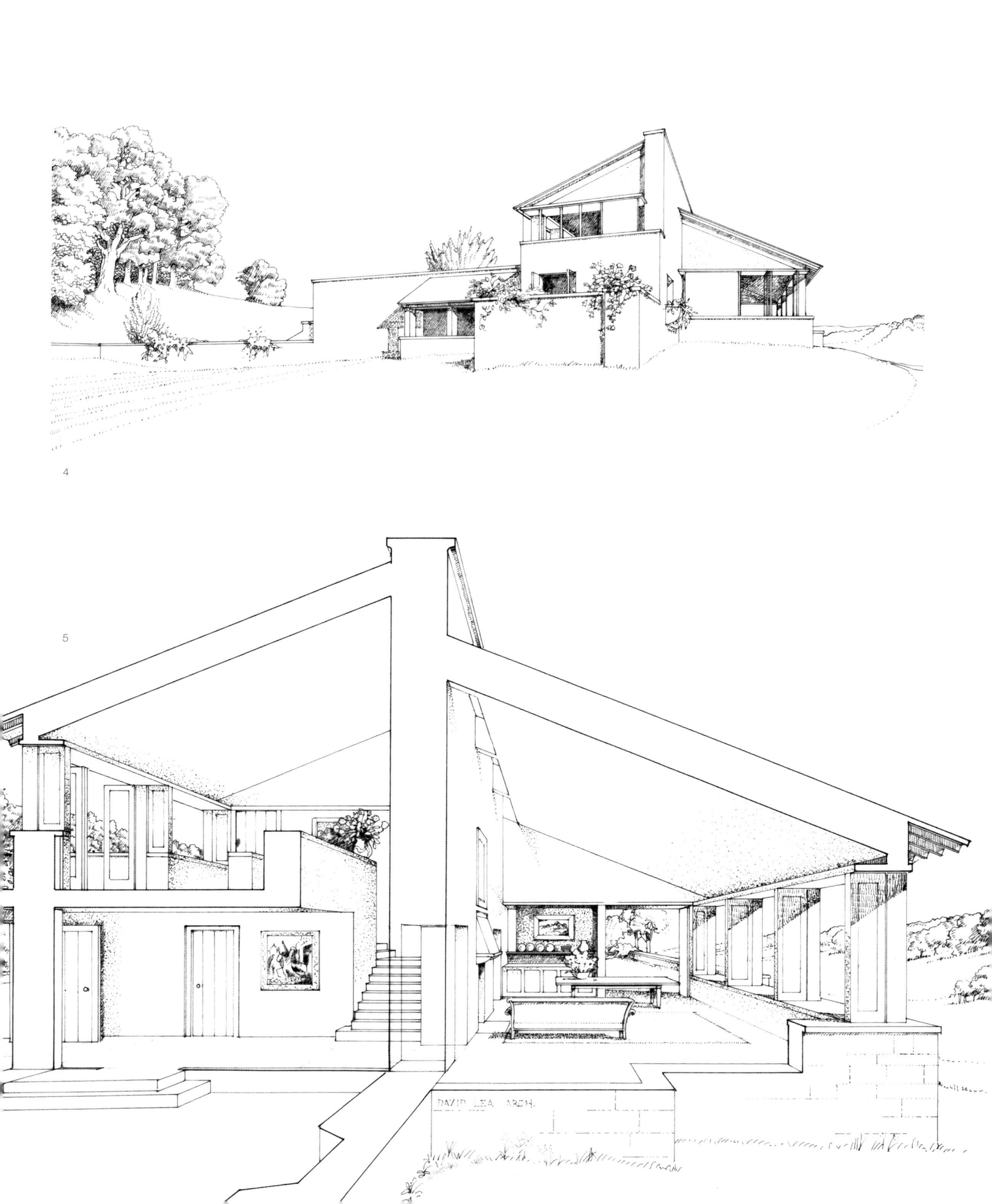

4

5

DAVID LEA ARCH.

Robinson College, Cambridge
1995

Though the college is a new one (built in 1977–1980), expansion for graduate accommodation was needed by 1994, and this was proposed in the gardens of two houses the college owned in Adam's Road, behind the main campus.

Lea's scheme consists of a three-sided courtyard on two floors, its rooms facing inwards with the circulation around the outside. The rooms are grouped in houses of eight rooms, each house has shared bathrooms (surprisingly) and a circular kitchen/common room placed in two back-to-back pairs at ground level next to the entrances. Each bedroom has a desk, bookcase and window seat incorporated as part of the window, one half a large sliding glazed light, the other a lattice screen of opaque glass panes—reminiscent of the Japanese *shoin* (a window seat/desk in a Buddhist monastery).

The walls are of red brick and the main roofs to the bedrooms of clay tile, mono-pitches abutting a spine wall. The flat corridor roofs, of stainless steel, hover over glazed upper passages that sit above a solid brick base; the circular common rooms have stainless steel skirts around a parapet behind which the domed ceiling rises to a small top-lit cupola. The large curved windows of the common rooms look out onto an existing preserved yew hedge which forms a top-lit, living, outer wall.

1: Model **2:** Common room
3: Perspective from west
4: Ground floor plan

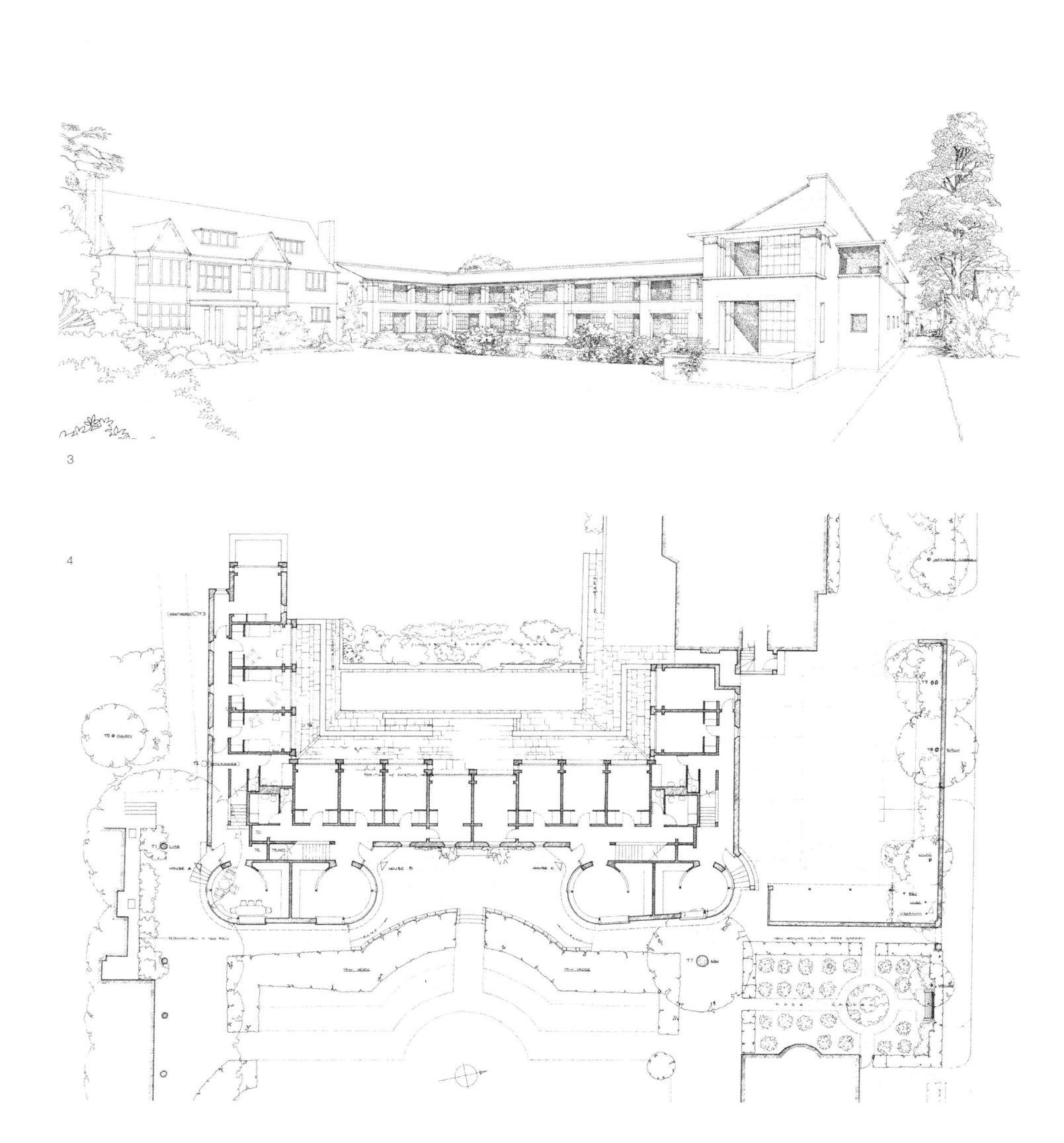

3

4

111

The Oasis of Peace, Porthmadog
1995

This scheme for the Catholic Centre for Healing in Marriage provides new counselling rooms, a library and a house for one of the two couples who ran the centre. The site was a tricky one: not large, near a main road and overshadowed by a steep hillside to the south.

The built design comprises three distinct parts. At the lower end is the house which divides the carpark to the north from the quiet garden to the south. It is arranged as a pair of parallel blocks, one for the main rooms each side of a recessed, partly roofed terrace (all with barrel-vaulted ceilings) and a narrower one for the service spaces and circulation. The relationship of the little terrace, the rooms within, and the garden was suggested to Lea by Filippo Lippi's *Annunciation*. The central part steps up to join the existing house, and contains the library on the first floor. The upper part breaks away from the rest, curling tightly around a pool of water and looking down over the lawn below. This intimate semicircle contains four counselling rooms and is accessed from a curving top-lit passage around the outside. The colonnade of four doors and the pool of water, were an idea of the clients', inspired by the presence of a spring on the site and verses from St John's Gospel. Unfortunately this little scheme has been much changed by its present owner.

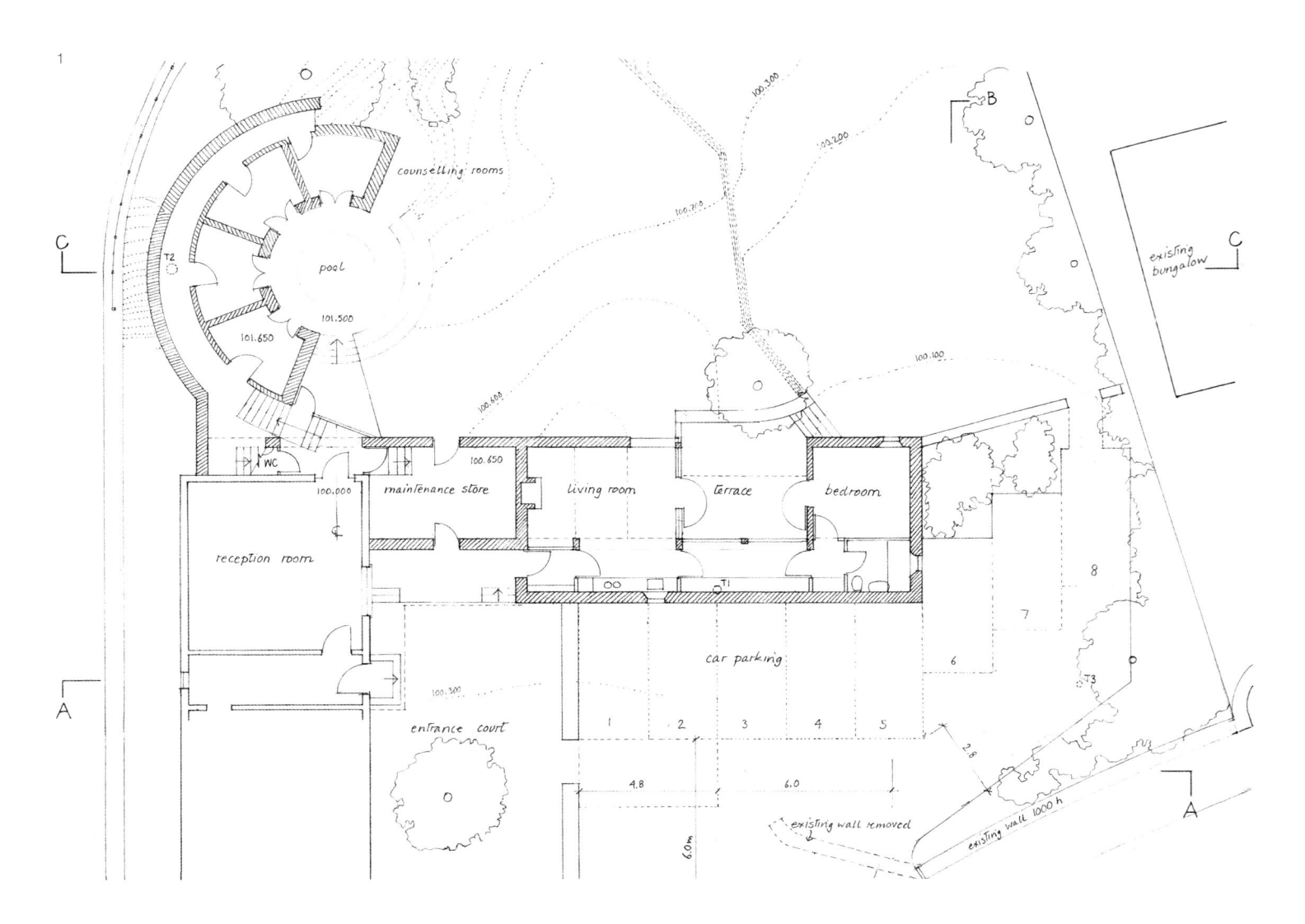

1: Ground floor plan **2:** Filippo Lippi, *Annunciation*, c 1445–1450 **3:** Living room **4:** Cut-away section through counselling rooms

1

2

3

1: Glazed passage around counselling rooms **2:** Healing pool
3: Glazed link from house
4: Doorway from bedroom to loggia
5: Loggia, view from the living room

Kingswood Project, Somerset
1998

The client intended to establish a small study centre in an ancient woodland in north Somerset. The accommodation must be flexible and eventually removable, so the buildings are based on 2m x 2m and 4m x 4m timber framed rectangles. These can be put together in various ways to form small laboratories or individual study huts. All joints are bolted or screwed. These small buildings form human nests in the woods, offering a feeling of shelter and warmth, but also allowing some walls to open fully to enjoy the life of the trees. They form one stage of Lea's ongoing exploration of minimal small houses.

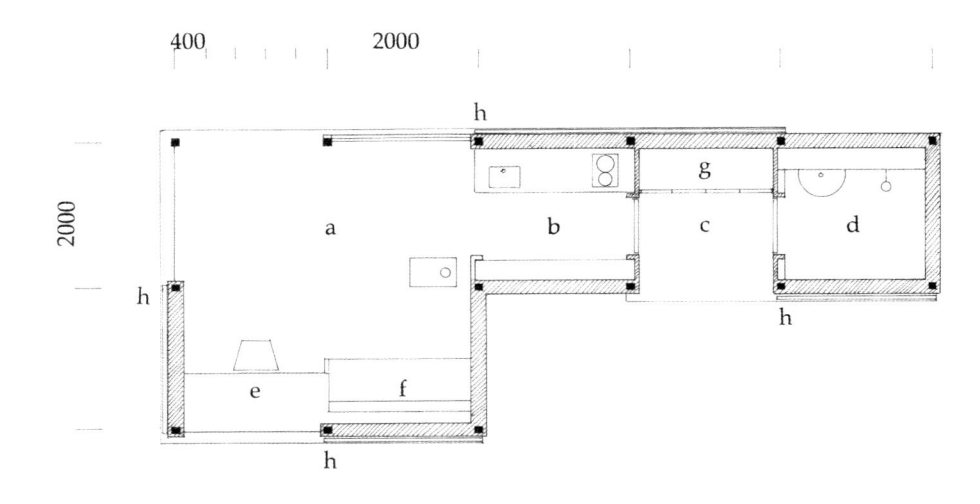

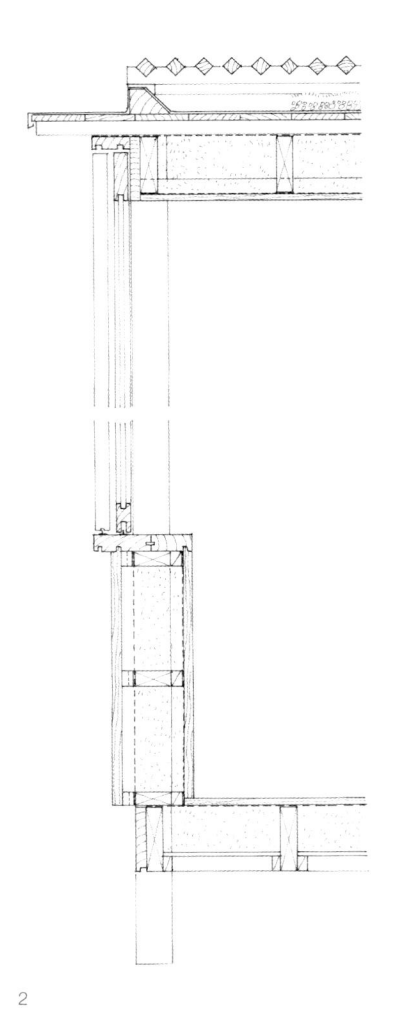

1: Plan of study hut **2:** Detail
3: Study hut in the woods
4: Living in the trees

Visitor Centre,
Sir Harold Hillier Garden and Arboretum,
Romsey, Hampshire
1997

1: Ground floor plan **2:** South elevation **3:** East-west section **4:** North elevation **5, 6:** Model of west window to restaurant

Like the Wakehurst Place competition project, the building proposed at Romsey forms a gateway to the garden, giving visitors a panoramic view of a lake to the north as soon as they enter the garden. But before they do this, they walk through a serene paved courtyard planted with a row of trees overhanging a channel of swiftly running water. To one side are the cafe and restaurant, to the other the shop, exhibition space and lecture room. Between them a loggia with the tantalising gateway to the garden, the wall given depth to accentuate its quiet monumentality (and to accommodate within it the ticket booth and toilets for the cafe).

The planning of the building offers a continual dialogue between inside and outside space. Sometimes you are securely inside and sometimes you are certainly outside, but often the space is less defined and you find yourself in that delicious in-between realm, both within and without at the same time. A flat roof hovers above, almost independent of the walls which tuck themselves back from a thin projecting eaves or thrust themselves out into the landscape.

The design is rich in its sources of inspiration: Japanese palaces and gardens, Mies van der Rohe's 1923 plan for a brick country house (and his Barcelona Pavilion), Luis Barragán's own house at Tucubaya, Mexico. It also has the atmosphere of a temple, not in a strict liturgical sense but in the way its simple architecture, reduced to bare essentials, provides a place of contemplation and spiritual nourishment. As Lea pointed out in his competition report, English gardens have become places of pilgrimage, even replacing, for many people, the traditional buildings of worship.

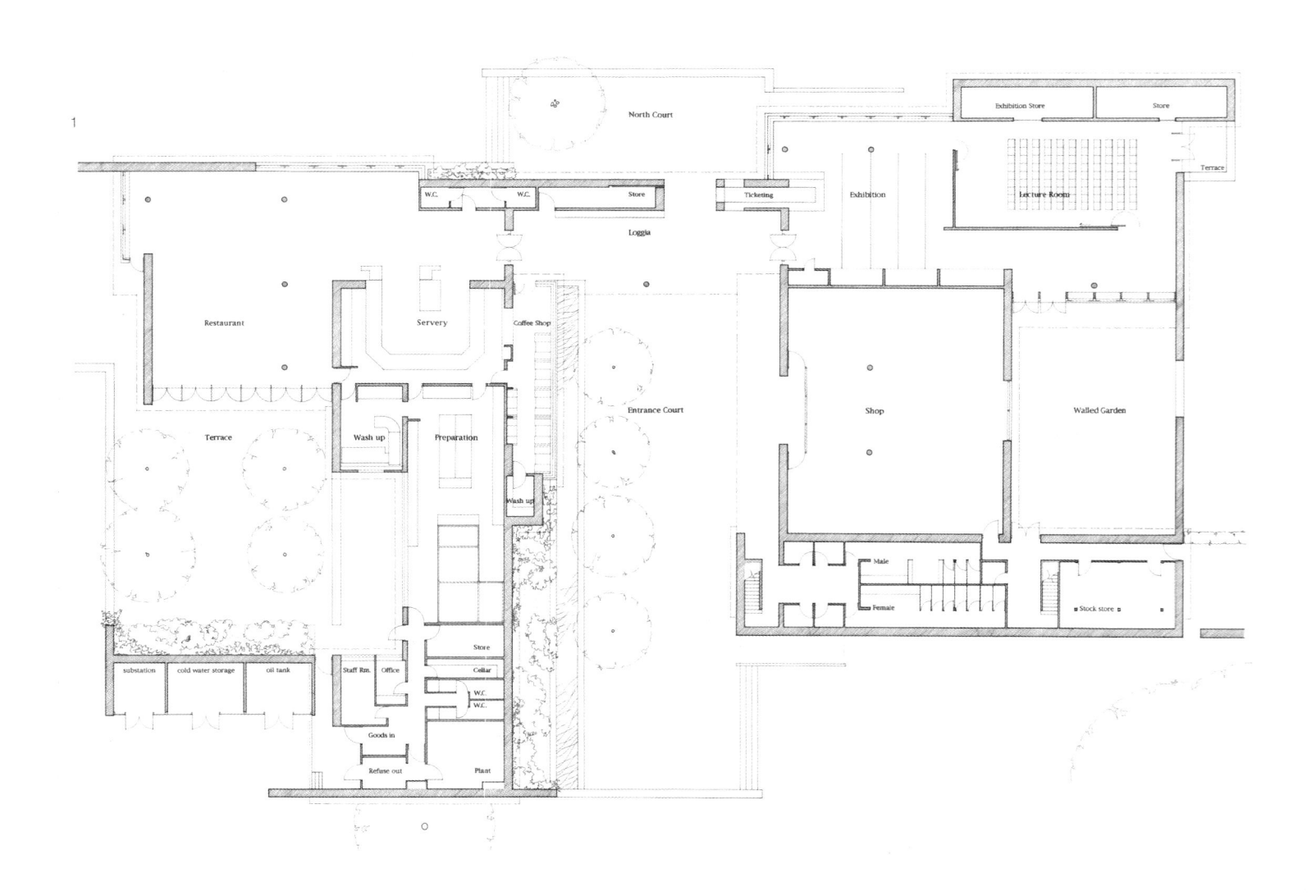

2

SOUTH ELEVATION

3

RESTAURANT GARDEN | WASH-UP | KITCHEN | COFFEE SHOP | ENTRANCE COURT | SHOP | LECTURE ROOM GARDEN

SECTION AA

4

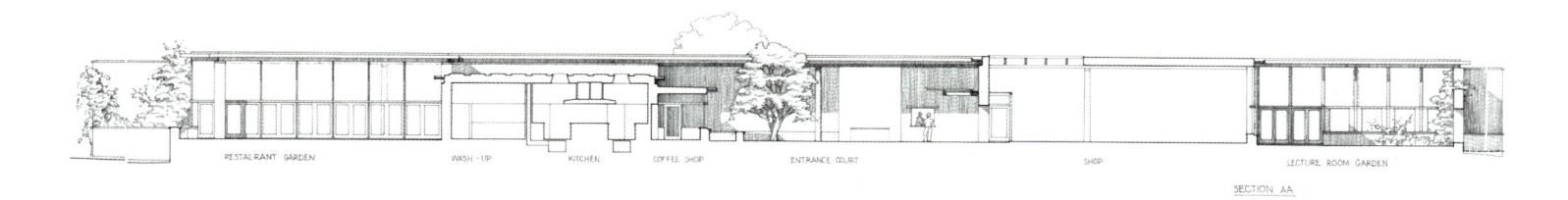

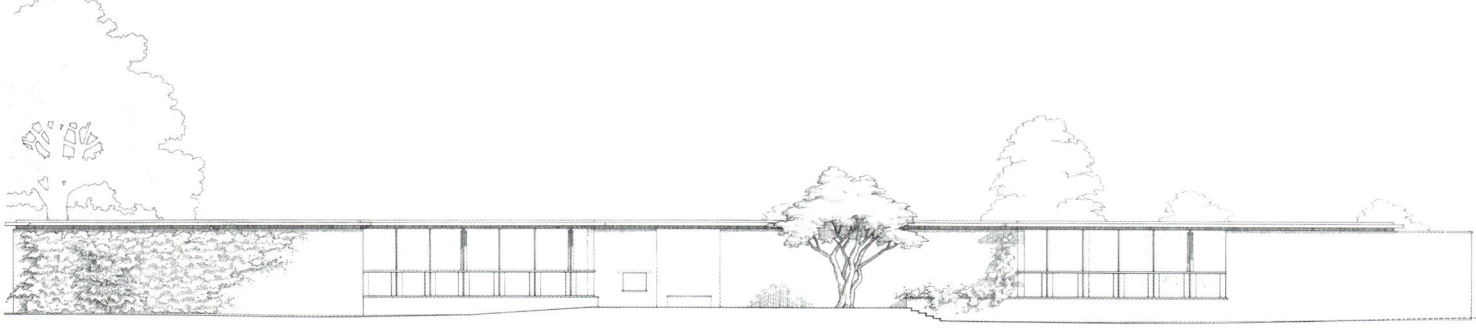

NORTH ELEVATION

5

6

119

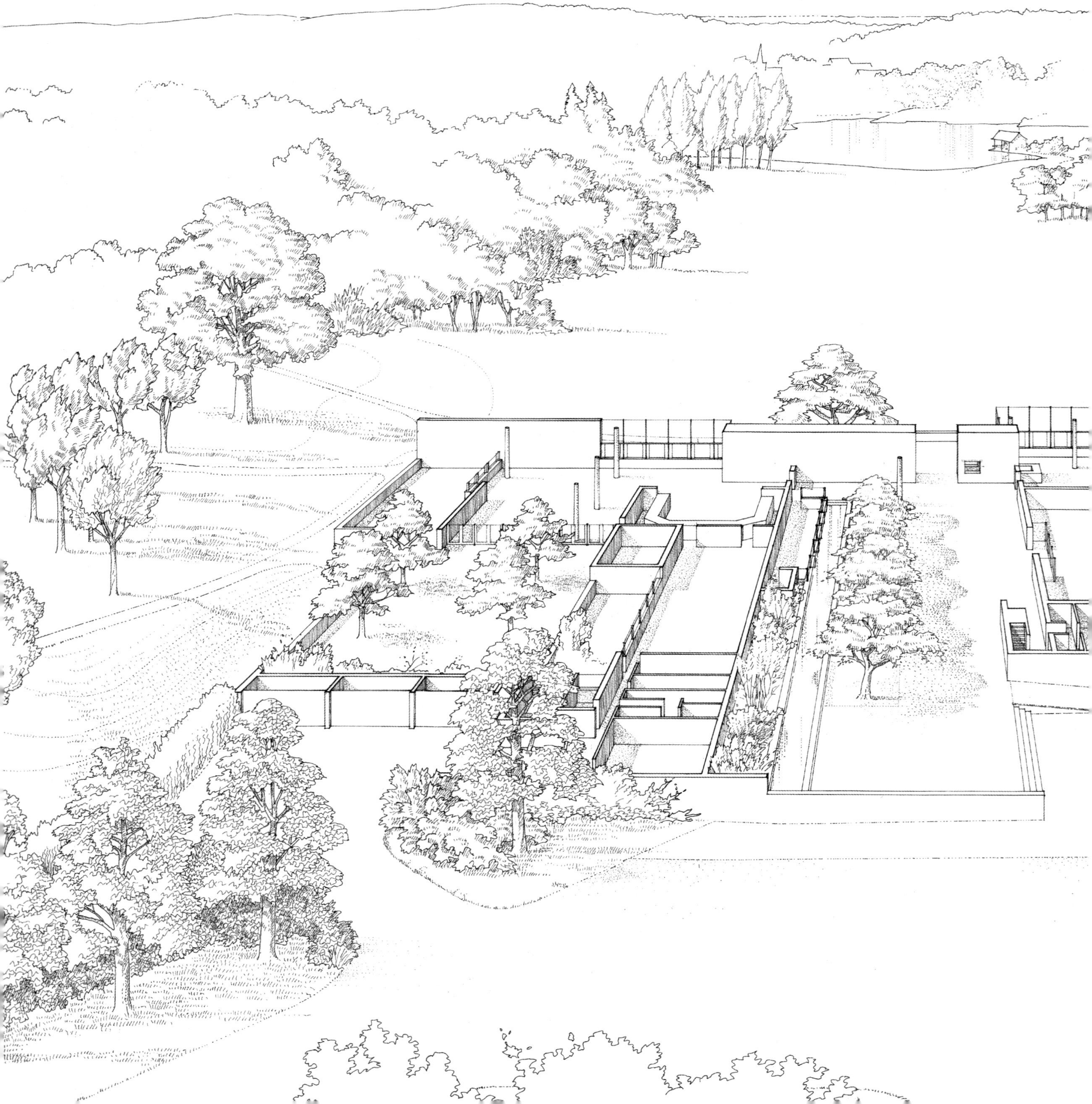

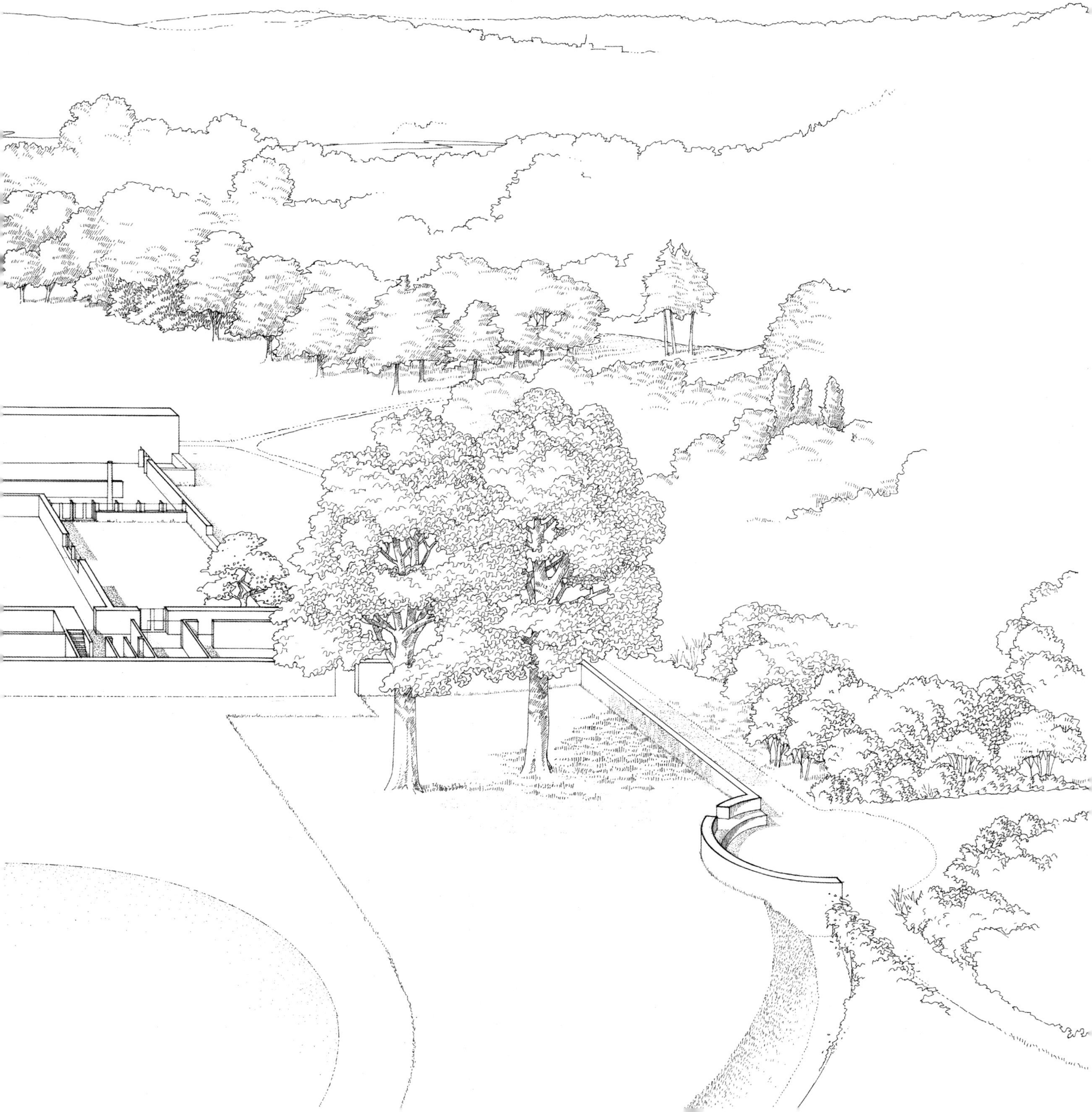

House Extension, Blaen Camel, Ceredigion
1998

1: View from south-east **2:** Living room **3:** Dining corner, showing bracing **4:** Fireplace seat

The clients are organic growers who wanted to extend their nineteenth-century house in a way that embodied the ecological concerns they share with Lea, and made use of materials from their own land.

The new accommodation comprises a living room, a master bedroom with bathroom, utility and back door, and an office/guest room, all placed on one level at the upper end of the existing house. The extension's pair of roofs run at right-angles to that of the house, and between them are strips of roof which combine gutter and continuous glazing next to each other. The structure is a frame of green oak arranged as a grid of wide and narrow bays, the wide ones generally coinciding with the main living spaces, the narrow ones defining circulation routes—a relaxed interpretation of Louis Kahn's served/servant space idea. The narrow bays also have a structural reason—their cross-panels provide bracing to the open, untied roofs of the main spaces.

The magic of the interior lies in the skilful manipulation of daylight, from above through the strips of glazing and through glazed sliding doors which open onto small walled courtyards. Although the glazed circulation routes are just as much internal as the main spaces which they join, somehow they give an extra degree of cosiness to the darker, main spaces. The bed alcove feels even warmer, with its timber platform raised half a step above the main floor and its own lower ceiling—a big box-bed.

Stone for the walls was quarried on the clients' land, the oak came from their trees and wool insulation was clipped from their sheep. Almost every component was designed and made specially, including the built-in furniture.

1

2

3

4

123

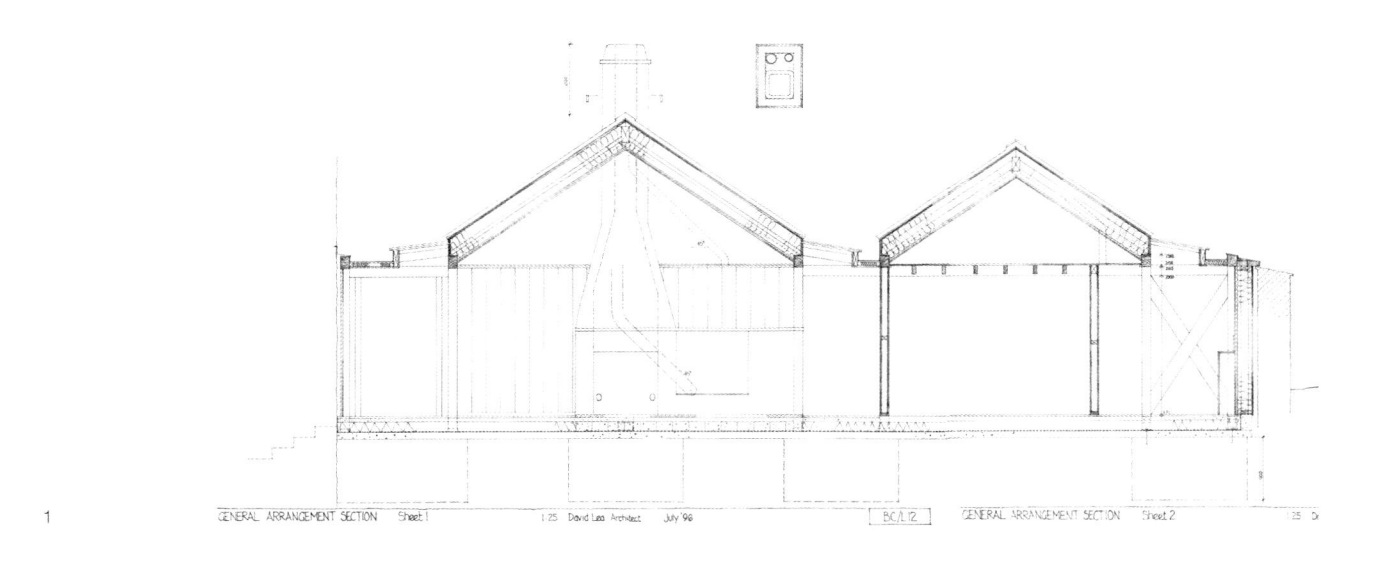

1

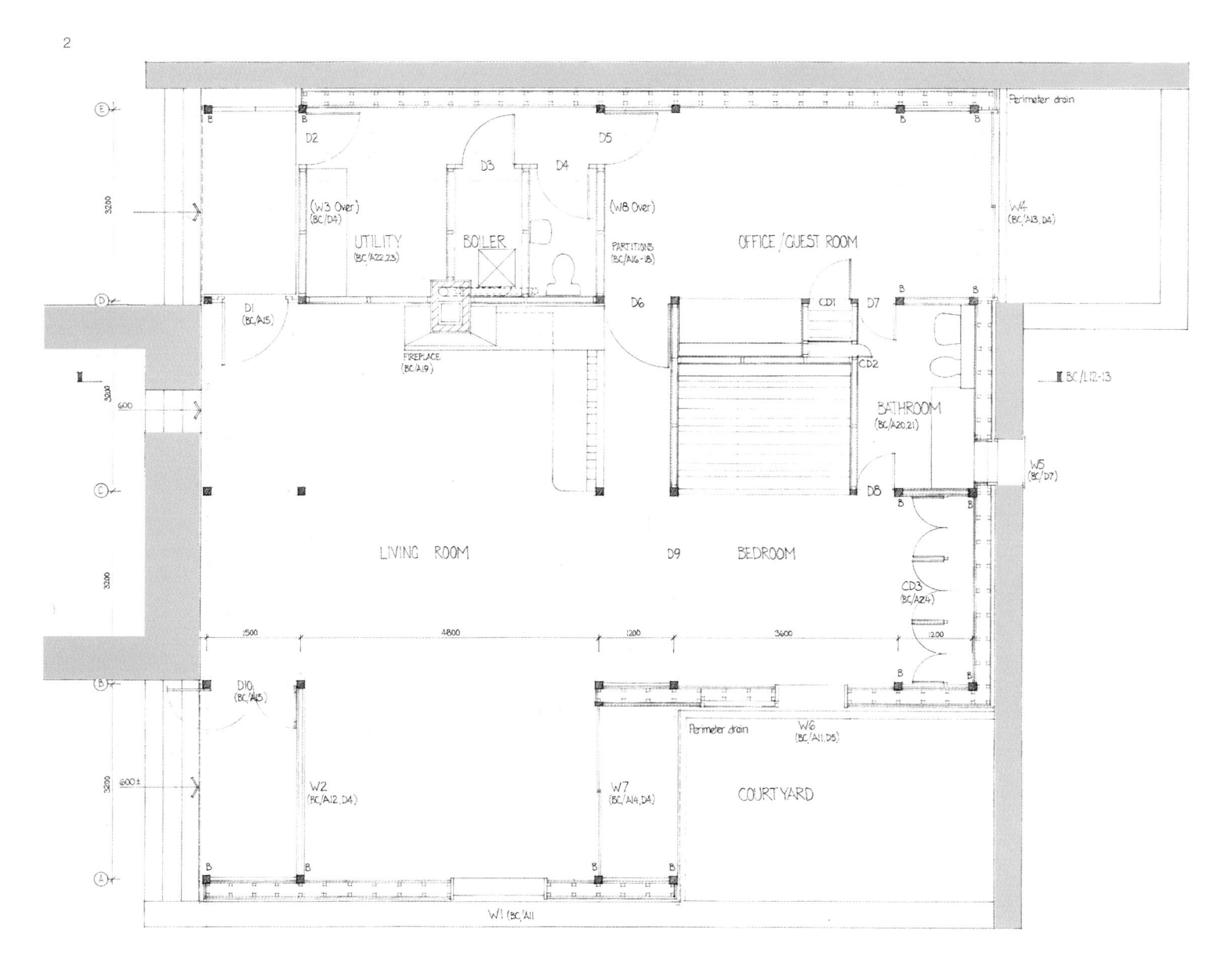

GENERAL ARRANGEMENT SECTION Sheet 1   1:25 David Lea Architect July '98   BC/L12   GENERAL ARRANGEMENT SECTION Sheet 2

2

UTILITY
(BC/A22,23)

BOILER

OFFICE / GUEST ROOM

PARTITIONS
(BC/A16-18)

FIREPLACE
(BC/A19)

BATHROOM
(BC/A20,21)

LIVING ROOM

BEDROOM

COURTYARD

Perimeter drain

1: Section **2:** Plan **3:** Oak frame
4 and **5:** Views from the east

Bridge Pottery, Cheriton, Gower
2000

Entrance veranda Floor plan and construction grids Gallery overlooking river Sections

It is scarcely credible that the local authority planners initially objected to this small building, a gallery and studio for a potter, because it was made of timber, not stone, and was so near to a river. That's precisely where the charm of the scheme lies. Mostly built of untreated larch, inside and out, it blends wonderfully in its woodland setting. With its large full-height gallery windows overlooking the river, frameless triangles of glass in the gables and strips of combined skylight and gutter running along the rear of each wing, the relationship to nature could not be more intimate.

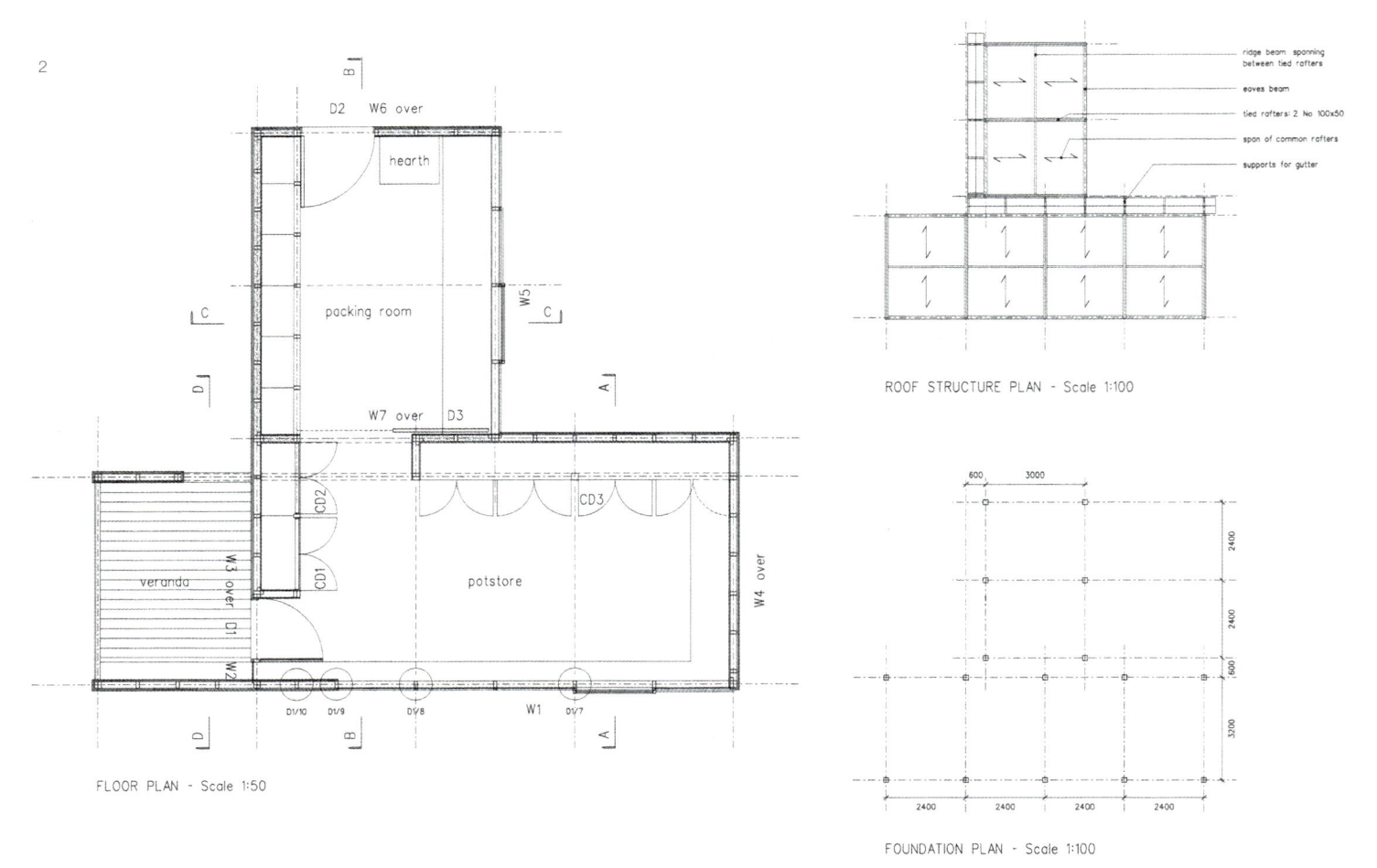

FLOOR PLAN - Scale 1:50

ROOF STRUCTURE PLAN - Scale 1:100

FOUNDATION PLAN - Scale 1:100

3

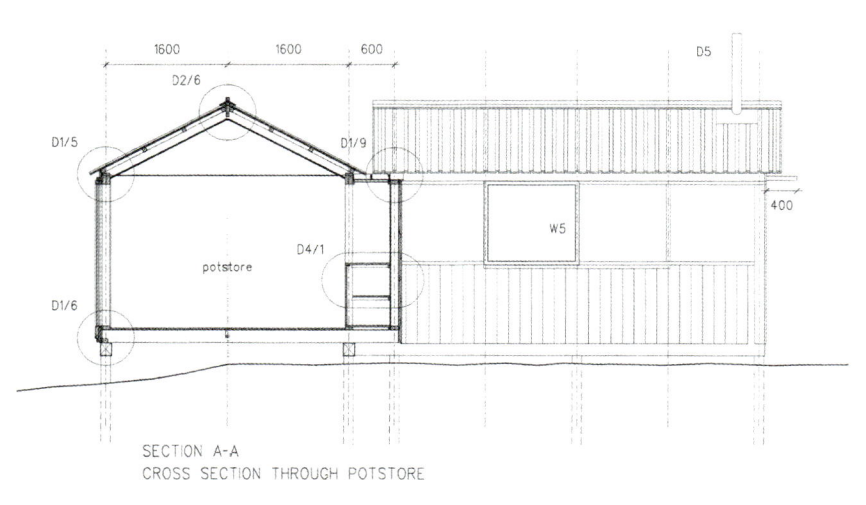

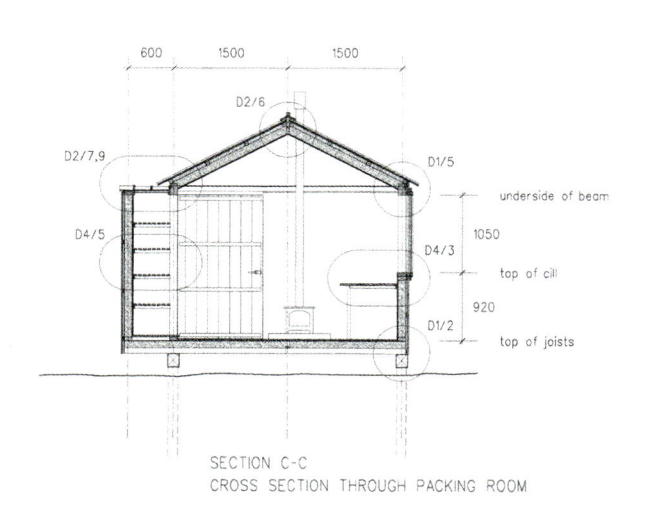

4

SECTION A-A
CROSS SECTION THROUGH POTSTORE

SECTION C-C
CROSS SECTION THROUGH PACKING ROOM

Magdalene College, Cambridge
2000

By 2000 Cambridge colleges could earn more from hosting conferences than from their regular academic functions. The brief for this project included a large independent suite of conference facilities in addition to new study bedrooms, and a full-size sports hall.

Lea's entry design, the last he did for a Cambridge college, can be seen as a valedictory homage to his teachers, Martin and Wilson, in its similarity to Harvey Court: the inward-looking courtyard plan with communal facilities at the centre, the stepped entrance loggia, the defensive exterior, the brick aesthetic. Because the site was across a busy main road from the main college, Lea was keen to forge a link between the two, proposing a tunnel below the road and angling the conference wing towards the college. The size and proportions of the new building were based on those of Magdalene's First Court, which Lea liked for its simplicity and its atmosphere of calm.

All study bedrooms are approached from the courtyard, giving it a liveliness that Harvey Court perhaps lacked. Internal circulation is round the perimeter, on the blank, rear side so that the rooms can look inwards. As in Lea's other student schemes, much thought was given to the "window place" (as he called it in his report, echoing Christopher Alexander's *A Pattern Language*), that transition point which connects student to community, inside to outside, as well as providing a place for work and contemplation.

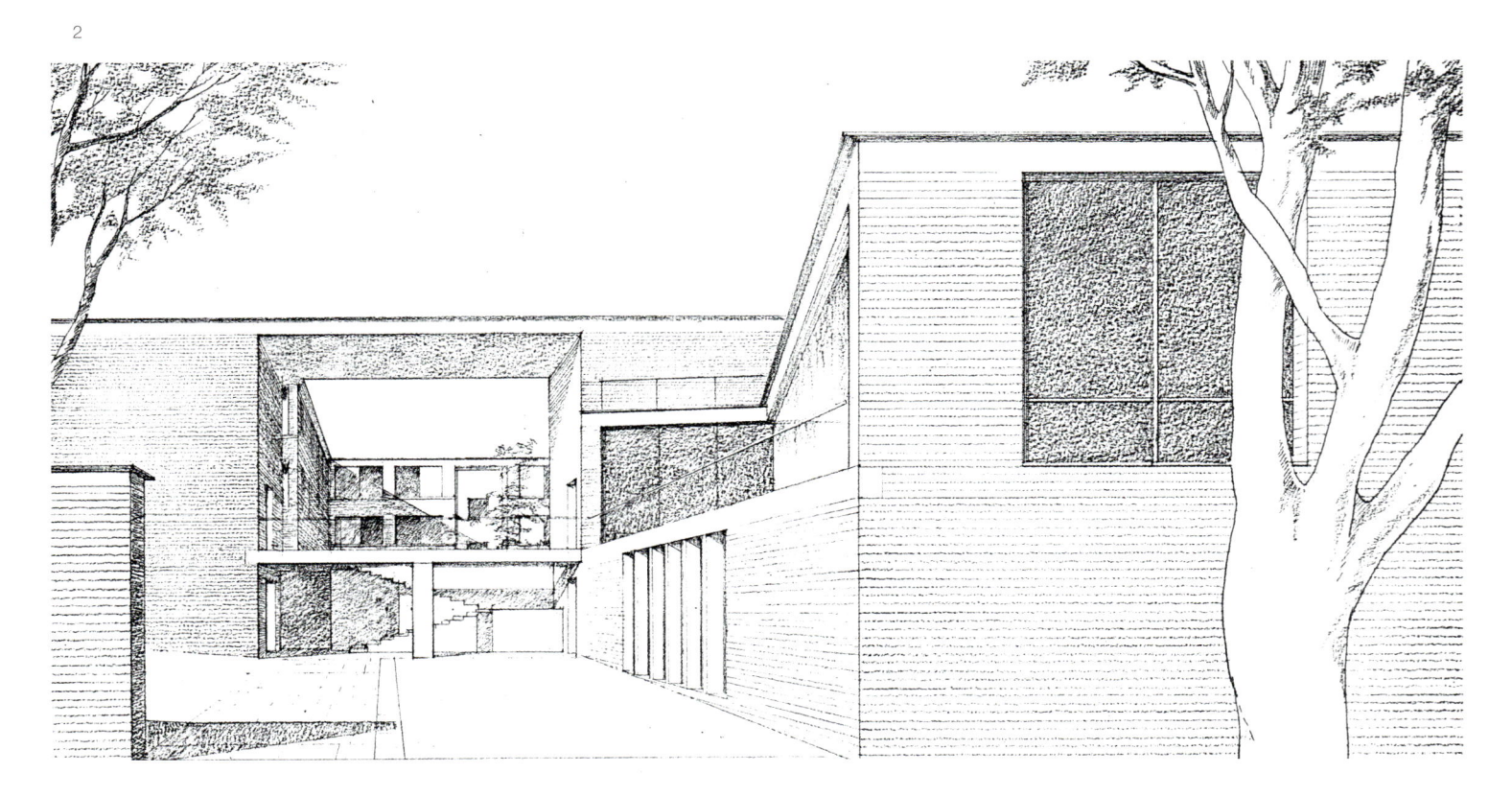

1: Precendents: Generalife, Grenada and Ducal Palace, Urbino **2:** Entrance **3:** Section **4:** Plan at entrance level **5:** Plan at courtyard level

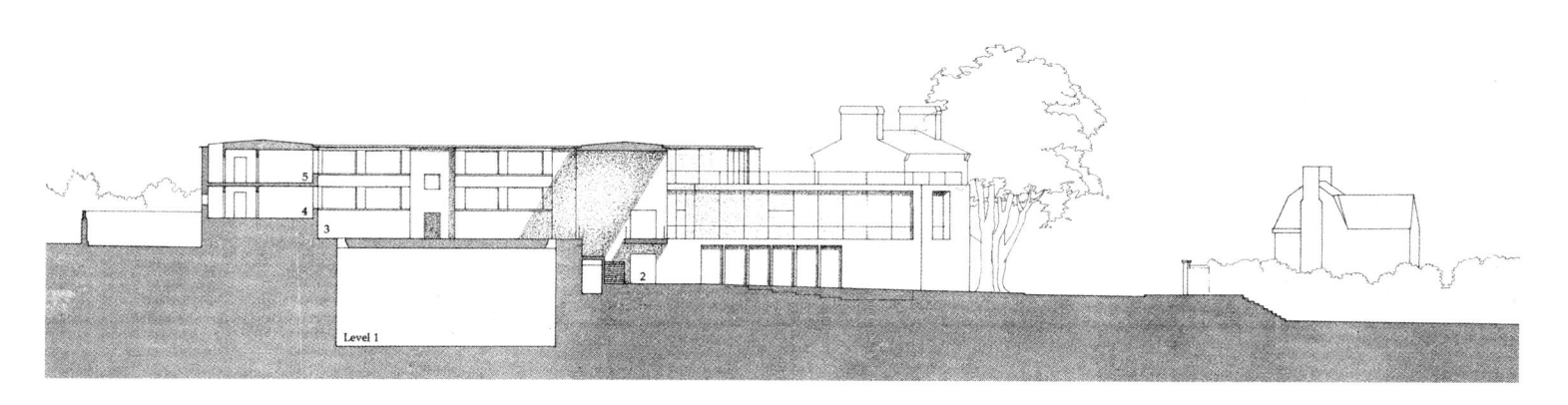

3

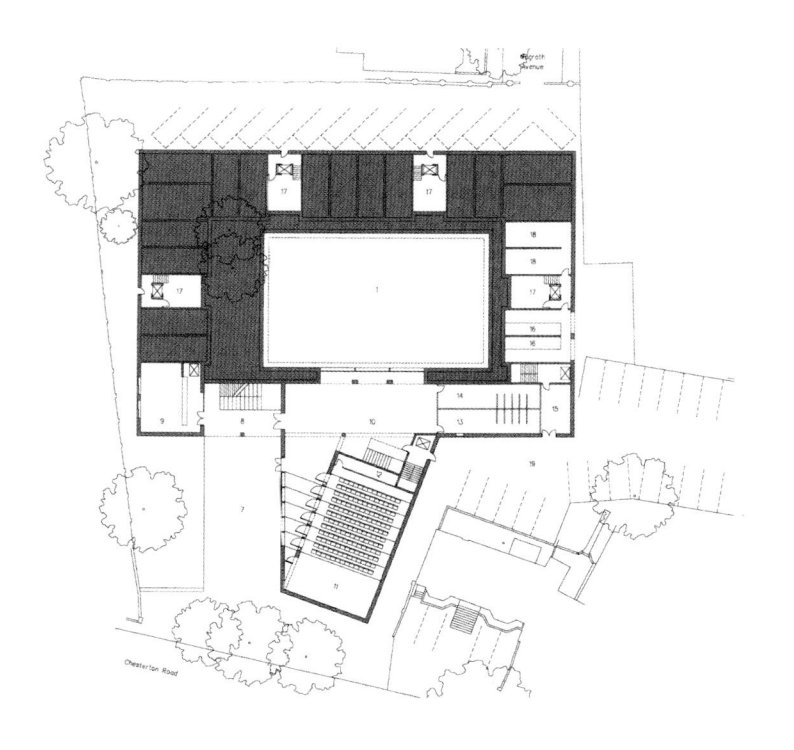

4

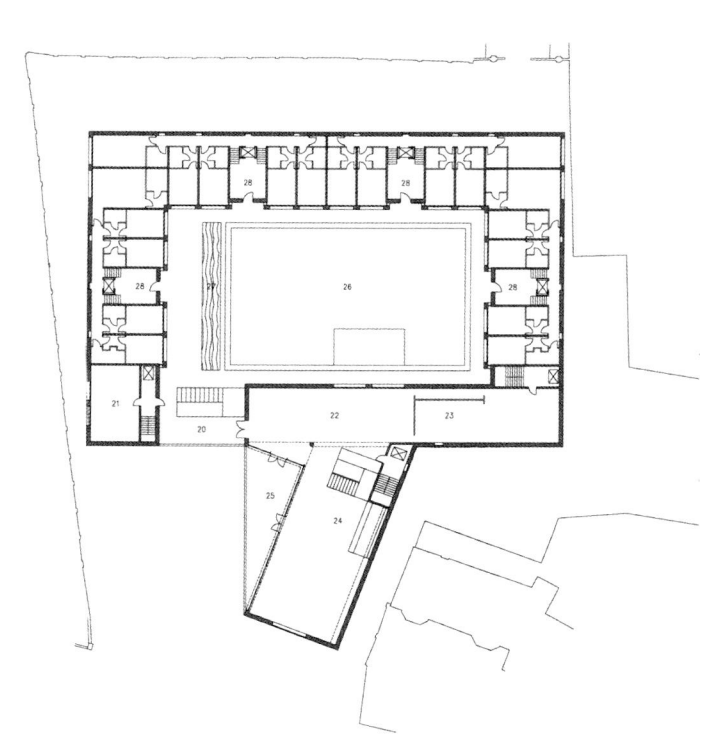

5

129

Community Centre, Slaidburn, Lancashire
2002

1: Model, with mock-up of ashlar sandstone wall (lower left) **2:** South elevation, facing village green **3:** Ground floor plan

The project was the brain-child of a wealthy client who moved to Slaidburn, a pretty village nestling amongst the fells north of Clitheroe. He wanted to create a social and cultural centre for the villagers as well as the wider community. Lea won the job in competitive interview.

The site borders the village green, below the main village, next to the Hodder river. A row of stone houses and the former Methodist chapel, used as the village hall, overlook the green. The area is generally very unspoilt; any new building being traditional in character.

The proposed building is atypical of Lea's work in its plan form: a single, compact block rather than a courtyard or a series of related wings. To overcome the static quality imposed by such a plan, Lea elaborated the circulation pattern, bringing visitors in at one end and taking them the length of the building before letting them turn back inside. The way in is through a tall doorway in the end wall, yet this doorway is not the entrance into the building, it is just a foretaste of the extended threshold that stretches along the front of the building, affording views of the river or a place to sit in the sun. The fine view down the river to the south is the reward once inside the building; or, if a winter evening, the fire in the inglenook between the staircase and a fixed seat.

The spaces inside would have been anything but static. With an upper level of rooms placed in two arms disposed diagonally from each other across a bridge, and the double-height hall and foyer taking up the remaining space on the opposite diagonal axis, Lea was able to regain the dynamic quality of his freer projects.

Lea wanted the walls to be built of warm cream sandstone ashlar and the flat roofs paved with slate slabs, but the local people preferred the more familiar rubble walls and pitched roofs. In the end, the project was abandoned and the existing chapel was reused and extended by another architect.

1

2

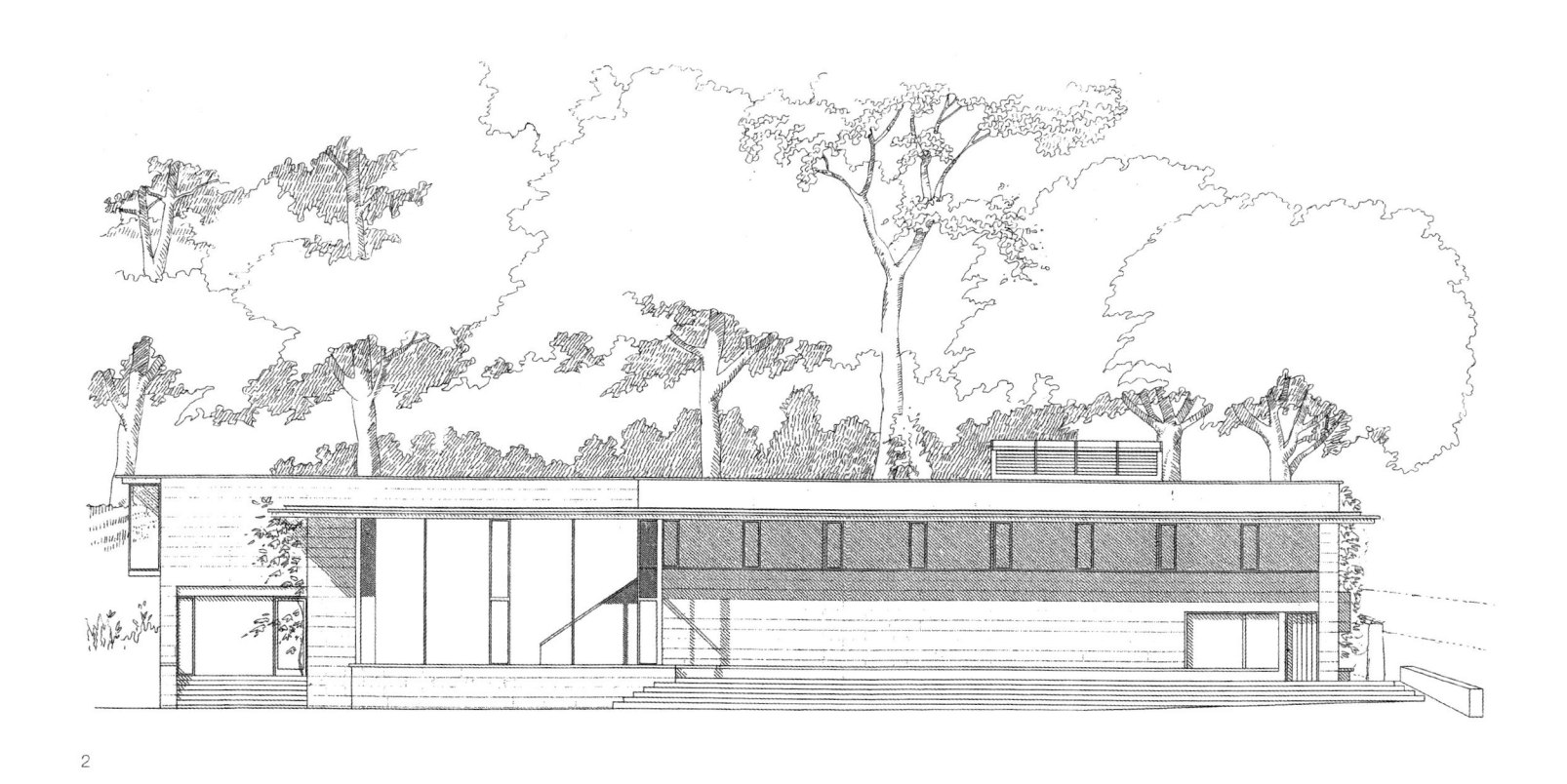

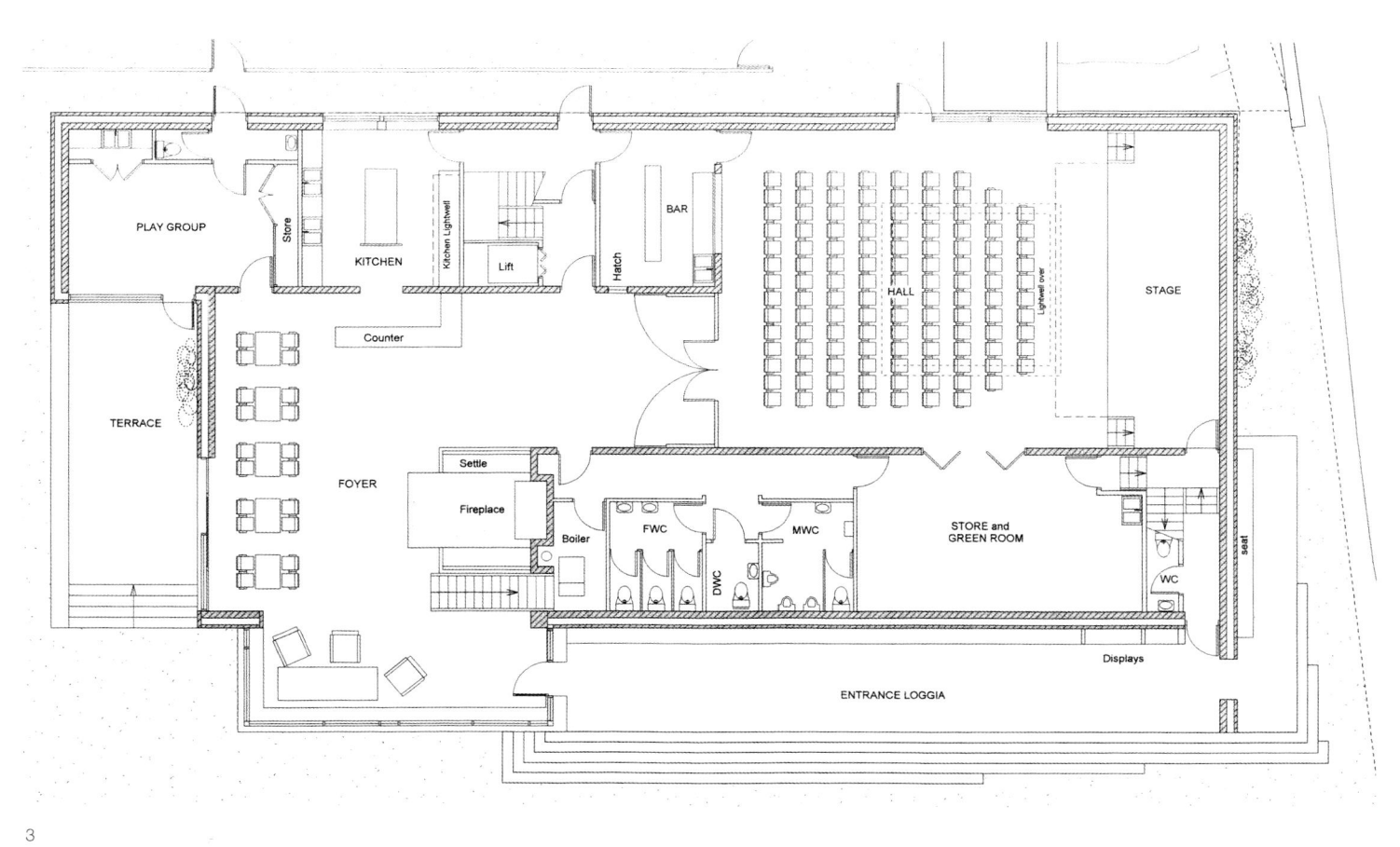

3

Penlee Quarry, Cornwall
2004

The quarry lies a short distance south of Penzance, separated from the sea by a narrow neck of land which carries the road to the little village of Mousehole. The quarry forms a vast amphitheatre. The scale is heroic. The client intended to cut through the narrow neck to allow the sea to flood the quarry, forming the first safe, 24 hour yacht haven after Land's End. A hotel, marina and associated chandlers and workshops, designed by MJ Long, occupied the north bank while the more precipitous south side was terraced for houses and flats for visitors and permanent residents, designed by Lea.

The site was extremely varied and intensely dramatic, suggesting both terraces along the contours, and buildings across the contours which gave lift access to all the levels, formed by massive retaining walls.

Two stonemasons from North Wales, Harri Pugh and Keith Jones, constructed a demonstration wall of 'cyclopean' blocks of up to 7 tons in weight, laid dry and backfilled with smaller rubble. The blocks were dressed by hand using a mason's hammer where necessary and lifted into place with a mechanical grab.

1: Perspective of south side
2: The quarry

House in North Wales
2005

The house was designed for a couple with three daughters on an awkwardly-shaped plot facing approximately north-west towards the sea. An existing stone wall, running the length of the site, provided the key to the plan. It suggested a glazed spine, used as a passage connecting the rooms either side of the entrance and adjacent courtyard, the girls' bedrooms one side, the living rooms and master bedroom the other. The kitchen and dining room are down a few steps from the entrance, and the living room down a few more. The roof remains at a constant level, however, so the rooms become gradually taller and more spacious as the climax is reached, a panoramic view towards the sea and the evening sun.

Despite the extended perimeter, which suggests high energy consumption, the quality of light within the house would have been as magical as it was at the Segger house, and the sequence of contrasting spaces sensually uplifting.

1

1: Preliminary sketch **2 and 3:** Plans showing views and sunlight **4:** Model

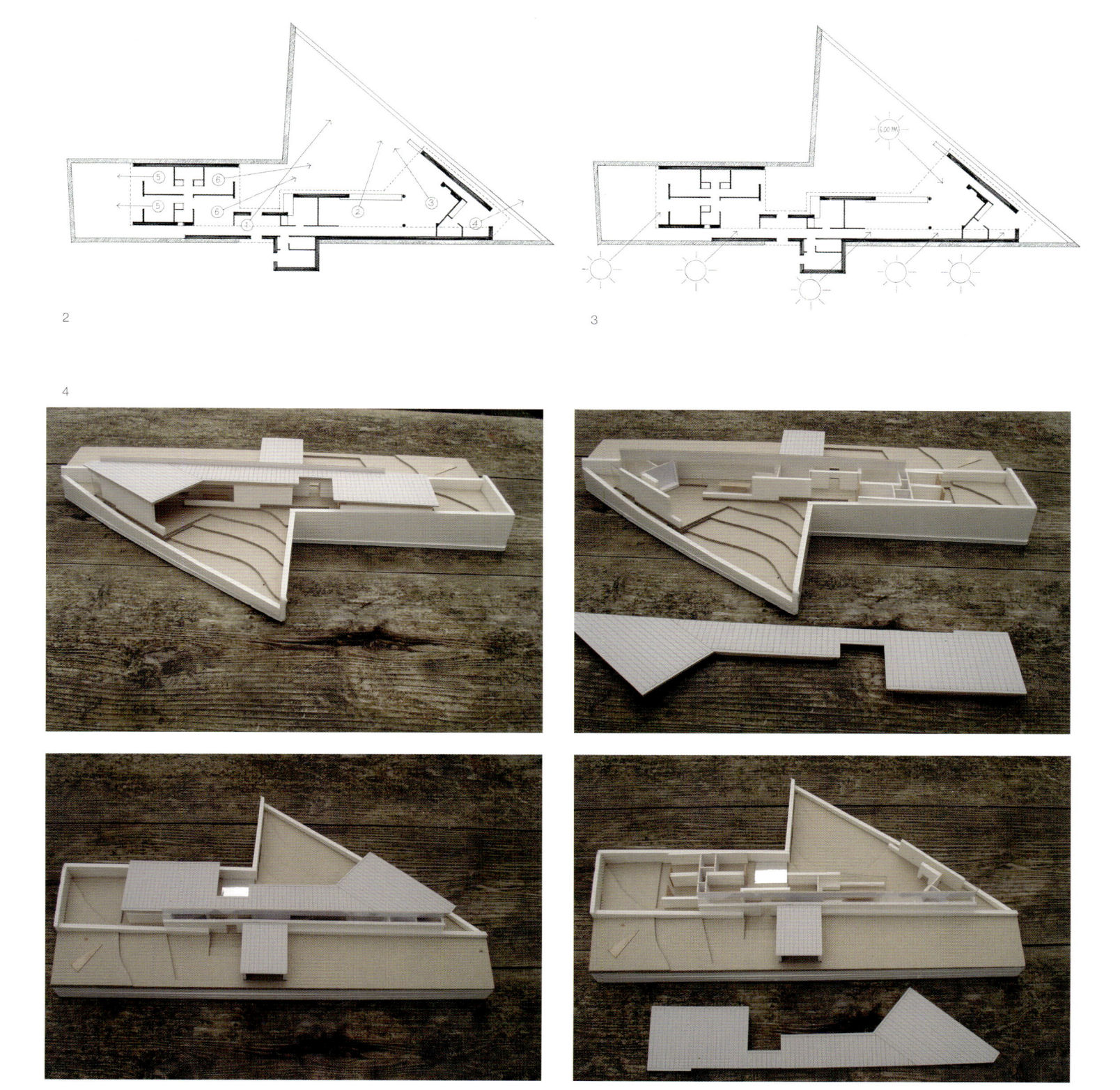

2

3

4

135

House in Dorset
2007

1: Model from south-east **2:** View from south **3:** Upper floor plan **4:** Ground floor plan

The site is a level terrace cut out of a north-facing wooded slope. The atmosphere is like a sacred precinct, a temenos, a partly enclosed space up under the sky. The panoramic view to the north is magnificent. The terrace is contained by the house to the south and west and by a garden wall and sheds to the east. The living room lies across the slope facing east onto the terrace garden so that it receives some sunlight in the morning even in winter. The north wall of the living room extends under the broad eaves into the garden making a warm, south-facing spot for an outside table.

A straight stair connects the living room to the bedrooms at first floor level and both bedrooms have outdoor terraces overlooking the garden at one end and the entrance at the other.

The walls are lightweight clay blocks (Ziegel) rendered outside and in. The roof was intended to be covered in western red cedar shingles but at the arbitrary insistence of the planners this was changed to slate.

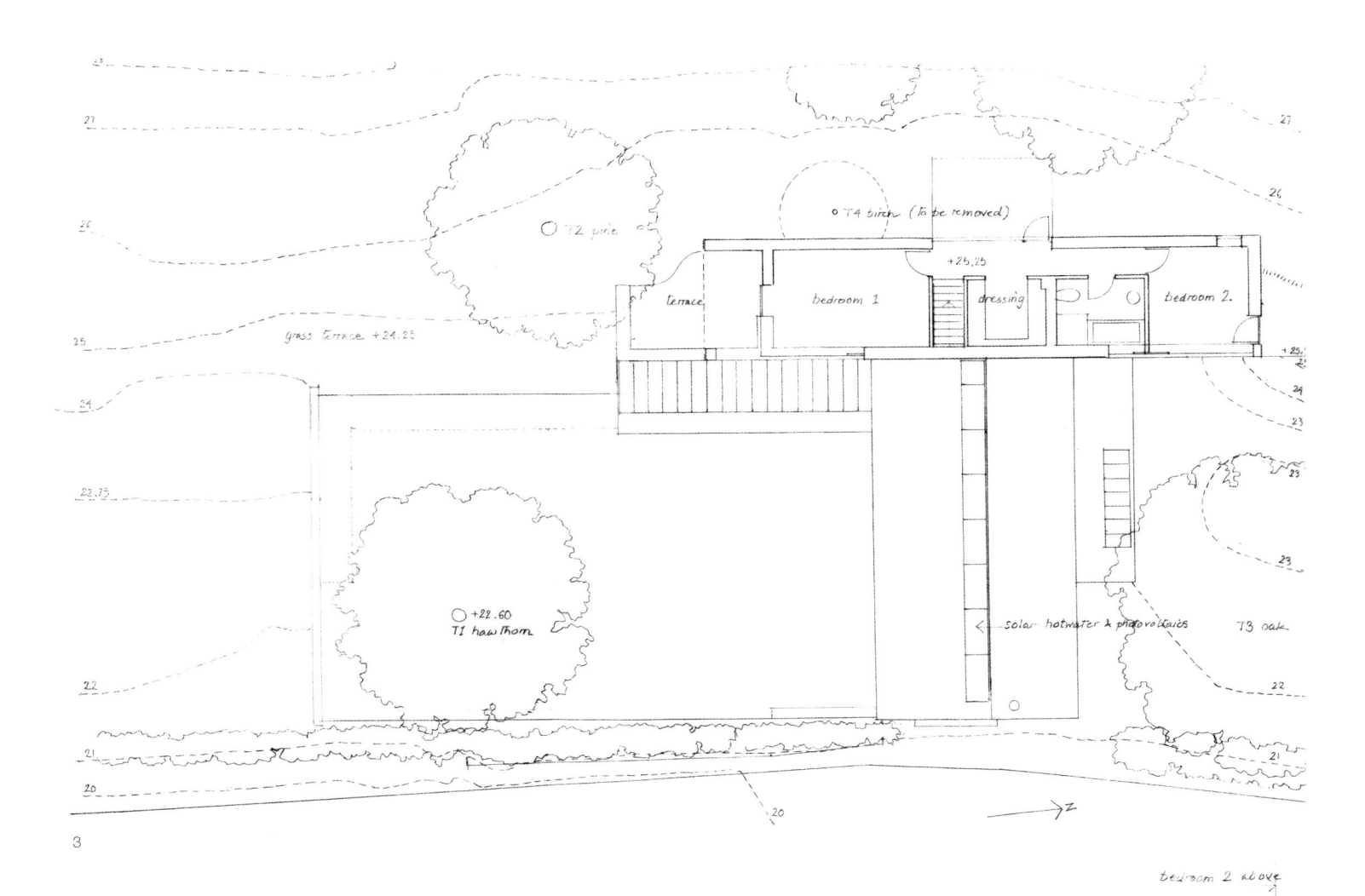

3

- T2 pine
- T4 birch (to be removed)
- terrace
- bedroom 1
- dressing
- bedroom 2
- grass terrace +24.25
- +25.25
- T1 hawthorn +22.60
- solar hotwater & photovoltaics
- T3 oak

4

bedroom 2 above

- store
- utility room
- boiler room/store
- retaining wall
- footpath
- conservatory
- +22.75
- entrance
- vegetable garden
- garden
- terrace
- living room
- T3 oak
- retaining wall

WISE Building, Centre for Alternative Technology, Machynlleth
2002–2010

1: Early scheme, showing movement through the building **2:** Lecture theatre, with oculus

The WISE building is the largest and most ambitious of built projects at CAT, conceived in Planning for Real sessions held during the early 2000s, started on site in 2006 and completed in 2010. Its purpose is to provide teaching and bedroom accommodation for students as well as suitable facilities for the conference trade.

An early scheme had the teaching and social accommodation located near the existing restaurant and the bedrooms on the steep, wooded hillside north of the restaurant where views and solar orientation were best and the rooms could be like tree-houses. However, for financial reasons, the two parts had to amalgamate, allowing the building to take on the character of a monastic establishment with its communal spaces and individual cells arranged around courtyards.

Access is from the west, through a dining room attached to the existing restaurant and then up half a level to a concourse that gives direct access to the circular lecture theatre and the bar as well as to the upper levels. It looks out to the lower part of a contained and calm courtyard of gravel, slate and water, through which the teaching rooms and workshops are reached. Above this, the courtyard opens out and is surrounded on the north and east sides by two floors of bedrooms, each with a generous sliding window. Further teaching and administrative rooms are provided in the east arm of bedrooms, which continues south past the lecture drum.

The layout of the building is clear and rational, the routes connecting the parts are self-evident, sometimes dramatic. The inside and outside are in continual dialogue. Rooms are reached sometimes internally, sometimes by open cloisters or galleries; large windows and doors allow rooms to expand out into sheltered man-made areas or offer views of the natural world beyond; sky lights let the sun penetrate right into the heart of the building, casting constantly changing streams of light on the walls, or, as in the case of the lecture room's 'oculus', "a pause for memories of the slow darkening of the world during a solar eclipse", according to Lea.

Water control is central to the story of CAT. Water from the reservoir in the hills above the quarry drove the wheel which powered the slate-cutting machinery. This is expressed dramatically in the rainwater system of the building. Rain falls, the run-off from the roofs and terraces cascades into shallow pools in the lower courtyard, and pours down between the slate walls of the old waterwheel pit to be conducted away to the river below.

The building is made largely from natural products—"80 per cent pre-industrial materials plus 20 per cent 'industrial vitamins'"(Pat Borer). The main structure is timber-framed, using FSC glulam elements. Footings and the ground floor are of limecrete, the roofs and upper floors of solid timber with appropriate insulation, finishes etc. External walls are formed in 500mm hemcrete sprayed over timber, finished externally with limewashed lime render (its rich ochre colour inspired by a mosque in Morocco). Other solid walls are made of sand-lime bricks or unfired earth blocks. The 7.2m-high wall of the lecture room is 500mm thick, formed in four sections from layers of rammed earth using a ply shuttering system, and left unfinished on both faces. Its diameter is similar to Agamemnon's tomb at Mycenae, built of huge, close-fitting blocks of ashlar in around 1750BC. "This building has tremendous power and we hoped that our space might share some of its predecessor's numinous quality" (Lea).

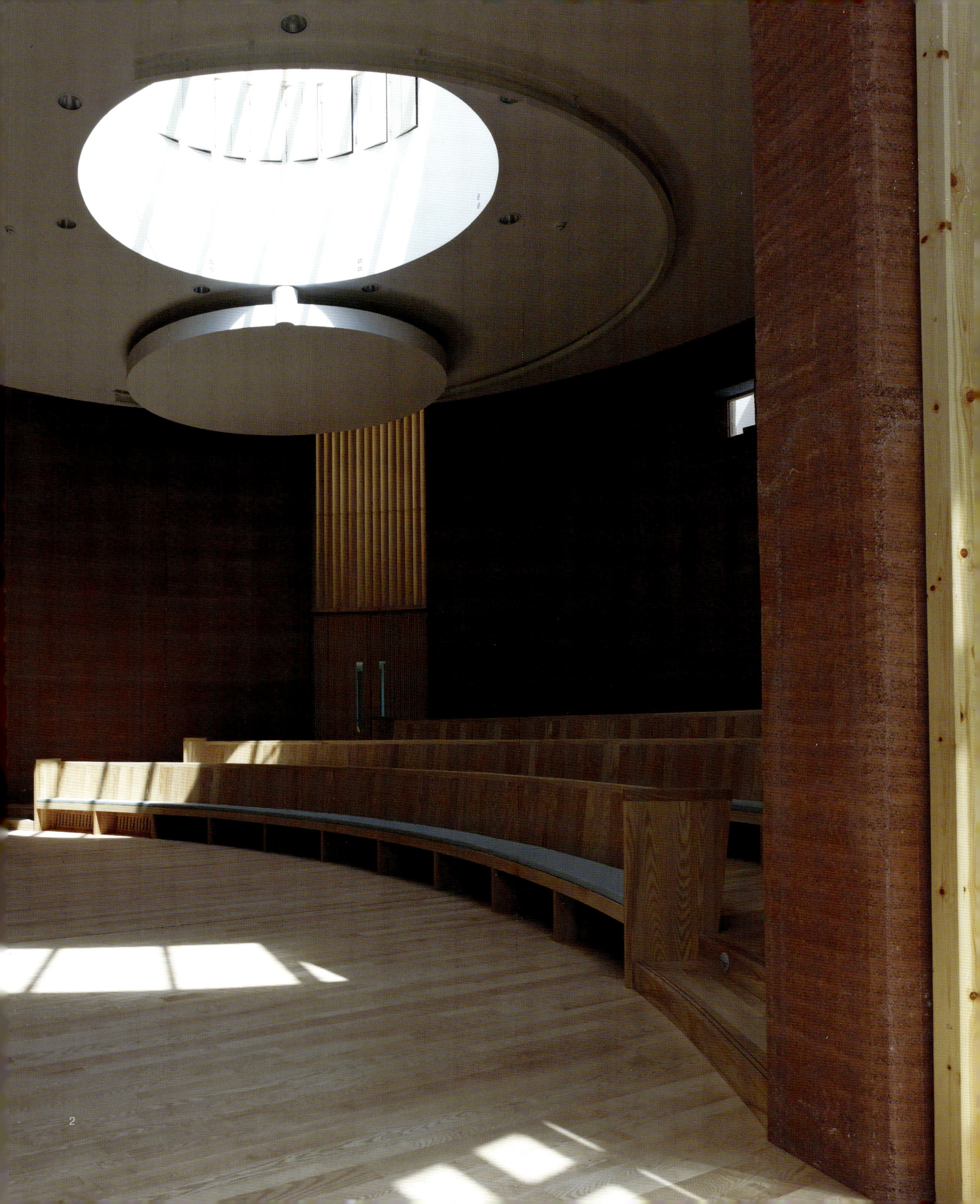

2

1

2

3

4

5

6

1: Entrance courtyard **2:** Restaurant extension and reception **3:** Foyer **4:** Lecture theatre **5:** Courtyard looking north **6:** Courtyard looking west **7:** Upper floor, bedrooms and seminar rooms **8:** Floor at foyer level

1
2
3
4
5
6

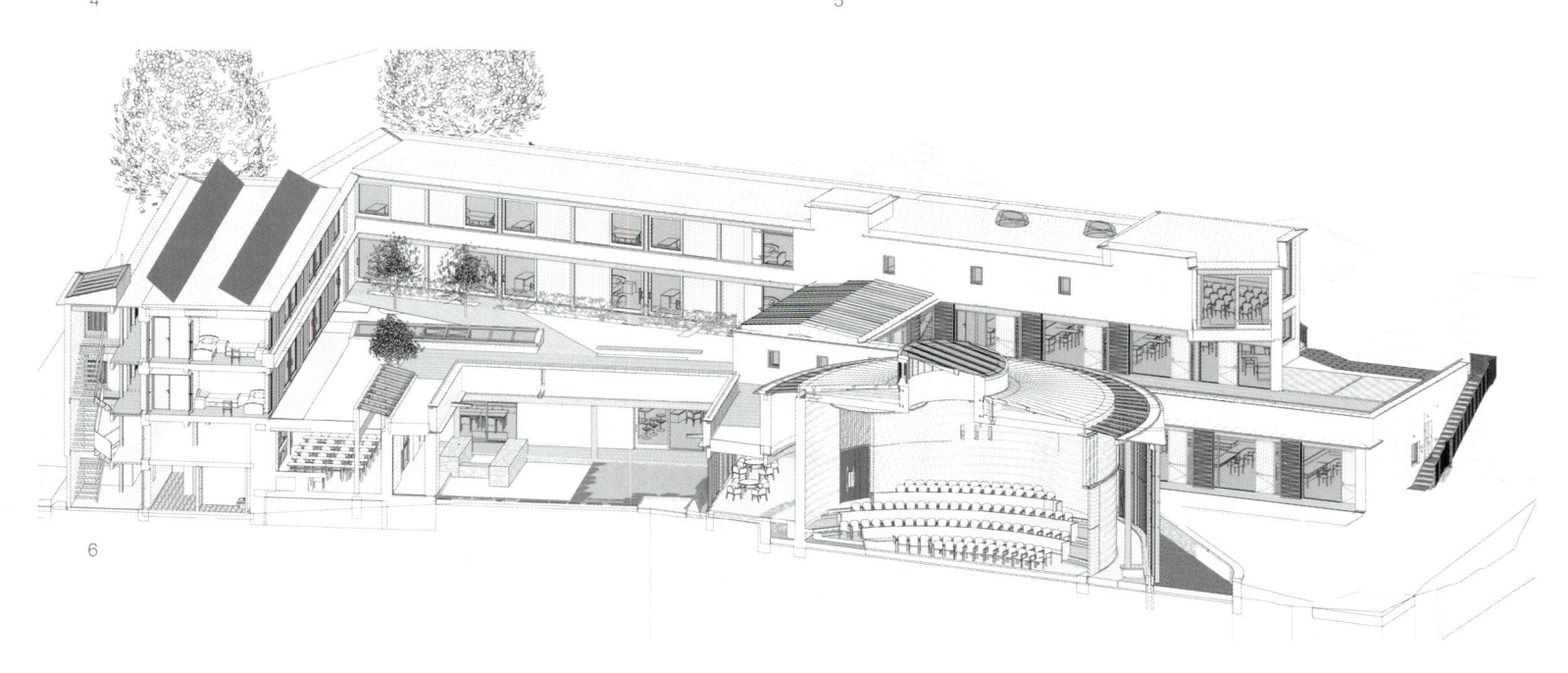

1 and 2: Ambulatory around lecture theatre **3:** Seminar room window **4:** View of slate tip of former quarry **5:** View from a bedroom, looking south **6:** Cut-away axonometric **7:** Bedroom gallery **8:** Seminar room window **9:** Terrace to bedrooms

Early scheme for bedrooms on separate site

CATBR Common Room
Site Conditions

Is this a column building – like a little temple on an acropolis?

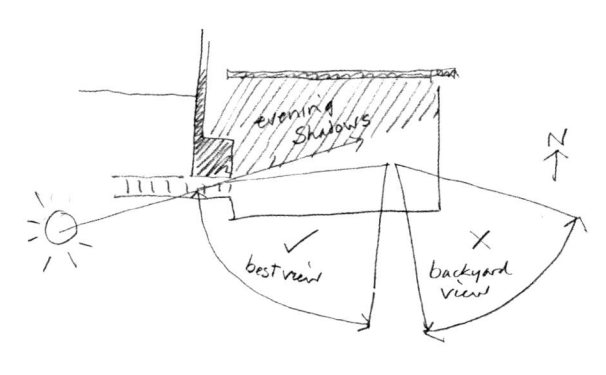

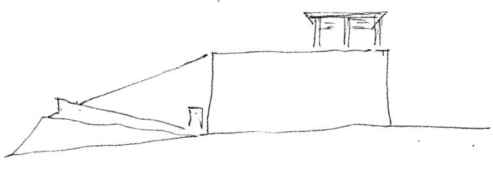

Or is it a wall building with sides enclosed? & big openings...

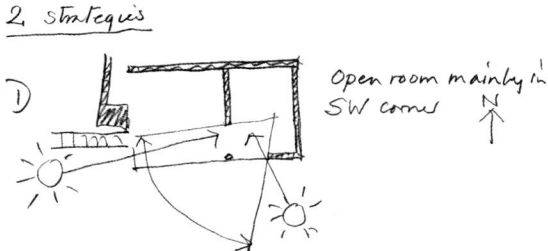

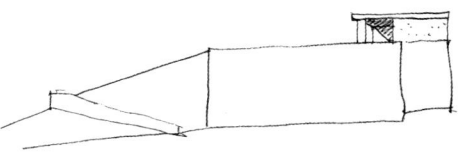

Or a mixture

2 strategies

1) Open room mainly in SW corner

2) Skew room & view & SW sun

Problem with columns & balustrades/handrails....

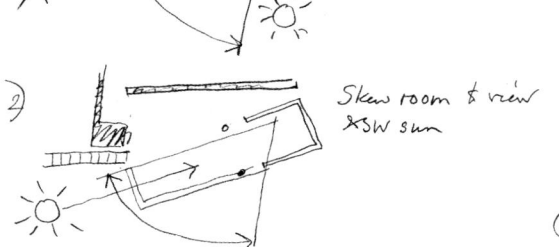

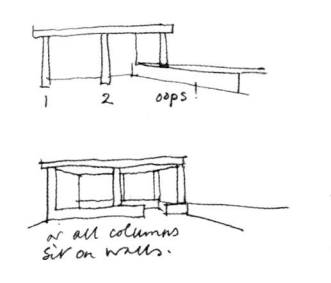

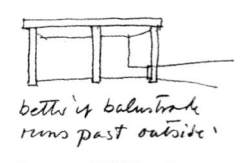

1 2 oops!

better if balustrade runs past outside

or all columns sit on walls.

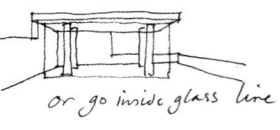

or go inside glass line

145

Schnapps

In 1947, on my father's return from the war, our family enjoyed our first summer holiday together… I was eight years old. My father introduced me to the art and craft of sailing, an activity which was to bring me great pleasure for the rest of my life.

A sailing boat is a microcosm of our life on earth: the individual or small community surrounded by impersonal nature whose powers we wish to harness, but to whose laws we must submit. It is solar powered via the wind and, if made of wood, it arises from a solar economy.

The economical integration of form and function are basic requirements for an efficient boat. Each boat has its own patterns of behaviour. That boats and ships have personalities, and are in some sense 'alive' is an ancient and continuing revelation.

It was not until 2001 that I bought a boat of my own. This was the 28ft Tumlare, 'Schnapps', designed by Knud Reimers in 1936. When it first appeared, Uffa Fox hailed the Tumlare as the most advanced yacht of its type, yet its canoe shaped hull and sweeping sheer suggest an ancient Nordic lineage.

Its form and proportions seem natural, harmonious and strong. The tall mast is set at a rake suggesting alertness and speed. Reimers often based the design of his hulls on two straight lines running from the bow and stern, meeting where the keelson joins the sternpost. This determines the Tumlare's characteristic shape beneath the waterline, the long bow and steeply raking rudder, all smoothly faired in to the wineglass cross section of the hull. Many people have commented on the sense of life in the Tumlare's form. To imbue matter with spirit is one definition of art.

You trust yourself completely to the power of nature when you set out to sea in a sailing boat, and the sea shows you visions which you cannot find in any other way. One night I was sailing home from Ireland. There was little wind at first and I could hear the chattering of guillemots on the surface nearby in the darkness as we moved slowly along. Later the moon floated up out of a bank of dark mist ahead and its light made a bright path on the sea. As it rose higher, a north wind began to blow, the boat heeled over and began to move faster and faster. I sat low in the cockpit, close to the water and steered straight for home down the path of light. The boat began to rush and sing, rising and dipping like a flying bird. Stars came out above and down in the water thousands of tiny bright sparks like diamonds flew from the hull. Astern a shining mist streamed up from the keel deep in the water. I put the palm of my hand on the surface of the water as it rushed past and drew silver fire from it. We sped through a magical world of sound and light, which grew more intense with each moment, until the night and the boat and her crew entered a different universe, a brief eternity, fading as clouds again covered the moon.

Afterwards I thought, maybe death could be like that, a magical flight into oblivion. And it seemed to me that this was an idea and a memory I should hold on to.

147

Quotation Sources

p 15 (Morris) "The Beauty of Life", in Thompson, E P, *William Morris: Romantic to Revolutionary*, New York, 1955 (1976)

(Zumthor) *Thinking Architecture*, Birkhauser: Birkhauser Architecture, 2006

p 17 (Kahn) quoted in Brownlee, David B and David G De Long, *Louis I Kahn: In the Realm of Architecture*, New York: Rizzoli, 1991

p 19 (Martin) *Buildings and Ideas, 1933–1983*, Cambridge: Cambridge University Press, 1983

(Kahn) in Brownlee and De Long, *Louis I Kahn,* 1991

(Wilson) in Stonehouse, Roger and Eric Parry, *Colin St John Wilson: Buildings and Projects*, London: Black Dog Publishing, 2008

p 20 (Pallasmaa) "Six Themes for the next Millennium", *Architectural Review*, July 1994

p 21 (Morris) letter to Mrs Alfred Baldwin (26 March 1874), in Briggs, Asa, *William Morris: Selected Writings and Designs*, London: Penguin, 1962

p 22 (MacCormac) *Architectural Design*, vol 47, no 9–10, 1977

p 25 (Engel) *The Japanese House: A Tradition for Contemporary Architecture*, Vermont: Tuttle, 1964

p 26 (Bryggman) in Pallasmaa, Juhani, Hapticity and Time, RIBA Discourse lecture, 1999

(Pugin) *The True Principles of Pointed or Christian Architecture,* London, 1841

(Segal) in McKean, John, *Learning from Segal*, Birkhauser: Birkhauser Architecture, 1989

p 27 (Morris) The Lesser Arts, lecture, 1878 in Briggs, *William Morris*, 1962

(Morris) "How I became a Socialist", *Justice*, 16 June 1894, in Briggs, *William Morris*, 1962

p 28 (Teiji) *Wabi Sabi Suki—The essence of Japanese beauty*, Hiroshima: Mazda Motor Corp, 1993

(Engel) *The Japanese House*, 1964

p 29 (Fukuoka) *The One-straw Revolution,* Emmaus, NY: Rodale Press, 1978 p 30 (Thoreau) *Walden*, 1854

p 31 (Fukuoka) *The One-straw Revolution*, 1978

p 32 (Fukuoka) *The One-straw Revolution*, 1978

p 34 (Morris) Shankland, Graeme, "Essay on Textiles", in Briggs, *William Morris*, 1962

p 35 (Voysey) "The English Home", *British Architect*, vol LXXV, 1911, in Davey, Peter *Arts and Crafts Architecture*, London: Phaidon, 1995

p 38 (Jewson) "By Chance I did Rove",1951, quoted in Drury, Michael, *Wandering Architects*, Stamford: Shaun Tyas, 2000

(Murcutt) from the *Dictionary of Contemporary Architects*, London: Thames and Hudson, 1930

p 41 (Pallasmaa) 'Six Themes for the next Millennium", *Architectural Review*, July 1994

(Kahn) letter to B V Doshi, 1961, in Brownlee and De Long, *Louis I Kahn*

p 49 (Yoshida) *The Japanese House and Garden*, London: Architectural Press, 1955

(Sedding) *Architecture–Old and New* (1881), in Drury, *Wandering Architects*, 2000

p 55 (Segal) in McKean, *Learning from Segal*, 1989

p 56 (Storey) letter dated 25 Feb 2000, in the college files

(Saint) in Davey, *Arts and Crafts Architecture*, 1995

p 58 (Pallasmaa) Hapticity and Time, RIBA Discourse lecture, 1999

p 59 (Pugin) *Contrasts,* London, 1841

p 60 (Pouillon) *The Stones of Le Thoronet*, London: Jonathan Cape, 1970

(Pärt) quoted in Kimberley, N, "Starting from scratch", *Gramophone*, vol 74, no 880, 1996

(Reich) from Wikipedia

p 61 (Morris) "The Beauty of Life", in Thompson, EP, *William Morris*, Romantic to Revolutionary, London: Lawrence and Wishart, 1955

p 98 (Hojoki) in Yoshida, *The Japanese House and Garden*, 1955

Catalogue of Works

NA   Nick Alexander
DC   David Cole
EC   Emlyn Cullen
BF   Benedicte Foo
HH   Helen Hollis
AH   Anthony Hudson
AK   Andrew Knox
LM   Liz Miller
TM   Tom Miller
KM   Kieran Morgan
AM   Ann Morris
FN   Frans Nicholas
NS   Nick Smith
AV   Adam Voelcker
FV   Frances Voelcker
EW   Ekkehard Weisner

Built schemes are shown in **bold**

"WHITEHALL: A PLAN FOR THE NATIONAL AND GOVERNMENT CENTRE"
1965
with Sir Leslie Martin and Lionel March

GRADUATE HOUSING
St John's College, Cambridge
1965
with Colin St John Wilson

LIVERPOOL CIVIC CENTRE
1966
with Colin St John Wilson

HOUSING
Eastfield, Mitcham and Pollards Hill, Mitcham
1967–1968
with Richard MacCormac, Peter Bell and Nick Alexander
with the London Borough of Merton, Architects' Dept

SHELTERED HOUSING (Houses 1–5)
Churt, Farnham, Surrey
Eddystone Housing Association
(1969) 1972
£13k

YOUTH CENTRE
Extension to tithe barn
Melling, Lancashire
Revd John Lumby
(1972) 1973

VICARAGE
Melling, Lancashire
Revd John Lumby
(1970–1972) 1975

SHELTERED HOUSING (Houses 6–10)
Churt, Farnham, Surrey
Eddystone Housing Association
(1973) 1974
£19k

HOUSING
Takeley Nursery, Takeley, Essex
Christopher Bailey
(1974)

GARDEN PAVILION
Howe Green House, Takeley, Essex
Christopher Bailey
(1975)

HOUSE RENOVATION
Four Mile Bridge, Holyhead, Anglesey
1978
FN

COMMUNITY CENTRE
St Dunstan's, Toxteth, Liverpool
1977
AH

NEW OFFICE
Ogoronwy, Llanfrothen, Gwynedd
David Lea
1978
AH, NS

SHELTERED HOUSING (Houses 11 and 12, and Warden's House)
Churt, Farnham, Surrey
Eddystone Housing Assocation
(1980) 1981
£24k
NS

LIBRARY EXTENSION
The Royal Agricultural College, Cirencester, Gloucestershire
(1980–1981) 1982
£160k
AV, FV, NS (and site architect Alan Drury)

NEW STUDY BEDROOMS (BLEDISLOE COURT)
The Royal Agricultural College, Cirencester, Gloucestershire
(1980) 1981
£514k
AV, FV, NS (and site architect Alan Drury)

HOUSE EXTENSION
Old Birmingham Road, Worcestershire
Peter Worsley
(1977) 1980

ARTIST'S STUDIO
Nettlecombe, Somerset
(1984) 1989
£4k

NEW HOUSES
Coates, Cirencester, Gloucestershire
Hastings, Coates, Mason, Russell, Chilton
(1985) 1986
£60–75k
NS

NEW HOUSES
Quaker Row, Coates, Cirencester,
Gloucestershire
The Royal Agricultural College
(1985)

PEMBROKE COLLEGE
competition design for new student rooms
Grandpont, off Marlborough Road, Oxford
(1986)
£2.7m
NS, EC

VISITOR CENTRE
Newborough, Anglesey
Forestry Commission
(1986)

NEW ACCOMMODATION
Rendcomb College, Rendcomb,
Gloucestireshire
(1987)

WOODWOOL HOUSE
(1987)
KM

CONVERSION OF SCHOOL
Penmon Old School, Penmon, Anglesey
1987

HOUSE
Pen y Rhiw, Ffestiniog
(1987) 1989
£60k

SPORTS HALL
Blaenau Ffestiniog, Gwynedd
(1987) 1989
£497k
EC, HH, AK, AV, KM, NS

HOUSE
Pen y Bryn, Blaenau Ffestiniog, Gwynedd
(1988) 1989
£35k

TIMBER-FRAMED HOUSE
project for constructing houses from timber
grown in Gwynedd
(1988)

RESTAURANT AND SHOPS
Conwy Quay, Conwy
(1988)

VILLAGE HALL (Neuadd Uhlman)
Garreg Llanfrothen, Penrhyndeudraeth,
Gwynedd
(1988)

DARWIN COLLEGE
competition design for new library
Silver Street, Cambridge
(1989)
EC

NEW STUDY BEDROOMS (COAD COURT)
The Royal Agricultural College,
Cirencester, Gloucestershire
(1989) 1991
£1.6m
AV, FV, BF

KING'S COLLEGE
competition design for new student rooms
Garden Hostel site, off West Road,
Cambridge
(1990)
£2.4m
NS, AV, EC

RESOURCE CENTRE
Centre of the Earth, Birmingham
The Wildlife Trust
(1990) 1993
£135k
BF, EC

EMMANUEL COLLEGE
competition design for new accommodation
Emmanuel College, Cambridge
(1991)

LOWER STATION
Centre for Alternative Technology,
Machynlleth, Powys
(1991) 1992
£73k
EC, BF
with Pat Borer

GONVILLE AND CAIUS COLLEGE
competition design for 149 study bedrooms
and other accommodation
Harvey Court site, off West Road,
Cambridge
(1992)
£10.5m
EC

MUSEUM
Rural History centre
Reading University
(1992)
£2.8m

VISITOR CENTRE – WAKEHURST PLACE
Ardingly, Haywards Heath, West Sussex
National Trust/Royal Botanical Gardens,
Kew
(1992)
£400k

CONVERSION OF BARN
Buarth Gwyn, Llanfrothen
Peter Marshall
(1993)

HOUSE RENOVATION
Higher Meerhay Farm, Bridport, Dorset
David and Georgia Langton
1993

THE OASIS OF PEACE
Extension to the Catholic Centre for
Healing and Marriage
Penamser Road, Porthmadog, Gwynedd
Mr and Mrs Dady, and Mr and Mrs Stewart
(1993) 1995
£140k
EC

HOUSE
Top Lane Farm, Stourton, Wiltshire
Mr and Mrs H C Hoare
(1994)
£200k
EC

HOUSE RENOVATION
West Greenridge, Northumberland
(1994)

ROBINSON COLLEGE
30 graduate bedrooms
behind 4–6 Adam's Road, Cambridge
(1995)
£1.1m
EC, TM

HOUSE EXTENSION
Blaen Camel, Cilcennin, Dyfed
Peter Segger and Anne Evans
(1997) 1998
TM

PRESTON FIELD BARN
House
Cirencester, Gloucestershire
William Chestermasters
(1997)
£197k
DC

VISITOR CENTRE
Sir Harold Hillier Garden and Arboretum,
Romsey, Hampshire
(1996–1997)
£2.1m
EW, TM, EC

COVER BUILDING
Chedworth Roman Villa, Gloucestershire
The National Trust
(1997)
£2.5m
LM, TM

HOUSE
Minard, Dingle, Co. Kerry
Brendan McNutt
1997

SHOP, Cafe AND WORKSHOP
Garreg Llanfrothen, Penrhyndeudraeth,
Gwynedd
Mentur Llanfrothen
(1995–1997) 1998
£260k
NA, LM, TM

AtEIC BUILDING
Centre for Alternative Technology,
Machynlleth, Powys
(1997–1998) 2000
£500k
with Pat Borer

COMMUNITY BUILDING
Bryn Melyn, Llangollen, Denbighshire
Bryn Melyn Community
(1997–1998)
£260k
EM
with Pat Borer

KINGSWOOD PROJECT
Feasibility study for a woodland education
and research centre
Kingswood, Nettlecombe, Somerset
(1998)
DC, AM

SUMMER HOUSE
Jasmine Cottage, Cornwall
Peter Marshall
(1998)

YOGA CENTRE AND FLAT
The Forge, Totnes, Devon
(1998)

POTTERY
Bridge Pottery, Cheriton, Gower Peninsula,
West Glamorgan
Micki Schloessingk
(1999) 2000
£34k

CONFERENCE CENTRE
The Stables, Trafford Hall, Cheshire
2000
with Pat Borer

MAGDALENE COLLEGE
competition design for new student
accommodation and conference centre
Castle Hill site, Chesterton Road,
Cambridge
(2000)
DC

COTTAGE RENOVATION AND
EXTENSION
Blaen Camel, Cilcennin, Dyfed
Peter Segger and Anne Evans
(2000) 2001
£70k

RIXTON CLAYPITS
Education centre
Warrington Borough Council
(2000) 2005
£241k
with Pat Borer

BUDDHIST RETREAT CENTRE
Kunselling, Llwydallt, Powys
(2000)
£241k
EC

COMMUNITY RESOURCE CENTRE
Slaidburn, Lancashire
Tony Moores
(2001)
£1.4m
NS
with Pat Borer

FEASIBILITY STUDY
Holme Lacy College, Holme Lacy, Hereford
(2001)
with Pat Borer

NEW HOUSES (competition)
Gunnislake, Cornwall
Devon and Cornwall Housing Association
(2004)
with Pat Borer

NEW ACCOMMODTION (THE WISE BUILDING)
The Wales Institute of Sustainable Education
Centre for Alternative Technology, Machynlleth, Powys
(2002) 2007–2010
£3.3m
with Pat Borer

MIXED DEVELOPMENT AND MARINA
Penlee Quarry, Newlyn, Cornwall
MDL (Marine Developments Ltd)
2004
with MJ Long

SHOP AND OFFICES
Rhug Estate, Corwen
(2005)
with Pat Borer

HOUSE
Y Felinheli, Gwynedd
(2005–2006)
£240k
EC

PRIVATE MUSEUM of Ming Dynasty pottery
Blandford, Dorset
Sir Michael Butler
(2006–2007)

HOUSE
near Bridport, Dorset
Georgia Langton and Giorgio Moltoni
(2007)

VILLAGE HALL
Norberry, Church Stretton, Shropshire
(2008)

List of Publications

JOURNALS ON LEA'S BUILDINGS

Architectural Design
Article on Pollards Hill housing at Merton (with MacCormac & Bell), October 1971.

The Architects' Journal
MacCormac, Richard, "Housing: lightweight timber system", 26 November 1975. Churt scheme, phases 1 and 2 appraisal.

Long, MJ, "Literate library", 24 November 1982. RAC/library extension appraisal.

Martin, Bruce, "Architecture as the art of construction", 16 March 1983. Churt scheme, phase 3 appraisal.

Brawne, Michael, "Cotswold Court", 16 January 1985. RAC/Bledisloe Court appraisal.

"A Cotswold stone roof", 16 January 1985. AJ Construction article.

Blundell Jones, Peter, "College collage", 11 June 1986. Pembroke College project.

Blundell Jones, Peter, "A modern vernacular", 17 September 1986. Coates houses.

Blundell Jones, Peter, "Traditional games", 20 September 1989. Blaenau Ffestiniog sports hall.

Blundell Jones, Peter, "Woodland retreat", 27 September 1989. Artist's studio in Somerset.

Blundell Jones, Peter, "Rooms with a view", 13 May 1992. Cambridge college competition projects.

Hannay, Patrick, "Housing students and conferences", 21 Oct 1992. RAC/Coad Court.

The Architectural Review
Article on Pollards Hill housing at Merton (with MacCormac & Bell), April 1971.

Blundell Jones, Peter, "Traditional Values", August 1993. RAC/Coad Court.

Blundell Jones, Peter, "Wales Institute for Sustainable Education", January 2011.

ARQ (Architectural Research Quarterly)
Blundell Jones, Peter and Jan Woudstra, "Hillier's visitor centre, Romsey: a project by David Lea" vol 4, no 3, 2000.

Blundell Jones, Peter and John Sergeant, "New Meanings From Old Buildings", vol 5, No 4, 2001.

Hawkes, Dean, "Necessity and Poetry: David Lea's Bridge Pottery", vol 6, no 2, 2002.

Architecture Today
Anderson, Will, "CAT's coming of age", no 209, June 2010. WISE/CAT.

Archithese
McKean, John, "Die Architektur des David Lea: Im Frieden mit der Natur", January/February 1987.

Building Design
Woodman, Ellis, "Welsh wizardry", 25 June 2010. WISE/CAT.

Woodman, Ellis, Review 2010, 17 December 2010. WISE/CAT.

Woodman, Ellis, "Life class", 28 January 2011. WISE/CAT. Short back-page interview/profile of Lea.

Building for a Future
(journal of the Association of Environmentally Conscious Builders)
Lord Smith, Chris, "Site Politics", vol 8, no 2, 1998. Segger house Blaen Camel.

Country Life
Powers, Alan, "Bridging the extremes", 9 May 1991.

Powers, Alan, "Houses that live and breathe", 12 December 2002.

Deutsche Bauzeitung
Dechau, Wilfried, "Cotswold Cottage", 2 February 1986. RAC/Bledisloe Court.

Eco-city and Green Building (ECGB)
"Wales Institute for Sustainable Education of Centre for Alternative Technology", no 12, 2012. (in Chinese)

Green Building
(journal of the Centre for Alternative Technology)
Borer, Pat, "Icons of eco-building", Summer 2011. WISE/CAT.

Homebuilding and Renovating
"Case study 3: Peter Segger and Anne Evans", Case study 3, August 2000. Interview between Peter Segger and David Lea.

Orszagepito
Gerle, Janos, "David Lea—Wales" (in Hungarian), 1997/3–4. Artist's studio and Darwin College.

RIBAJ
Hannay, Patrick, "Ground force", Nov 2000. AtEIC/CAT.

Spazio e Società
Blundell Jones, Peter, "Between Tradition and Modernity: The Reticent Architecture of David Lea", no 55, 1991.

Blundell Jones, Peter, "The Fragrance of Timber", no 89, 2000.

Touchstone
(journal of the Royal Society of Architects in Wales)
Hannay, Patrick, "The Oasis of Peace", issue 3, October 1997. CAT.

Hannay, Patrick, "The Ecology of Elegance", issue 5, April 1999.

Blundell Jones, Peter, "A sense of material", issue 5, April 1999. Segger house Blaen Camel.

Hawkes, Dean, "Contemplating tea and pots", issue 10, Spring 2002. Bridge Pottery.

The Observer
Moore, Rowan, "Creative ways with cow dung", 18 July 2010. WISE/CAT.

Ville Giardini
Biagi, Marco, "Ecologia di luogo", no 370, June 2001. Blaen Camel.

Book articles about Lea's projects
Cherry, Monica, *Building Wales/Adeiladu Cymru,* Cardiff: Cardiff University Welsh School of Architecture, 2005. Bridge Pottery.

Stungo, Naomi, *The New Wood Architecture,* London: Gingko Press, 1998. Artist's studio, Somerset.

Wines, James, *Style, Not Sustainability,* Los Angeles: Taschen, 2000. Thatched Artist's studio.

Published articles written by Lea
Lea, David, "Churt, Surrey, England. Housing scheme for elderly people, *International Asbestos-cement Review*, AC88, October 1977.

Lea, David, "Architectural essence—modernist or natural", *Architects' Journal*, 2 June 1982.

Lea, David, "*One Earth: William Morris's vision*", *William Morris Today,* exhibition catalogue, London: ICA, 1984.

Lea, David, "Passport to Paradise", *Perspectives on Architecture*, issue 6, vol 1, October 1994

Lea, David, "Blaen Camel", *Building for a Future*, AECB, 1998.

Lea, David, "Fake or Real?", *Planet*, January 2000.

Lea, David, "Drawn back to nature", *Selfbuild and Design*, October 2001.

Lea, David, "Language, space and meaning", *Touchstone*, December 2011. WISE/CAT.

Lea, David and Wayne Forster, "Two-way conversation", *Touchstone,* issue 18, December 2011, WISE/CAT.

Lea, David, "Move to the light" in Blundell Jones, Peter and Mark Meagher eds, *Architecture and Movement: the dynamic experience of buildings and landscapes*, London: Routledge, 2015.

Index

Aalto, Alvar 5, 59
Agriculture 15, 28, 32, 61
Alexander, Christopher 19, 128
Alexander, Nick 21, 55, 150
Artist's studio, Somerset 11, 48, 95–99, 150
Arts and Crafts 4, 5, 10, 11, 36, 37
Arup Associates 39
AtEIC building (see Centre for Alternative Technology)
Authenticity 33, 34, 82

Bailey, Christopher (RAC bursar) 22, 32, 34, 36, 150
Baillie Scott, M H 36, 37, 92
Barcelona Pavilion 12, 18, 44, 59, 118
Barragán, Luis (house in Mexico) 45, 118
Bartlett (School of Architecture) 21
Bell, Peter 18, 20, 23, 150
Berry, Bill (RAC mason) 34
Birmingham
    land use studies 21, 68
    new library 59
Blaen Camel (house extension) 47, 48, 122–125, 134, 152
Blaenau Ffestiniog sports hall 9, 151
Bledisloe Court (see Royal Agricultural College)
Blundell Jones, Peter 13, 35, 154, 155
Boats 16, 17, 61, 146, 147
Borer, Pat 11, 12, 45, 49, 50–52, 54, 138
Brick 17, 22, 23, 36, 39, 40, 42, 59, 128
Bridge Pottery 47, 50, 126, 127, 152
British Museum Library 18, 19
Bryggman, Erik 26

Cambridge
    School of Architecture 17, 58
    Colleges (generally) 5, 7, 8, 19, 39, 82, 128
Centre for Alternative Technology (CAT): 5, 12, 41, 50, 52
    AtEIC building 51, 152
    cliff railway stations 51, 151
    masterplan 51
    WISE building 27, 41, 44, 49, 51–54, 138–145, 153
Chicago 17, 18
China 28, 29
Churt (timber-framed sheltered housing) 4, 11, 23, 32, 36, 40, 50, 69–75, 150
Cirencester (see Royal Agricultural College)
Clegg, Peter 54
Clients (generally) 47, 55–57
Clifton College, Bristol 15, 16, 29
Clifton-Taylor, Alec (*The Pattern of English Building*) 33
Coad Court (see Royal Agricultural College)
Coates houses, nr Cirencester (see Royal Agricultural College)
Competitions 35, 38–42
Cooper, Phil (structural engineer) 45
Cooper, Tim (friend) 16
Cotswolds, influence of 4, 33, 34, 36, 100
Courtyards 7, 8, 10, 12, 19, 24, 28, 35, 36, 39, 40, 41
Cullen, Emlyn 30
Cullinan, Edward 4, 33

Darwin College, Cambridge 39, 94, 151
Day, Chris(topher) 48, 49
Dorset, house in 56, 136, 137, 153
Douglass, Ruth 23, 24, 69
Downing College, Cambridge (new library by Q Terry) 37

Eddystone Housing Association (see Churt)
Engel, Heinrich 25, 28
Erskine, Ralph 41

Feltrino 36
Fox, Richard (builder) 47
Fukuoka, Masanobu 28, 30–32

Gayford, Martin 5
Goetheanum (see Steiner)
Gonville and Caius College, Cambridge (see Harvey Court)
Goodfellow, Terence 30
Greek (see Roman)

Harper, Peter (CAT) 51
Harris, Sylvia 57
Harvey Court (Gonville and Caius College, Cambridge) 17–19, 39, 42, 104, 128, 151
Haward, Birkin, and Joanna van Heyningen 35
Hemp, hemp lime 11, 52, 57
Hillier Garden visitor centre 11, 39, 44, 45, 118–121, 152
Hines, Jonathan (Architype) 55
History 17, 38, 41, 54, 58, 60
Hodgkinson, Patrick 19, 22
Holme Lacy Agricultural College 54, 55, 153

International Style (see Modernism)
Insall (Donald Insall Associates) 40
Irene, Awel 32
Italy 36, 42, 76, 108

Japan
    agriculture 31
    buildings 10, 24, 25, 27, 36, 49, 59, 70, 74, 76, 88, 110, 118
    philosophy 27, 28, 59, 62, 98
James, Rod (CAT) 51
Jewson, Norman 38

Kahn, Louis 17–19, 41, 42, 44, 47, 48, 106, 122
Kimbell Art Museum 44, 47, 48
King's College, Cambridge 39, 42, 151
Kingswood project 116, 117, 152
Koolhaas, Rem (CCTV building) 59

Lea Family
    Fiona (sister) 15
    parents 15, 16, 146
    Irene (see Irene)
Le Corbusier (La Tourette) 60
Leicester Engineering Faculty building 18
Lethaby, W R 10, 61
Lewisham (housing by Walter Segal) 25, 26
Liverpool Civic Centre project 18, 19, 150
Llanfrothen (shop) 46, 152
Long, M J 18, 56, 132, 133, 153, 154
Lutyens, Edwin Landseer 50
MacCormac, Richard 4, 17, 20, 21–23, 39, 44, 59, 150
Magdalen College, Oxford 37
Magdalene College, Cambridge 40, 53, 128, 129, 152
March, Lionel 21, 28, 66
Martin, (Sir) Leslie 17–19, 21, 22, 39, 66, 104, 128, 150
Medieval/Middle Ages 7, 9, 23, 35, 38, 49

Melling vicarage 28, 150
Menin, Sarah and Stephen Kite (book) 22
Merton, London Borough of (housing) 20–23, 28, 32, 33, 66, 67, 150
Mies van der Rohe, Ludwig 12, 18, 48, 59, 118
Miller, Tom and Liz 44
Model-making 16, 23, 55
Modernism 22, 34, 38, 44, 45, 54
Monastic, monasteries 7, 40, 60
Moore, Henry 18
Morris, William 13, 15, 21, 26, 34, 36, 37, 61, 88
Murcutt, Glenn 38, 48
Music 57, 60
Mycenae, Agamemnon's tomb 138

Nant Pasgen Fawr 28
Nelson, Jeremy 36, 48
Nitschke, Gunter 28
North Wales, house in 134, 135, 153

Oasis of Peace, Porthmadog 47, 112–115, 152
Ogoronwy 5, 12, 28, 30, 57, 78–81, 150

Pains Factory site (see Merton)
Pallasmaa, Juhani 20, 41, 58
Pärt, Arvo 60
Pears, Peter 57
Pembroke College, Oxford 7, 35, 38, 86, 87, 151
Penlee project, Cornwall 56, 57, 132, 133, 153
Perimeter planning 19, 21, 66, 68, 69
Peterhouse College, Cambridge 17
Planners 35, 50, 53, 126, 136
Planning for Real process 46, 52, 138
Pollards Hill (see Merton)
Porphyrios, D 37
Pouillon, Fernand 60
Powers, Alan 4, 154
Prince Charles, H R H 35, 53, 54
Pritchett, Ian (Lime Technology Ltd) 52
Pugin, A W N 26, 58

Rammed earth 11, 51
Reich, Steve 60
Reimers, Knud 61, 146
Rietveld, G (Schroeder House) 53
Rievaulx 7

Rixton Claypits 54, 153
Robinson College, Cambridge 39, 44, 110, 111, 152
Roman (influence of Roman and Greek architecture) 42, 43, 104, 106
Roofs (flat versus pitched) 11, 42–44, 46, 50, 70, 130
Rowe, Colin 17, 58
Royal Agricultural College, Cirencester: 4, 7, 9, 27, 32
  Bledisloe Court 27, 33, 35, 37, 38, 82, 83, 86, 100, 150
  Coad Court 38, 53, 100–103, 151
  Coates houses (Walled Garden) 10, 27, 36, 76, 88–91, 151
  Library extension 33, 44, 84, 85, 150
  Masterplan 103
Ruskin, John 26

Sailing (see Boats)
Saint, Andrew 56
Schildt, Göran 5, 59
Schinkel, Karl Friedrich 42, 43
Schnapps (see Boats)
Scott, Giles Gilbert 42
Sedding, J D 49
Segal, Walter 11, 21, 24–27, 33, 43, 50, 55, 70, 74
Segger, Peter and Anne Evans (see Blaen Camel)
Sergeant, John 27
Self-build 24, 26, 49, 95
Seymour, John 28, 49
Shaker 18, 82, 84
Shaw, R Norman 36
Slaidburn community centre 39, 45, 54, 130, 131, 153
Smith, Nick 57, 86
Snowdonia 12, 32
Steiner, Rudolf 49
Stirling, James 18
St John's College, Cambridge 19, 20, 150
Storey, Sir Richard 56
Stourton (see Wiltshire)
Strang, Tim (builder) 47
Students 30, 31, 57, 58

Takeley 32, 36, 76, 77, 150
Taliesin (see Wright)
Taut, Bruno 59
Teaching (see Students)
Teiji, Itoh 28
Terry, Quinlan 37
Thatch (artist's studio in Somerset) 11, 48, 49
The Limits to Growth 24, 28
Thomas, RS 27
Thoreau, Henry David 30
Thoronet, Le 60
Timber-framed building 23, 24, 28, 47, 48, 50, 125
Timber-framed house project, Gwynedd 37, 92, 93, 151
Timelessness 7, 35, 54, 59

Usonian houses (see Wright)
Utzon, Jørn 23, 69

Voelcker, Adam and Frances 31, 32, 78, 159
Voysey, C F A 10, 35, 36

Wakehurst Place visitor centre 42–44, 106, 107, 152
Walled Garden, The (see Royal Agricultural College)
Weese, Harry 17
Weisner, Ekkehard 11, 45, 55
Westwood Manor, Wiltshire 33
Whitehall project 21, 150
Willmott, Peter 20
Wilson, Colin St John (Sandy) 17–20, 22, 39, 40, 55, 104, 128, 150
Wiltshire, house in 42, 44, 108, 109, 152
WISE building (see Centre for Alternative Technology)
Wright, Frank Lloyd 10, 18, 27, 30, 32, 37
  Taliesin 30
  Prairie house(s) 18
  Usonian house(s) 18, 27, 32, 37, 70, 76, 88
Yeats, W B 28
Yoshida, Tetsuro 49

Zen 28, 59, 95
Zumthor, Peter 15, 58

Image Credits

Julian Bishop: 49 (3); Peter Blundell Jones: 47, 82, 98, 99, 103 (5), 125 (5); Jon Broome: 26; Nick Bullock: 110; Martin Charles/RIBA Library Photographs Collection: 74 (2); Emlyn Cullen: 104, 108 (1); © Sam Lambert: 17 (1); David Lea: 6, 8, 9 (figs 3 & 4), 12, 13, 18, 20, 22, 24, 27–29, 31, 32, 34, 37 (3), 42, 44 (1), 46, 55, 57, 59 (1), 68 (1), 69 (2), 70 (1 & 2), 74–75 (1, 4 & 5), 76–79, 83 (2 & 3), 87, 88, 93, 94 (4), 95–97, 100, 101 (4), 102 (1, 2 & 3), 103 (4 & 8), 105–117, 120, 121, 123, 125 (3 & 5), 128 (2), 131 (2), 132–134, 135 (4), 136–138, 144–145; Trystan Lea: 5; MJ Long: 17 (3 & 2); © Andrew Metcalf: 48; Tom and Liz Miller: 119; Nasa, 63; © Porphyrios Associates: 36, 37 (5); Armando Salas Portugal/Barragan Foundation: 45; John Sergeant: 37 (3); Timothy Soar: cover, 14, 64, 65, 103 (6 & 7), 139, 140–143; Nick Smith, 86; Bill Toomey: 70; Bill Toomey/RIBA Library Photographs Collection: 72; Adam Voelcker: 30, 36, 39, 40, 49 (4), 51 (1), 59 (3), 84 (2), 85.

Acknowledgements

Many people helped me in my research for this book, and I thank them all. In particular, I must thank those listed below. They contributed financially towards the cost of the book so their help is much appreciated—without it, the book could not have gone ahead.

Nick Alexander
Allies and Morrison
Graciela Artola De Williams
Julia Ayling
Skip Belton
Nick Bullock
Robert Camlin
Nick Carey-Thomas
Peter Carolin
Peter Clegg
Emlyn Cullen
Ted Cullinan and Cullinan Studio
Feilden Clegg Bradley Studios
Benedicte Foo and Mike Jones
Jo van Heyningen and Birkin Haward
Gaunt Francis
Glenn Howells
Anthony and Jenny Hudson
Peter Jamieson
Fiona Lea
Thomas Lloyd
Chris Loyn
Jonathan McDowell
Tom and Liz Miller (Haysom Ward Miller)
Frans Nicholas
Robin Nicholson
Huw Meredydd Owen
Robert Sakula
Gareth Scourfield
Peter Segger and Anne Evans
Ruth Selig
Nick Smith (Nicholas Merton)
Robin Webster
Ekkehard Weisner
Richard Weston

In addition, I must thank Patrick Hannay for helping to raise financial contributions from architectural practices across Wales, and Anthony and Jenny Hudson, who gave the final push in the direction of the publisher.

Biography

Adam Voelcker is an architect, living and working in North Wales. He trained at the Cambridge University School of Architecture from 1971 to 1977, did his year out with MacCormac and Jamieson and, after a year working in India with his wife Frances, they both joined David Lea to work on new buildings for the Royal Agricultural College, Cirencester. More recently he was co-author of the Gwynedd volume in the Buildings of Wales (Pevsner) series and has written a monograph on the Arts and Crafts architect Herbert Luck North, also based in North Wales.

Colophon

© 2015 Artifice books on architecture, the architect and the authors. All rights reserved.

Artifice books on architecture
10A Acton Street
London
WC1X 9NG

t. +44 (0)207 713 5097
f. +44 (0)207 713 8682
sales@artificebooksonline.com
www.artificebooksonline.com

All opinions expressed within this publication are those of the authors and not necessarily of the publisher.

Designed by Matthew Boxall at Artifice books on architecture.

British Library Cataloguing-in-Publication Data.
A CIP record for this book is available from the British Library.

ISBN 978 1 908967 74 9

No part of this publication may be reproduced, stored in a retrieval system, or transmitted, in any form or by any means, electronic, mechanical, photocopying, recording, or otherwise, without prior permission of the publisher.

Every effort has been made to trace the copyright holders, but if any have been inadvertently overlooked the necessary arrangements will be made at the first opportunity.

Artifice books on architecture is an environmentally responsible company. *David Lea: An Architect of Principle* is printed on sustainably sourced paper.